AF564627

Agro-Based Industries and their Prospects

Agro-Based Industries and their Prospects

Prof. Sriniwas Puri

RANDOM PUBLICATIONS
NEW DELHI (INDIA)

Agro-Based Industries and their Prospects

ISBN 978-93-5111-767-4

Published in 2016 in India by

RANDOM PUBLICATIONS

4376-A/4B, Gali Murari Lal, Ansari Road
New Delhi-110 002
Phone : +9111-43580356, 011-23289044, 011-43142548
e-mail: sales@randompublications.com,
info@randompublications.com, randomexports@gmail.com

Type Setting by : Friends Media, Delhi-110089
Digitally Printed at : **Replika Press Pvt. Ltd.**

Preface

Agro based industries play a vital role in the development of India's rural economy which has been receiving increasing attention from the central as well as state government in view of its importance to the national reconstruction. The economic prosperity of a developing country like India depends largely on the development of agro based industries which in turn leads to the creation of forward and backward linkages to the development process on large scale by making mutual complementarity of agriculture and industries.

Agro based industry refers to an industry that adds values to agricultural raw materials through processing in order to produce marketable and usable products that bring forth profits and additional income to the producer. The development of the agro industry can help stabilize and make agriculture more lucrative and create employment opportunities both at the production and marketing stages. The broad based development of the agro products industry will improve both the social and physical infrastructure of India. India is one of the largest producers of food, and is the second largest producer of rice, wheat, fruits, and vegetables in the world. Nearly 70% of the population depends on agriculture and agro-based industries. Since it would cause diversification and commercialization of agriculture, it will thus enhance the incomes of farmers and create food surpluses. It is a well recognized fact across the world, particularly in the context of industrial development that the importance of agro industries is relative to agriculture increases as economies develop. It should be emphasized that food is not just produce. Food also encompasses a wide variety of processed products. It is in this sense that the agro-industry is an important and vital part of the manufacturing sector in developing countries and the means for building industrial capacities. The development of agro-based industries commenced during pre-independence days. Cotton mills, sugar mills, jute mills were fostered in the corporate sector. During the post-Independence days, with a view to rendering more employment and using local resources, small scale and village industries were favored.

The book deals with the operational conditions of agro based industries. Agro based industries units are very much varies in their size cost structure scale of production pattern of financing and problems faced. The difference is inter industry as well as intra industry.

– Author

Contents

1

The Agro-based Industries in India

This group of industries depends on the raw material produced by the agricultural sector. The products comprise mostly consumer goods. Agro- based industry is important from the point of view of contribution to industrial production and employment generation. A survey of various agro- based industries is given below.

TEXTILE INDUSTRY:

The textile industry plays predominant presence in the Indian economy. It is the only industry which is self-reliant, from raw material to the highest value added products, viz., garments/made-ups.

COTTON TEXTILES:

Cotton accounts for a major portion of the total fabric produced. The first successful cotton textile mill was set up at Mumbai by Parsi entrepreneurs.

The following factors favoured the development of cotton textiles industry at and around Mumbai:

1. Location of port facilitated import of capital goods, chemicals, etc., and the export of finished goods.
2. Mumbai got progressively well connected through rail and road links with cotton growing areas of Gujarat and Maharashtra in the interior.
3. The humid coastal climate favoured textile- making without breaking the thread.
4. Development of chemical industry around Mumbai made available the necessary inputs.
5. Availability of capital and financial resources helped the industry grow.
6. Cheap labour was available for the industry.

Ahmadabad grew as another cotton textile centre. The size of cotton mills is small here, but they produce high quality goods. The raw materials for the industry come from cotton growing areas of Maharashtra and Gujarat.

Since cotton industry is not a weight losing industry, it does not make much difference if either raw material or the finished product is transported.

Hence, the industry tends to be located at sites with favourable transport links with the market. The most notable feature of the distribution of cotton textiles industry is that even within a state, it tends to get localised within particular areas and regions, to the complete seclusion of others.

GEOGRAPHICAL DISTRIBUTION:

The major centres of cotton textiles production are given below state wise. It will be noticed that they are generally in cotton growing regions.

1. Andhra Pradesh: Dharmavaram, Venkatagiri, Anantapur, Secunderabad, Vijayawada, Guntur are important centres.
2. Maharashtra: With Mumbai as the focal point, the industry has spread to Sholapur, Kolhapur, Pune, Jalgaon, Akola, Sangli and Nagpur.
3. Gujarat: Besides Ahmedabad, other cotton textiles centres are Surat, Vadodara, Bharuch, Bhavnagar, Nadiad, Porbandar, Rajkot and Navsari.
4. Tamil Nadu: Coimbatore, Tirupur, (which has some of Asia's largest garment manufacturing units), Chennai, Tirunelvelli, Madurai, Tuticorin, Salem, Virudhnagar and Pollachi are the major cotton textile industry centres.
5. Karnataka: Bengaluru and its hinterland have attracted cotton textiles industry. Hassan, Harihar, Mangalore and Belgaum are other centres.
6. Uttar Pradesh: The state has the advantage of a large home market, cheap and efficient labour, excellent transportation facilities and of the homegrown raw material from Rajasthan, Haryana and Punjab. The major cotton textiles producing centres in Uttar Pradesh are Kanpur, Etawah, Modinagar, Moradabad, Bareiley, Hathras, Agra, Meerut and Varanasi.
7. Madhya Pradesh: Indore, Gwalior, Mandsaur, Dewas, Ujjain, Nagda, Bhopal, Jabalpur and Rajnandgaon.
8. Rajasthan: Kota, Jaipur, Sriganganagar, Bhilwada, Bhavanimandi, Udaipur and Kishengarh.
9. West Bengal: Kolkata, Howrah, Serampore, Shyamnagar, Murshidabad and Saikia.

The Indian cotton textiles industry has a complex three-tier structure:

1. Handspun and hand woven khadi sector,
2. Intermediate, labour intensive sector of handlooms and powerlooms,
3. Mill sector, which is large scale, capital intensive and sophisticated.

The bulk of the cotton cloth comes from handloom and powerloom sector. The cotton textiles industry in India is the single largest organised industry. It gives employment to a large number of workers and supports a number of ancillary industries. Partition had created problems for supply of raw material, because 22 per cent of the cotton growing area went to Pakistan. This deficit was gradually made up through imports and by expansion of area under long staple cotton.

One-third of the looms in the country are in the states of Tamil Nadu, Andhra Pradesh, Assam and Uttar Pradesh. Three-fourths of the looms produce cotton, while the rest produce silk, staple fibre, wool, composite fabric, artificial silk and synthetic fabrics.

Problems of Cotton Textiles Industry:

1. There is shortage of raw material, particularly of long staple cotton.
2. The industry faces constant threats of sickness and consequent closure, on account of (i) uncertainty of raw material, (ii) low productivity of machine and labour; (iii) increasing competition from power-loom sector; (iv) lack of modernisation; (v) management problems.
3. A majority of the spindles and looms are of the olden type. India has the lowest percentage in the world of automatic looms to total loomage.
4. There is a danger of loss of foreign markets due to (i) continued increase in cost of production, (ii) development of cotton textiles industry in other developing countries, (iii) protectionist policies abroad.
5. Inadequacy of power and machinery is another problem of the industry.

The increase in number of closed mills is indicative of a structural transformation in the textiles sector. The weaving mills in the organised sector are losing ground to the decentralised sector or the powerlooms, on account of greater cost-effectiveness of the latter.

WOOLLEN TEXTILES:

The first woollen textiles mill was set up in 1876 at Kanpur, because Kanpur was the principal depot for the British Indian Army. But the industry did not flourish because of a short winter and long summer in India leading to an inadequate demand. Also, the textiles produced were of poor quality. After independence, there was rapid development of the industry mainly as an export oriented industry.

The woollen textiles industry in India is partly a cottage industry and partly a factory industry.

The organised sector has three sub-sectors:

(i) Woollen (superior yarn for fabrics and hosiery);

(ii) Worsted (medium quality goods—blankets, tweeds, suitings, etc.);

(iii) Shoddy (for blankets).

Geographical Spread Most of the woollen textiles mills are situated in Punjab along the Amritsar-Gurdaspur-Ludhiana belt, and at Patiala and Dhariwal . The concentration in Punjab is due to its proximity to the high demand region in northern India in general and the hilly areas in particular.

Also, because Punjab is close to the sheep-rearing regions of Jammu and Kashmir (where the Bakerwals are associated with sheep-rearing) and Himachal Pradesh (where the Gaddis rear sheep). A statewise survey of other centres in the country is given below.

Uttar Pradesh: Kanpur, Agra, Mirzapur

Rajasthan: Jaipur, Jodhpur, Bikaner

Madhya Pradesh: Gwalior Gujarat Jamnagar, Ahmeda- bad, Vadodara

Maharashtra: Mumbai Karnataka Bengaluru Jammu and Kashmir The state is a large producer of handloom woollen goods (tweeds, carpets) and manufacturing is centred around Srinagar.

Problems of the Industry:

1. The size of the mills is small and productivity is low.
2. Nearly half the capacity remains idle for want of adequate raw-wool. Also, the wool is of poor quality.
3. Obsolete technology is still in use.
4. There is stiff competition from terrywool and synthetic yarn- wool mix items.

SILK TEXTILES:

Sericulture is a labour- intensive industry. It provides employment to nearly 55 lakh people, most of them being small and marginal farmers, or working in tiny and household industry mainly in the hand reeling and hand weaving sections. This sector of the Indian industry got great patronage during the medieval period. The famous 'Silk Route' passed through India, and Indian silk found markets worldwide. India is the second largest producer of natural silk, after China, and is the only country producing all varieties of natural silk. The demand for Indian silk dress materials and scarves comes from the USA. Europe, Kuwait, Saudi Arabia and Singapore.

However, the competition from Japan, China and Italy has resulted in shrinking markets, and the problem has been further compounded by introduction of artificial silk and synthetic fibres, which provide stiff competition, as they are cheaper and easy to maintain.

Geographical Spread Karnataka produces most of the silk in the country. Major silk producing centres in the state are Tumkur, Dodballapur, Bengaluru and Mysore . Other silk producing states and centres therein, are as follows.

Tamil Nadu: Dharmapuri, Salem, Coimba-tore, Tirunelveli

Andhra Pradesh: Karimnagar, Warangal, Mahbubnagar, Kurnool, Ongole, Adilabad

Maharashtra: Chandrapur

Chhattisgarh: Raigarh

Uttar Pradesh: Varanasi, Mirzapur

Bihar: Katihar, Bhagalpur Jharkhand Ranchi

West Bengal: Malda, Murshidabad, Bankura Assam Assam has received a geographical indication for the production of muga silk. Sualkuchi in the Kamrup district is considered the silk village of Assam. Dibrugarh, Sibsagar and Jorhat are other famous silk centres. Kashmir Silk weaving is an important industry in and around Srinagar. The Kashmiri silk is known for its fine texture.

SYNTHETIC TEXTILES:

Although weaving of synthetic fibres began around 1920, the first rayon plant was set up at Rayonpuram, Ernakulam, in Kerala. The raw materials used in manufacturing of synthetic textiles, include cellulose pulp which produces viscose Or acetate rayon yarns, and petrochemicals such as naphtha, caprolactum which produce nylon, polyester, terelene and acrylic yarns.

The handlooms and the powerlooms were the first to use synthetic yarn; weaving mills came later. Now, most of the synthetic fibre is produced by cotton weaving mills.

During the last four decades or so, the capacity and production of synthetic textiles industry has gone up by more than 100 times. With the growth of petrochemicals, more raw material is available and there is more scope for growth in production. Also, because of paucity of raw cotton, the mills are going in for blended materials. But, high prices of synthetic fibres are a problem.

Mumbai, Ahmedabad, Delhi, Surat, Kolkata, Amritsar and Gwalior are the centres of this industry.

JUTE TEXTILES:

The first modern jute mill was set up at Rishra near Kolkata in 1855. It was powerloomed in 1859 and included both spinning and weaving. After independence, this sector made rapid progress as an export-oriented industry. But a peculiar problem arose due to the partition of the country, 80 per cent of the jute growing areas went to East Pakistan (now Bangladesh), while all the mills remained in India. Imports from Bangladesh were not possible due to political reasons. This problem was overcome to a large extent by extending the area in India under jute and mesta.

The jute products include gunny bags, canvas, pack sheets, jute webs, hessians, carpets, cordage and twines. Now, jute is also being used, in one form or the other, in plastic furniture, insulation, bleached fibres to blend with wool, and is being mixed with cotton to make carpets and blankets.

The jute sector has been playing an important role in the economy of the country in general and the eastern region in particular. The socio-economic significance of the jute sector stems not merely from the contribution it makes to the national exchequer as earnings from exports and through taxes and levies, but also from the sizeable employment it provides in the agricultural and industrial sectors. Besides, providing a livelihood' to millions of farmers, most of them small and marginal, and employment to some 2 lakh workers, the jute sector also provides indirect employment to a considerable number of people. India tops in production of raw jute and jute goods and second in export of jute goods.

Geographical Location:

Nearly 90 per cent of the manufacturing capacity is located in a narrow belt about 100 km long and 3 km wide along river Hooghly . This concentration in the Hooghly region is because of the following reasons.

(i) Soil and agronomic conditions suit jute cultivation here.

(ii) The East India Company's initial efforts in and around Kolkata were of great advantage for the industry.

(iii) This belt is well connected through waterways and rail with the jute growing areas.

(iv) There is ample availability of water for jute processing.

(v) There is close proximity to coal producing areas of Bihar and Orissa. Also, power is readily available from the Damodar Valley Corporation.

(vi) The presence of the port and a humid climate favoured the industry. Import of machinery and export of finished products were easy.

(vii) Capital and financial services were easily available.

(viii) Ready market in the vicinity promoted sales.

(ix) Cheap labour was easily available.

In the recent past, there has been a slight dispersal of the industry to Uttar Pradesh and Andhra Pradesh because of the increasing demand for gunny bags in Uttar Pradesh and Bihar, due to rapid development of sugar and cement industry, and because of availability of local fibres like mesta and Bimlipatlan jute.

Problems of the Industry:

1. The industry is facing stiff competition from modern packing material from the West, bulk handling capacities developed in the West, and development of jute substitutes like sisal (East Africa), caroa (Brazil), linseed fibre (Russia and Argentina) and the Manila hemp.
2. Newly established factories and improved machines in Bangladesh are posing a tough competition.
3. There is shortage of raw material. To overcome this problem, acreage is being expanded in Uttar Pradesh, Madhya Pradesh and Kerala. New hybrid varieties like JRO-632, JRO-753 are being grown.
4. Obsolete machinery, shortage of power and industrial sickness affect production.

Thus, what is required is modernisation and diversification of production, reduction of costs and introduction of new products.

SUGAR INDUSTRY:

Sugar production is known in India since ancient times, but modern sugar industry in the country developed in first decade of the twentieth century. Indian sugar industry is the second largest agro- based industry in India.

The basic raw material is sugarcane, which has some specific qualities:

(i) It is a weight losing raw material;

(ii) It cannot be stored for long, because in that case, it loses the sucrose content;

(iii) It cannot be transported over long distances, because that results in higher production costs and in drying up of sugarcane.

Because of these considerations, the sugar factories tend to be located near the sugarcane cultivation area. And since the harvesting is done in a particular season, the crushing is confined to a limited period, and the sugar factories keep lying idle for the rest of the period. This restricts sugar production.

Geographical Distribution:

Uttar Pradesh, Maharashtra and Tamil Nadu account for about 70 per cent of the total production of sugar in the country. A survey of sugar producing centres in India is given below.

Uttar Pradesh: There are two belts—one in western Uttar Pradesh and the other in eastern Uttar Pradesh. The western belt includes Meerut, Saharanpur, Muzaffarnagar, Bijnor and Moradabad, and the eastern belt includes Gorakhpur, Deoria, Basti and Gonda.

Bihar: There is an extension of the eastern Uttar Pradesh belt, which includes Darbhanga, Saran, Champaran and Muzaffarpur.

The reasons for concentration of sugar industry in Uttar Pradesh and Bihar are—

(i) Fertile alluvial soil, rich in lime and potash;

(ii) Level topography—suitable for irrigation;

(iii) Abundant water for washing and processing;

(iv) Sugar industry is relatively independent of coal and electricity, because bagasse is enough to run steam;

(v) Densely populated market in the surrounding regions, coupled with excellent transport links;

(vi) Availability of cheap labour;

(vii) Cultivation is done in compact blocks, which ensures ready availability of fresh cane to factories.

Maharashtra: Nasik, Pune, Satara, Sangli, Kolhapur, Sholapur are the centres well integrated in the cooperative sector in terms of cultivation ^ and sugar factories. Punjab: Centres exist mainly in the eastern side, in Phagwara, Dhuri.

Karnataka: Munirabad, Shimoga and Mandya are the main centres here.

Tamil Nadu: In this state Nalikupuram, Pugulur, Coimbatore and Pandyarajpuram are famous for producing sugar.

Andhra Pradesh: Nizamabad, Medak, west and east Godavari, Visakhapatnam and Chittoor produce sugar.

West Godavari, East Godavari, Vishakhapatnam, Bargarh, Rayagada, ,Shimoga, Mandya Chittoor, Nalikupuram, Pugulur, Coimbatore, Pandyarajpuram .

Orissa: Bargarh and Rayagada in Orissa produce sugar.

Madhya Pradesh: Sihor is the sugar-producing centre here.

Differences in Sugar Production in North India and Peninsular India:

1. Yields are higher in south India.
2. The southern sugarcane, being of the tropical variety, has more sucrose content.
3. The crushing season is longer in the south, where it lasts from October to May-June. In the north, it lasts from November to February.

In spite of the tropical climate, good irrigation and transportation facilities, there is not overall comparable growth in the peninsula, because (i) other cash crops are more lucrative, which include cotton, groundnut, tobacco, coconut etc.; (ii) cost of production is higher in Maharashtra, because of high irrigation rates and costly manuring practices; (iii) the peninsular sugarcane is not grown in compact blocks, as in Uttar Pradesh and Bihar.

Problems of Sugar Industry:

1. There is a paucity of good quality sugarcane—the Indian sugarcane has low sucrose content and gives poor yields.
2. The high costs of production are due to (i) uneconomic nature of production; (ii) short crushing season; (iii) heavy excise duties; (iv) manipulation of stocks and hoarding, etc.
3. Small, uneconomic units with obsolete technology are still functioning.

VEGETABLE OIL INDUSTRY:

Vegetable oil is a major source of fat in Indian diet and a widely used cooking medium. Vanaspati' is hydrogenated vegetable oil. Different regions use different raw materials for oil, depending on the technology used.

There are mainly three types of technologies used:

(i) Ghani: This is used mainly in the rural areas and uses local materials like coconut (in Kerala), groundnut (in Gujarat) and mustard (in Uttar Pradesh, Punjab, Rajasthan).

(ii) Intermediate: Technology This is used by the factories located in towns, and uses region- specific raw materials.

(iii) Sophisticated Technology: This is used by units located in large towns. The acquisition of raw materials is from a larger area and the units cater to a larger market.

The vegetable oil industry is widely scattered and the sizes of the units differ from location to location. Maharashtra has the largest number of vanaspati units, followed by Gujarat, Uttar Pradesh, West Bengal, Karnataka, Tamil Nadu, Andhra Pradesh, Madhya Pradesh, Rajasthan and Punjab.

New emerging raw materials for edible oil include sunflower, safflower, soyabean, cottonseed, rice bran, etc.

TEA INDUSTRY:

Tea cultivation in India first started in the mid- 19th century in Darjeeling, Assam and the Nilgiris. Nearly 98 per cent of the tea production comes from Assam, West Bengal, Tamil Nadu, Kerala and Karnataka. Some tea is also grown in Himachal Pradesh, Arunachal Pradesh, Manipur and Tripura.

The tea estates are generally set upon cleared hill slopes, while in Assam, tea cultivation is done in the lowlands, above the flood level. The production of tea has more than doubled since independence mainly through increase in yield by improved varieties and optimum use of inputs.

The tea industry provides direct gainful employment to more than one million workers mainly drawn from the backward and socially weaker sections of the society. It is also a substantial foreign exchange earner and provides significant contribution to the state and central exchequer. Tea plantations in India are mainly located in rural, hill and backward areas of north-eastern and southern states.

COFFEE INDUSTRY:

Coffee was first grown in Bababudan Hills in Karnataka during the 17th century, but on a plantation scale, it was cultivated in Chikmaglur (Karnataka) in 1826. Later, coffee cultivation was extended to Wynad, Shevaroy and the Nilgiris.

Among the plantation crops, coffee has made significant contribution to the Indian economy in the last few decades. Although India contributes only a small percentage of the world production, Indian coffee has created a niche for itself in the international market, particularly Indian robustas, which are highly preferred for their good blending quality. Arabica coffee from India is also well received in the international market.

More than half of the country's coffee production comes from Karnataka, of which 80 per cent comes from Coorg and Chikmagalur. Hasan is the third largest producer in the state. In Kerala, coffee is produced in Wynad (Palghat region), Kozhikode and Cannanore. In Tamil Nadu, coffee comes from the Nilgiris, Annamalai (Coimbatore region) Shevaroy hills (Salem district), Palani hills, Tirunelveli and Madurai. Small quantities come from Orissa, Andhra Pradesh and the north-eastern states.

LEATHER GOODS INDUSTRY:

The importance of this sector lies in wide dispersal, vast employment and export potential. Hides and skins are the basic raw materials which come from pelts of cattle and large animals and small ones like goat and sheep. India has a large livestock population.

West Bengal and Tamil Nadu are the largest producers of cattle hides and Uttar Pradesh and West Bengal of the goat skin. Rajasthan and Madhya Pradesh also produce substantial quality hides. Major footwear production centres in the country include Kanpur, Agra, Lucknow, Kolkata, Chennai, Mumbai, Bengaluru and Jaipur.

Leather is a highly labour-oriented industry in India, and has been identified as one of the major thrust areas for export. It is one of the traditional industries of India spread over organised and unorganised sector. The small-scale, cottage and artisan sector account for over 75 per cent of the total leather production. India has traditionally a rich advantage in this industry both in terms of raw material and skilled manpower. People employed in this sector are predominantly from the minorities and disadvantaged sections of the society.

The leather industry has made significant strides during the 1990s and early twentieth century.

2

Forests, Source of Life for the Forest-Based Industries

INTRODUCTION

Timber industry in India was initially confined to produce building materials, agriculture implements, bullock carts, and railway sleepers. Forest based industries were encouraged because of its rural identity and its ability to solve the problem of unemployment and poverty. In addition, the policy makers had also perceived that natural resource based industrial development is a pre-requisite for the economic development of less developed countries like India. Hence, the Government, both at the Centre and State encouraged establishment of small, medium, and large-scale forest based industries in the region. Due to this policy, the country witnessed heavy pressure of industries on forests for raw material purpose.

This paper attempts to fill this void by exploring some important issues relating to growth of forest industries and their reliant on forests for survival. The major objective of the present study is to analyse and understand the relative dependency of different forest based industries on forests and their survival strategies in the context of shrinking forest cover and non-availability of timber. Shimoga and Uttar Kannada (hereafter referred to as UK) districts of the Western Ghats of Karnataka was selected for the present study.

MATERIALS AND METHODS

The study was based on both primary and secondary data. The secondary data pertaining to forest dependence, intake, and outturn of logs and timber supply to local industry and other related data were collected from forest department, statistical bureau, and the Karnataka Industrial Development Corporation. In order to assess the extent of industrial dependency on forests, primary data was collected from two types of respondents. The respondents who directly depend on forests for their survival, such as the small scale industries form first category and the higher officials from medium and large scale forest based industries represent as second category of respondents.

Stratified sampling technique was adopted to select small-scale industries and census method was used to collect data from medium - and large-scale industries. All the registered small enterprises in the District Industrial Centre (DIC) were considered for selection. 10 per cent (124) of the total units registered at the DIC was selected for the present study. Using the census method two large and one medium scale selected industries. A well framed and pre-tested interview schedule was used to collect the primary data from the sample respondents. The fieldwork was carried out during the year 1993 and the secondary data was collected for a period of two decades, 1973-74 to 1991-92. The collected data was analysed with the help of simple statistical tools such as ratio's, growth rate - linear and compound, and co-efficient of variation.

RESULTS AND DISCUSSION

Forests have always played a significant role in shaping the life of mankind and the economy. Perhaps, forests have contributed much to man's comfort and enjoyment as well as to his economic development down to ages. They provide wood and other products to meet the domestic and industrial requirements of men. Forests also serve as a source of life for forest industries.

TRENDS IN FOREST UTILISATION AT MACRO LEVEL

Forest covers about 19 per cent of the total geographical area of India. The area under forests has come down from 640134 Sq.kms to 639182 Sq.kms. between 1988-89 to 1989 -90. On an average, the country is loosing about 47600 hectares of forest area per year.

The loss was due to deforestation for industrial and firewood purpose and diversion of forestland for non-forestry purpose.

As against the loss of forest cover at the all India levels, the area under forests have shown an increasing trend in the study area. On an average 10536 hectares of forest area was being afforested every year in Karnataka. The increase was owing to regeneration and conservation measures adopted by the State, transfer of non-wooded district forests, and 'C and D' class revenue wastelands from the revenue department to forest department for afforestation purpose.

TRENDS IN OUTTURN OF FOREST PRODUCE IN KARNATAKA

Table 1 explains an overview of outturn of forest produce in the State as well as in select districts. A cursory view of the table reveals a downward trend in the production of major and minor forest produce in the State as well as in the select districts. The extraction of major forest produce had declined from

1320829 cu.m to 339832 cu.m in 18 years period in the select districts. Similarly, the extraction of minor forest produce also declined from 57065 tonnes to 5847 tonnes between 1973-74 and 1990-91. The trend remains same for the State as well. The decline in the production of forest produce was owing to strict enforcement of forest policy, namely less exploitation and sustainable management of forest resources.

Among the forest produce, the extraction of firewood was found to be higher. It is due to higher dependency of people on forests for firewood purpose. Bamboo shares a majority in the minor forest produce because it is used as raw material in paper industry and cottage industry such as basket weaving. Since bamboo produces quality pulp, the paper mills located in this region have consumed more bamboo than any other softwood. Furthermore, subsidised rate of supply of bamboo is also a reason for higher outturn. A noteworthy aspect of the above table is that the industries located in the study area had extracted more than 50 per cent of major and 30 per cent of minor forest produce from the select districts alone. Thus, forest is an instrument for growth of industries in the districts.

Table. Trends in Outturn of Forest Produce

Year	Major Forest Produce			minor forest produce			
	Timber	F.W	Total	Bam.	Cane	Other	Total
Out-turn of forest produce in the State							
1973-74	1069067	1481970	2551037	385295	701	10521	396517
1977-78	1472260	1323802	2796012	143745	569	23948	168262
1981-82	636809	677889	1314698	170737	1093	13871	185701
1985-86	452622	499029	951651	68815	1528	11565	81908
1990-91	148232	358885	507073	47316	2500	12499	62315
Out-turn of forest produce in the Select Districts							
1973-74	52204	798788	1320829	55542	120	1403	57065
1977-78	549992	690628	1240620	54962	396	2209	57567
1981-82	241436	335566	577002	98559	474	2149	101182
1985-86	151390	474445	625835	28985	319	1366	30670
1990-91	96653	243179	339832	5296	252	299	5847

TRENDS IN INDUSTRIAL REMOVAL OF FOREST PRODUCE

It is found from the Table 2 that industrial removal has shown a negative growth rate. Among the forest produce, the extraction of softwood was found to be more homogenous than the removal of other forest produce by the forest based industries in the State. The higher extraction of softwood and bamboo was due to the existence of two paper mills in the districts.

Within the two paper mills, the private owned West Coast Paper Mill (WCPM) has extracted more softwood (107106 tonnes) and bamboo (640363 tonnes) than the Government managed Mysore Paper Mill (MPM), which has extracted 68759 tonnes of Eucalyptus and 202036 tonnes of bamboo during the study period.

Table. Industrial Removal of Forest Produce

Year	Industrial Removal in the State			Industrial Removal in the select districts		
	Timber	Bamboo	other Softwood	Timber	Bamboo	Other Softwood
1982-83	187599	243649	109260	80846 (43)	71095 (29)	44136 (40)
1984-85	56177	77476	84097	41765 (74)	32110 (41)	28949 (34)
1986-87	71750	59421	34950	52569 (73)	28372 (48)	18479 (53)
1987-88	86096	67772	40425	43407 (50)	34862 (51)	13502 (33)
1988-89	9468	35244	58806	6992 (74)	20341 (58)	32816 (56)

Notes: (i) Eucalyptus is included in other softwood (ii) Figures in Parentheses indicate per cent share of industrial removal in the select districts to State

The industries located in select districts have removed 63 per cent of timber, 45 per cent of bamboo, and 43 per cent of softwood to the total removal of forest produce in the State during the study period.

The higher quantity of removal of forest produce in the districts was due to the location of a large number of wood based industries in the districts. Hence, forest act as a source of life for large number of traditional as will as modern forest based industries.

FORESTS, SOURCE OF LIFE FOR THE FOREST BASED LARGE AND MEDIUM SCALE INDUSTRIES

Forest serves as a source of livelihood for the large and medium scale industries located in the study area. Several industries were operating in the study region. However, few forest-based industries have got the privilege to extract forest products on their own.

The Indian Plywood Manufacturing, MPM, Western Indian Match Company, Harihar Polifibres, WCPM, and Karnataka State Veneers are a few worth mentioning. Taking advantage of this Policy decision, many private industrialist have got long-term agreement with the forest department and started to exploit the forests in a haphazard manner.

Although the raw material received from forest department was considered to be permanent, the supply is declining year after year. Industries located in the select districts have received 16 per cent of timber in 1982-83, which has been reduced to 4 per cent in 1988-89. Similarly, the supply of bamboo to industries also declined from 31 per cent in 1986-87 to 25 per cent in 1988-89 . The trend remains same for the State as well. The forest department supply of bamboo is found to be more homogenous than the supply of any other raw material. The department supply of other raw material shows a negative growth rate.

Table. Forests, Source of Life for Large and Medium Scale Industries

(Timber in cu.m and Bamboo in tonnes)

Year	Total Removal in the State		Industrial Removal in the State		Industrial Removal in the select Districts	
	Timber	Bamboo	Timber	Bamboo	Timber	Bamboo
1982-83	502883	371492	187599 (37)	243649 (66)	80846 (16)	71095 (19)
1984-85	477234	163715	56177 (12)	77476 (47)	41765 (9)	32110 (20)
1986-87	488935	92370	71750 (15)	59421 (64)	52569 (11)	28372 (31)
1987-88	395399	108253	86096 (22)	67772 (63)	43407 (11)	34862 (32)
1988-89	189126	81924	9468 (5)	35244 (43)	6992 (4)	20341 (25)

Note: Figures in Parentheses indicate per cent share of forest industries dependency on State forests.

As forest department has reduced its supply, the forest based medium and large-scale industries are depending on private source for their raw material requirement.

In addition, industries are meeting their raw material requirements through industrial captive plantation and also by importing it from other States and other countries.

The industries have also substituted bagasse, pine trees, eucalyptus and acacia for bamboo. Nonetheless, the forest is a sole dependable source of raw material, required by industries and also the only major level player for the survival of large and medium scale industries in the study area.

DEPENDENCY OF SMALL SCALE INDUSTRIES ON FOREST PRODUCTS

The small-scale industries in the study area consume teak, rosewood, sandalwood, bamboo, cane and other jungle woods for their survival. These raw materials can be broadly grouped as major and minor forest produce. The small-scale industries like Wood Timber Sawing and Furniture and Cart Manufacturing require major forest produce. On the other hand, the Bamboo and Cane Manufacturing and sandalwood Carving enterprises require minor forest produce.

Based on the survey, the 124 sample industries were grouped under six sub-groups, namely Wood and Timber Sawing (WTS), Wooden Furniture (WFU), Cart Manufacturing (CMG), Rose and sandalwood Caring (RSC), Miscellaneous Wood Industries (MWI), and Bamboo and Cane Manufacturing

(BCM).

FORESTS, SOURCE OF LIFE FOR THE SMALL SCALE INDUSTRIES

The small-scale industries purchased wood and timber from two main sources, namely from the forest department or Government and from private parties. Almost all our respondents have purchased wood and timber from the forest department. About 54 per cent of major forest produce and 67 per cent of minor forest produce were exclusively supplied by the forest department to the small-scale industries. Table 4 further explains the role of different agencies in supplying wood, timber, bamboo, and cane to the small-scale industries. Among the sources, the smuggles have also supplied all kinds of forest produce except sandalwood.

The small-scale industries depend on this source to the extent of 16 per cent for minor forest produce and six per cent for major forest produce. Although the quantity supplied by bootleggers is less when compared to other sources, their role may become intensified in case of heavy demand for forest products by the small-scale industries in future.

Table. Forests, Source of Life for the Small Scale Industries

(Wood and Timber in cu.m; Sandal wood in Kg; Bamboo and Cane in no.)

Source	Major Forest Produce				minor forest produce			
	Teak	Rose	JungleWood	Total MFP	Sandalwood	Bamboo	Cane	Total mfp
Government	425(44)	719(72)	4360(52)	5504(54)	2630(100)	8150(57)	99850(68)	108000(67)
Malki Holders	215(22)	146(15)	1630(20)	1991(19)	-	-	22000(15)	22000(14)
Farmers	50 (5)	-	1589 (19)	1639(16)	-	5100 (36)	-	5100(3)
Saw Mills	195(20)	84(8)	278(3)	557(5)	-	-	-	-
Smugglers	89(9)	46(5)	458(6)	593(6)	-	1080(7)	25950(17)	27030(16)
Total	974(100)	995(100)	8375(100)	10284(100)	2630(100)	14330(100)	147800 (100)	162130 (100)

The Government or the forest department was the only authorized dealer for extraction and supply of sandalwood. Therefore, no middlemen were found here, however, the bootleggers play substantial representation in supplying other forest produce to small-scale industries.

Particularly, the CMU industry is completely depend on smugglers for hard and softwood. Nonetheless, the forest is the main source of supply of rose wood in the Western Ghats. Since rose wood is a national property, the forest department alone can extract it from forests and supply the same to the small-scale industries, especially RSC. The table clearly explains the role of forests for continuous survival of small-scale forest industries. Almost 60 per cent of small and cottage entrepreneurs have depended on forest department for its sustained raw material supply.

IMPACT OF WOOD SHORTAGE ON FOREST BASED INDUSTRY

Almost all small-scale industries have informed to the researcher that they face shortage of wood and many have lost their occupation. They are slowly migrating to some other occupation. The deforestation coupled with shortage of wood had severely affected the small scale industries, particularly CMG and RSC industry.

It was also found that deforestation and non-availability of forest produce was mainly responsible for the closure of many traditional industries like Ayurvedic and woodcraft industries. As far as medium and large-scale industries are concerned, they try to fulfill the wood requirement either through their own captive plantation or through private supply, sometime by importing wood from foreign countries. As an alternative, the wood based large scale industries have already started to replace a few raw materials like bamboo by other substances, such as bagasse pulp from sugar industry, unfamiliar soft wood such as acacia, pine and eucalyptus. Since the supply of wood and timber is scarce, the small scale industries have started to combine synthetic nylon wires, plywood, sunmica, and steel along with wood, timber, bamboo, and cane products.

Conclusion

Forests no doubt serve as a source of life for the forest based small, medium, and large-scale industries in the Western Ghats of Karnataka, India. However, due to the shrinking forest area the industries are facing wood famine since 1985-86.

Interestingly, they have tried to meet the demand on their own through industrial captive plantation. Nonetheless, long term plan is needed such as planting trees on wasteland, encouraging farmers to grow trees on farm lands, mixed captive plantation, and optimum utilisation of wood resources seem to be an immediate and wise solution for solving the present problem and for sustained life of all forest based industries in the study area. To conclude, the Government should supply raw materials for the survival of small-scale industries than the medium and large-scale industries. Because the small scale industries play a pivotal role in creating employment, reducing regional disparities, increasing avenues to use locally available resources, and their eco-friendly nature.

FOREST BASED INDUSTRIES

Timber production:

- No green or commercial felling is being carried out in the State in areas which are more than 1000 metres above msl.
- Only uprooted, wind-fallen, dry, dead, dying, diseased trees are removed.

- First preference is given to meet the demand of local people through their recorded rights, concessions and petty demands.
- Timber in excess of such demands is extracted through Uttarakhand Forest Development Corporation (UAFDC)

Plantation:

To bring uniformity in plantation activities, Plantation Policy has been formulated and issued in 2005. Main features of the Policy are as under:

- 'Land Banks are to be formed at the district level as per the classification of All India Soil and Land Use Survey.
- Site Specific Planning (SSP) is to be done for all plantation sites.
- Involvement of Public, Government Departments, NGOs, villages, Van Panchayats, private institutions etc. in plantation activity, particularly in after-care of the plantations
- Village and Van Panchayat land is also to be taken up
- Agro-forestry to be re-activated by planting more of the plants giving Non Timber Forest Produce, medicinal, aromatic substances etc.
- Green belts will be developed in the cities with the help of the local bodies/local residents
- Soil binding and conserving species will be planted along the banks of rivers and rivulets.
- Monitoring and evaluation will be conducted through departmental as well as external agencies with a fixed time frame to develop and maintain quality plantations
- A Plantation Manual will be prepared and made available to all agencies carrying out plantations.

Resin Production:

Resin tapping is one of the more important activities of the Forest Department as Uttarakhand has substantial area under Chir pine which exudes resin. Resin extraction not only earns revenue for the State, it also provides employment to a large number of people in the hills. Some facts about resin production are listed below.

To ensure transparency in allotment of resin to different agencies, resin policy has been formulated and issued on 30 April 2003. Main features of the policy are :

- 25% of the resin will be sold by open auction on all India basis..
- 50% will be sold by open auction to units registered in Uttarakhand according to their processing capacity.
- Balance 25% will be sold by open auction amongst the units of Khadi-Gramodyog, Co-operatives, Kumaon Mandal Vikas Nigam and Garhwal Mandal Vikas Nigam according to their processing capacity.
- If some quantity of resin is left unsold as per the above arrangements it will also be sold by all India open auction.

- Resin production has increased from 15.8 million Kgs in 2002-03 to 19.3 million Kgs in 2007-08.

CIRCLEWISE DISTRIBUTION OF FOREST BASED INDUSTRIES

Uttarakhand Forest multiplicity state which has total forest area of 65 percent of total geographical area which consists of Cedar, Kyle, fur Sprus, Suri, oak, pine, sal, teak, well, rosewood, Eucalyptus, Poplar, Bamboo forests. While laying emphasis on protection of the environment,with the help of scientific research crores of revenue is generated from forests. On other hand the general public from various forest based industries receive direct and indirect employment.

Most of Eucalyptus paper mill is used in paper making. Currently the Century Paper Mill situated in Uttarakhand and Star Paper Mill in Uttar Pradesh are using largest quantity of it. Plywood industries and fuel is also used in it.

Circlewise distribution of forest based industries is as following :-

SNo	Circle	No. Of Sawmill	Plywood/ वेनियर इकाईयां	Working	Not working currently
1	North Kumaun	26	-	48	56
2	South Kumaun	3	-	10	2
3	Western kumaun	132	26	31	1
4	Garhwal	8	-	4	-
5	Bhagirathi	12	-	15	-
6	Yamuna	27	-	-	-
7	Shivalik	174	7	-	-
8	NDBR	2	-	-	1
9	Rajaji National Park	-	-	-	-
	Total	**384**	**33**	**108**	**60**

EXTRACTION OF MINOR MINERALS

Perennial rivers, rivulets and rivers originates from mountains in Uttarakhand and enters various places in plain regions. Because these rivers are due to seasonal rainfall therefore a lot of debris (due to heavy landslide) in form of gravel, sand and stone drains down through mountains.

Revenue generated since 2002-03 is as following:-

Year	Volume (in lakh m^3)		
	Sand	Bazri	Boulder
2002-03	15.38	7.97	19.55
2003-04	15.71	5.94	21.28
2004-05	16.58	10.12	27.36
2005-06	18.14	13.43	52.27
2006-07	14.83	6.41	68.48
2007-08	15.84	5.13	71.59
2008-09	14.86	3.67	74.50
2009-10	10.55	1.44	60.17
2010-11	10.33	1.14	65.37

The debris is used in industries for various industrial use such as the construction industry, glass industry, for road construction, water treatment and for park path. these cause excessive demand of the debris.

Collection and marketing of minor minerals (sand, boulder and Bazari) from the river beds of reserved forest areas has been undertaken (Indian Forest Conservation Act, 1980) in order to protect the forest lands, agricultural crops, inhabitations from the havoc of floods. The collection and marketing system is being converted from volume base to weight basis for the disposal of minor minerals, in the Gaula, Sharda, Nandhaur, Kosi, Dabka, Ganga, Yamuna and Song rivers of the State.

ROYALTY OBTAINED FROM FOREST DEVELOPMENT CORPORATION

Removal of dead, dying, uprooted trees along with harvesting of the industrial plantations of Poplar and Eucalyptus in the State. These operations are carried out by the trained and experienced personnel with technically sound methodology suiting to the conservation of environment and ecology.

PINE RESIN EXTRACTION

The pine resin is an important non-timber forest produce from Pine forests of Uttarakhand. Viroja and turpentine oil is made from pine resin which is used in production of soaps, paper and paint etc. Pine resin in Uttarakhand is a key means of self-employment and the rural economy and currently employs 173 pine based industries (According to year 2010 – 2011 census) out of which 90 pine resin units are working and remaining 83 are non-working. Lisa extraction was started on experimental basis in 1890 and by the year 1920 it was made aregular practice. "Fanc cup and lip" method has been used for pine resin extraction till 1993

FOREST BASED INDUSTRIES

Agroforestry is a potential approach to minimize unsustainable withdrawals from forests and instead promote production of fuelwood, fodder and timber in conjunction with agricultural crops on non-forests land. Highly adopted trees species have been identified for each agro ecozone to encourage high productivity and diversify the products for use. Agroforestry is to be promoted on wood catchment basis to support a large number of wood/pulp based industries. Following are the major agroforestry systems, which are economically beneficial.

SOME IMPORTANT AGROFORESTRY SYSTEM

The poplar based agroforestry system as proved more profitable over the most intensive cropping systems of rice-wheat in the northern region. Poplars are an excellent source of fibres for various grades of paper, fine paper, and packing papers and newsprint paper. Poplar wood is used for making match splints, plywood, sports goods, toy, pencil-making, packing cases and crate-making. Teak is one of the most popular and highly valued timber trees. Attracted by the economic advantages of teak culture, many private companies in India had ventured into establishing commercial plantations of teak. Teak tree is graded in India as first, second, third, fourth and fifth quality as per the girth and height attained at maturity (50-60 years). The market price of timber reduces progressively from the bottom to the top end of the tree. The crown and branch wood of trees is sold at about Rs. 1,000 per m^3 as fuel wood. The average price of the timber obtained for the entire tree can, therefore, be only about 20% of the highest price obtained, for the best quality of timber.

Bamboo extensively traded throughout the country a good quality bamboo of about 6-meter length and 18 cm girth sales for about Rs.30. In the northeastern states bamboo's are abundant commercial uses of bamboo are Bamboo parquet (Block Flooring), laminated bamboo, bamboo reinforced concrete, artificially shape bamboo viz. handicrafts, decoration items and cottage industries, and medicine. Also bamboo charcoal in electric batteries. It is used in deodorizing fish oil in Asian Countries.

Sandalwood yields maximum heartwood with a good amount of sandal wood oil. The sandal wood oil is in great demand all over the world for its use in perfumery products. Sandalwood is also in demand for use in perfumery products. Sandalwood is also in demand for use in wood carvings. Sandalwood fetches a very high price, 1 kg of sandalwood fetches an astronomical price of Rs. 1000 in the market. Apart from these agroforestry system the most important multipurpose trees are viz. *Populus deltoides, Acacia spp., Dalbergia spp., Morus alba, Anthocephalus cadamba, Casuarina equisetifolia, Prosopis spp., Bamboos, Grevillea robusta, Leucaena leucocephala* etc.

Trees in agroforestry systems are used for making agricultural implements, furniture, bark yields gum/tannin, softwood, mats, and thatches, turpentine and for oil purpose. The tree species in agroforestry can be used for sericulture and apiculture also. Thus tree species in agroforestry systems are useful for many forest-based industries.

3

The Impact Of Agriculture and Agro-Based Industries on Economic Development

The role of agriculture and agro-based industries in Nigeria cannot be over emphasized. Agriculture is a source of food for consumption by man, foods for animals and raw material for the agro-based industries. Agriculture contributes to the growth of the economy and also provides employment opportunities for the teaming population and eradicates poverty in the economy. An articulated agricultural revolution and increased value addition activities in the downstream agro-processing sub-sector present a potential platform for effective wealth generation and consequently, sustainable poverty eradication.

Ukeje (2003) put it that before and immediately after independence in 1960, agriculture contributed up to 64% to the total GDP, but during the 1970s, the contribution of agriculture to the GDP decline to 48%. The decline continued in 1980 to 20% and 19% in 1985. The uncertainty associated with the oil glut of the 1980s, which has great negative impact on the Nigerian economy, resulted in increased Federal and State government attention toward the development of agriculture. However, during the 1990s, the contribution of agriculture to the GDP increased due to the shift of emphasis to agricultural development.

This study attempts to examine the impact of agriculture and the agro-based industries on the development of the Nigerian economy for the period 1985 to 2005.

THEORETICAL ISSUES

The physiocrats laid more emphasis on agriculture in the development of an economy. In their views, the development of an economy depends on the growth of the agricultural sector. The source of national wealth is essentially agriculture. The physiocrats believe that the fate of the economy is regulated by productivity in agriculture and its surplus is diffused throughout the system in a network of transactions. The agricultural sector to the physiocrats is the only genuinely productive sector of the economy and the generator of surplus upon which all depends. Todaro and Smith (2003), while looking at Lewis theory of development, assume that the underdeveloped economies consists of two sectors. These sectors are the traditional agricultural sector characterized by zero marginal labour productivity and the modern industrial sector. The primary focus of the model is the labour transfer and the growth of output and employment in the modern sector. Tombofa (2004), states that the state of agriculture is of paramount importance to the development process. He pointed out that agriculture provides the basis for the world's great civilization in the past and the increase in agricultural productivity in England laid the basis for, and sustained the first industrial revolution. The agricultural sector is known to employ over 75 percent of the labour force in developing countries and provide the purchasing power over industrial goods. Rostow (1960) as cited in Tamuno (1996), argued that in the process of economic development, nations pass through several stages namely; traditional stage, the precondition for take off, the take off stage, drive to maturity and the high mass consumption stage. Agriculture played crucial roles in the first three stages.

Again, Todaro and Smith (2003) put it that if development is to take place and become self-sustaining, it will have to include the rural area in general and the agricultural sector in particular. "Traditionally, the role of agriculture in economic development has been as passive and supportive". Based on the historical experience of Western countries economic development was seen as requiring a rapid structural transformation of the economy focused on agricultural activities to a more complex modern industrial and services society. As a result, agriculture's primary role is to provide food and manpower to the expanding industrial economy.

AGRICULTURE AND ECONOMIC DEVELOPMENT

THE NATIONAL ACCELERATED FOOD PRODUCTION PROGRAMME (NAFPP)

This programme was established in 1973 with the aim of distributing to those who involve themselves in packaging information and raw materials in order to improve the production of wheat, sorghum, millet, rice, maize and cassava.

THE NIGERIAN AGRICULTURE AND CO-OPERATIVE BANK (NACB)

The establishment of this bank owes to the fact that the agricultural sector lacked finance. The bank is charged with the responsibility of disbursing loans to agricultural projects. As a programme the bank faced some problems such as;

(a Inadequate financial resources to meet with agriculture loan demand,

(b non-fulfillment of security or collateral requirements necessitated bad debt, which could not be recovered at the time of maturity,

(c) lack of disposition of the bank to modern loan appraisal techniques which resulted in poor loan management,
(d) diversion of fund by the bank for non-agricultural purposes, and
(e) late disbursement of agricultural loan arising from bureaucratic impediment.

OPERATION FEED THE NATION (OFN)

This programme was established in 1976 which was aimed at self-sufficiency in food and to ensure that the objective was realized. Some of the products of this programme include; subsidized supplies of fertilizers, seeds, insecticides and pesticides.

Every one was encouraged by this programme to cultivate their back gardens intensively and to keep chickens, whose eggs and meat would provide an important source of protein and whose dropping could be used as fertilizer. However, the success of this programme was limited because about two-third of the entire funds were spent on student wages, living little for farmers. The programme also collapsed because of timing related inadequacies.

AGRICULTURAL CREDIT GUARANTEE SCHEME FUND (ACGSF)

In 1979 the ACGSF was established by the Federal Government of Nigeria as an inducement to commercial and merchant banks to increase credit purveyance on their part to actively engage in agricultural lending. The Fund was under the management of the Agricultural Credit Scheme Fund Board with the CBN acting as managing agent for its day-to-day administration. It is worthy to note that though ACGSF had limitations, its operation improved significantly in 1994.

THE RIVER BASIN DEVELOPMENT AUTHORITIES (RBDA)

The RBDA were also established in 1978. The authorities were established to provide all year round water through irrigation to farmers. This period also witnessed the establishment of various other programmes such as the Grain Boards and the World Bank Assisted Agricultural Development Projects (ADP).

THE GREEN REVOLUTION (GR)

This programme was established at the wake of the third republic after the Operation Feed the Nation (OFN) in 1983. This programme was managed by the National Council for the Green Revolution. It was operated on green revolution principles that is, the use of high yielding varieties of seed, high inputs of fertilizers, irrigation, etc.

NATIONAL AGRICULTURAL LAND DEVELOPMENT AUTHORITY (NALDA)

NALDA was established in 1990 for the purpose of making land available to those interested in farming. The Authority was intended to reduce the prevalence of subsistence agriculture in the country and in its place infuse large-scale commercial farming by assisting farmers with inputs and developing land for them to the point of planting at subsidized rates. On its establishment, the government allocated a take off grant of N30million in order to acquire 50,000 hectres of land in each state of the federation for agricultural activities.

SPECIAL PROGRAMME FOR FOOD SECURITY (SPFS)

This programme was introduced in 2002 by the Federal Government and the Federal Ministry of Agriculture and Rural Development was given the responsibility of its implementation through its project coordinating unit. The size of the programme, the general capital outlay channeled to it and the built in implementation and monitoring mechanism made this programme a potent weapon for heralding a meaningful agrarian revolution in the country within the shortest period of time. A critical look at the programme reveals that the success of this programme had been minimal because the government had failed to maintain consistency in its investment, implementation and monitoring the activities in the agricultural sector in general.

CONTRIBUTIONS OF AGRICULTURE TO ECONOMIC DEVELOPMENT

Agriculture helps to provide food for the teeming population of the country. When output increases, the incomes of the farmers increase thereby leading to an increase in the standard of living. Similarly, agricultural development is of vital importance due to the fact that a rise in rural purchasing power as a result of the increase in the agricultural surplus is a great stimulus to industrial development and expansion in the size of the market. The market size for manufactured goods in Nigeria is very small because a large proportion of the population is poverty ridden. However, the demand for such input like fertilizers, better tools, farm implements, tractors, irrigational facilities in the agricultural sector is relatively low which lead to the expansion of the industrial sector.

Again it is known that the LDCs in general and Nigeria in particular mostly specialized in the production of a few agricultural products for export.

Furthermore, agriculture creates employment opportunities in rural areas. As agricultural productivity and farm income increase, non-farm rural employment expands and diversifies. Nigeria needs large amount of capital to finance the creation and expansion of infrastructure and for the development of basic and heavy industries. In the stage of development, capital can be provided to increase the marketable surplus from the rural sector without reducing consumption.

Finally, an increase in rural income as a result of the agricultural surplus tends to improve rural welfare. The rural people build better houses fitted with modern amenities like electricity, furniture, radio farm, etc. They also receive direct satisfaction from schools, health centres, irrigation, banking, transport, and communication facilities, which forestall rural-urban migration.

DATA COLLECTION AND ANALYSIS

This research work used secondary data. Data were sourced from Central Bank of Nigeria's publications, journals, books and unpublished materials. The method of data analysis is the ordinary least square (OLS) multiple regression method. We made use of MICROFIT 4.1 (2001) econometric software.

SPECIFICATION OF THE MODEL

Gross Domestic Product (GDP) is a function of agriculture and ago-based industries.

where;

GDP = Gross Domestic Product

AGRQ = Agricultural output

INDQ = Industrial output

= Random term

, , and are the parameter estimates

$a_0 > 0$, $a_1 > 0$ and $a_2 > 0$

ESTIMATION AND RESULTS

We used both linear and log linear specification of the model and discovered that the log linear specification explained the impact of the agricultural and industrial sector on gross domestic product in terms of goodness of fit, precision of the estimates of the slope and tolerable level of multicollinearity. The results of the regression are presented in econometric compact form as:

The standard error values and t-values of each parameter are shown in parentheses, with the standard errors coming before the t-values.

The results of the regression show that there is a positive relationship between the dependent variable (GDP) and the independent variables (AGRQ and INDQ). A unit change in agricultural output and industrial output will cause 5.6 percent and 34.1 percent change in GDP respectively. The estimated model shows F-ratio of about 45.62 as compared with the F-table value of 3.55 with 5 percent level of significance. This implies that agricultural and industrial production for the period of analysis have significant influences on macroeconomic output level.

The explanatory power of the regression model with an adjusted R^2 of 0.82 is impressive. This indicates that 82 percent of GDP is explained by the agricultural and industrial sectors. The remaining 18 percent is explained by variables outside this model. From our results the standard errors for each parameters are statistically significant being that .

CONCLUSION

On the whole, the agricultural and industrial sectors contribute significantly to Nigeria's GDP. The employment base of the Nigeria economy is largely dependent on these two sectors. However, the agricultural sector contributes only 5.6 percent to the economy while the industrial sector's contribution is about 34 percent. This level of disparity is due to the neglect of agriculture when oil was discovered in a commercial quantity in the 1970s. It is well over due for the Nigerian economy to diversify. The negative perception and orientation of the average Nigerian about agriculture and agro-based industries should be disabused so that these sectors can contribute optimally to GDP.

RECOMMENDATION

In order to improve the agricultural and industrial sectors in Nigeria, the following should be considered.

- Government should provide funds to acquire sophisticated farm tools.
- Special incentives such as tax holidays should be given to those who engage in agriculture and agro-based industries.
- The Export Promotion Council should create markets for the exportation of agro-based industry's products and agricultural outputs.
- Economic co-operation among regions and state should be encouraged. The benefit of such cooperation is the ability to pool resources together in order to embark on projects that are adjudged to be beyond individual's states and regions. It also allowed the cooperative states to reap the benefit of economies of scale thereby improving the welfare of the people. The ultimate goal of the cooperating states should be to achieve accelerated rate of economic development and industrialization.
- Extension programmes aimed at educating farmers and bringing to their knowledge modern production techniques should be faithfully pursued by the government.

4

Wheat Flour Industry

Wheat is one of the world's most important field crops and the third most produced after maize (corn) and rice (1). It belongs to grass family, Gramineae, and the genus Triticum (2). Globally wheat is grown in 122 countries producing nearly 700 million metric tons. India is 2nd largest producer of wheat and is maintaining the position from last eight years (3). India accounts for 12.05% of the total world wheat production, which is next to China accounting 18.41%. Wheat production for major wheat growing countries for the year 2011 is shown in Table1 (4).

WHEAT

STRUCTURE AND COMPOSITION OF WHEAT

Kernel of wheat is divided in three main parts viz. endosperm, bran and germ. The endosperm, or, as, it is sometimes termed, the food bag of the grain of wheat, contains approximately 82-85% by the weight of the grain, bran 14% and germ 2-3%. Endosperm gives energy for plant growth and carbohydrates & protein for people. Bran protects seed and is rich in fibre, B-vitamins, minerals; whereas germ nourishes seed, future wheat plant and is excellent source of antioxidants, vitamin E and B-vitamins . Wheat consists of about 7.8-18% moisture, protein 8.3-19.3%, crude fibre about 1.2%, fat about 1.5% and ash content 1.17-2.96% .

WHEAT IN INDIA

Wheat is the second most important cereal in India after rice. Wheat provides more than 50% of the calories to the people who mainly depend on it. India has witnessed a significant increase in the wheat production over the years and has touched 93.9 MMT in 2012. There has been linear increase in the production from 44.3 MMT in 1987 to 86.87 MMT in 2011 with moderate growth rate of 2.27 .There were significant ups and downs between 2001 and 2007 due to unfavourable weather conditions. However from 2007 there has been a steady rise .

About 91% of the Indian wheat is produced in six states viz., Uttar Pradesh (34%), Punjab (22%), Haryana(13%), Madhya Pradesh(10%), Rajasthan(9%) and Bihar(6%). Uttar Pradesh, with 24.3 MMT is the highest producer of wheat followed by Punjab (14.7 MMT) and Haryana (9.1MMT). Wheat productivity in India is 2.8 tons/hectare. Punjab (4.3t/ha) and Haryana (4t/ha) have the highest productivity than other wheat producing states. Contribution of Uttar Pradesh and Madhya Pradesh is due to relatively large area (about 50% of total area) sown to wheat .

WHEAT MILLING PROCESS

The U.S. grain processing industry has evolved to efficiently co-mingle and move vast quantities of grain from rural America to population centers so consumers can have safe, healthful products with consistent quality.

Each year the U.S. wheat milling industry consumes more than 900 million bushels of an approximately two billion bushel crop. U.S. wheat mills of average size produce about one million pounds of flour daily, and the largest produce between 2.0 and 3.2 million pounds per day

Wheat is not just wheat. Six classes and several hundred varieties of wheat make possible the hundreds of wheat foods made worldwide. For example, hard wheat flours provide for a variety of bread products; durum semolina and flour are used in pasta. Soft wheat flours produce an array of crackers, cookies, cereals, cakes, pancakes, breading and pastries. Many mills specialize in the type of wheat they process and this specialization can be based, in part, on mill location.

GRAIN DELIVERY

Grain is delivered to mills by covered trucks and hopper railcars. The distance the grain has traveled varies greatly. In some cases it has traveled hundreds of miles in a 110-car unit train. In other instances it is being delivered from a local farm in the same county. Grain deliveries will frequently have gone through a number of aggregation steps prior to arriving at the mill (farmer, country elevator, terminal elevator etc.). The number of conveyances making deliveries of grain can vary depending on the time of year with more deliveries at harvest time.

GRAIN STANDARDS

Before wheat is unloaded at a facility, samples are taken to ensure it passes inspection. Grain is tested for moisture content, test weight, unsound kernels, and foreign material. Grain is graded according to the US Grain Standards and is also subject to commercial specifications set by the miller. Typically wheat used in milling is #2 grade or better. At unloading, product control chemists begin their tests to classify wheat and determine end-use qualities. The results from these tests determine how the wheat will be handled and stored.

The U.S. Grain Standards Act facilitates trading in grain. Administered by the USDA's Grain Inspection, Packers and Stockyards Administration (GIPSA) it provides criteria for determining the kind, class, and condition of grains and oilseeds. Standards define quality and condition factors and set grade limits based on those factor determinations. Mills, however, must use commercial specifications that are even more rigorous than the U.S. Grain Standards when testing for natural toxins, evidence of pest exposure, stress cracks, etc. Sampling, grading and testing of grade and quality factors continues throughout the storage, handling and milling processes.

GRAIN STORAGE

Once the grain has passed inspection it is unloaded directly from the delivery vehicle into pits and moved via conveyors and bucket elevators into large bins or silos. Storing grain is a science. The right moisture, heat and air must be maintained or the wheat may mildew, sprout, or ferment. During storage the grain may go through a fumigation process to eliminate insect pests. Wheat is stored according to protein level and other quality considerations. Storage times vary. Many mills will clean the wheat at this time to obtain better storage results. Millers frequently draw from different silos to blend different types of wheat with distinct performance properties to achieve the desired end product.

HACCP

Using their written Hazard Analysis and Critical Control Point (HACCP) plan, grain millers identify potential food safety hazards so that key actions can be taken to reduce or eliminate the risk of those hazards. Millers are working to eliminate critical control points before they become problems. This increases the reach and impact of precious food safety resources.

Milling pre-requisite programs consist of inspection and testing of raw grain as it arrives at the mill, sanitation programs, pest control programs, current Good Manufacturing Practices (GMPs), traceability and recall programs, shipping and receiving procedures that cover truck and railcar inspections and sealing, chemical control programs, allergen control programs, customer complaint responses, and lab testing procedures as well as many others. These programs also cover preventative maintenance programs, machinery and equipment programs, supplier programs, grounds and facilities programs.

A NUMBER OF STEPS IN THE MILLING PROCESS ENHANCE PRODUCT INTEGRITY

When it is time to mill the grain it moves from the bottom of the silo/bin through conveyors to the top floor of the mill where the cleaning process begins.

Cleaning the wheat -The first milling steps involve equipment that separates grain from seeds and other grains, removes foreign materials that might have originated during the farmer's harvest such as metal, sticks, stones and straw; and scours the kernels of wheat. It can take as many as six steps. The machines that clean the grain are collectively called the cleaning house.

Magnetic separator – The grain first passes by a magnet that removes ferrous metal particles. It will pass through other metal detectors after milling to ensure that no metal pieces are in the finished product. Magnets are also positioned throughout the milling process and at the last step prior to load-out.

Separator – Vibrating or rotating drum separators remove bits of wood, straw and almost anything else too big or too small to be the desired grain.

Aspirator – Air currents act as a vacuum to remove dust and lighter impurities.

De-stoner – Using gravity, the machine separates the heavy material from the light to remove stones that may be the same size as the desired grain.

Disc separator – The grain passes through a separator that identifies the size of the kernels even more closely. It rejects anything longer, shorter, more round, more angular or in any way a different shape. Scourer – The scourer removes outer husks, dirt in the kernel crease and any smaller impurities with an intense scouring action. Currents of air pull all the loosened material away.

Impact Entoleter – Centrifugal force breaks apart any unsound kernels or insect eggs and aspiration rejects them from the mill flow. From the entoleter, the sound wheat flows to grinding bins, large hoppers that control the feeding of the wheat to the actual milling process.

Color Separator – Newer mills may also utilize electronic color separators to simplify the cleaning process.

TEMPERING WHEAT

Now the wheat is ready to be conditioned for milling. This is called tempering. Moisture is added in precise amounts to toughen the bran and mellow the inner endosperm. This makes the parts of the kernel separate more easily and cleanly. The length of soaking time can range from 6-24 hours. The time and temperature depend on the type of wheat and its moisture level. Temper water may be treated with ozone or chlorine to maintain sanitation in this wet environment during the tempering process.

GRINDING WHEAT

The wheat kernels are now ready to be milled into flour. The modern milling process is a gradual reduction of the wheat kernels through a process of grinding and sifting. The millers' skill is analyzing the wheat and then blending it to meet the requirements of the end use. This science of analysis, blending, grinding, sifting and blending again results in consistent end products. Wheat kernels are measured or fed from the bins to the "roller mills", corrugated cylinders made from chilled steel. The rolls are paired and rotate inward against each other, moving at different speeds. Passing through the corrugated "first break" rolls begins the separation of bran, endosperm (starch) and germ.

There are about five roller mills or breaks in the system. Again, the goal is to remove the endosperm from the bran and the germ. Each break roll must be set to get as much pure endosperm as possible. The "break" rolls, each have successively finer corrugations. After each trip through the break rolls, the grist is sent back upstairs to drop through sifters. The system reworks the coarse stocks from the sifters and reduces the wheat particles to granular "middlings" that are as free from bran as possible.

In some mills double high roller mills eliminate elevating and sifting the product between two successive passages in the milling process, thus increasing efficiency.

SIFTERS

The broken particles of wheat are elevated through pneumatic tubes and then dropped into huge, vibrating, box-like sifters where they are shaken through a series of bolting cloths or screens to separate the larger from the smaller particles. Inside the sifter, there may be as many as 27 frames, each covered with either a nylon or stainless steel screen, with square openings that get smaller and smaller the farther down they go. Up to six different sizes of particles may come from a single sifter. Larger particles are shaken off from the top, or "scalped," leaving the finer flour to sift to the bottom.

The "scalped" fractions of endosperm called middlings are reduced in a smooth roller system to the particle size of flour. In hard wheat mills, the product is then subjected to a purifying process. A controlled flow of air lifts off bran particles while at the same time a bolting cloth separates and grades coarser fractions by size and quality.

The process is repeated over and over again, sifters to purifiers to reducing rolls, moving up and down and across the mill in a series until the maximum amount of flour is separated, about 75 percent of the wheat kernel.

BLEACHING THE FLOUR

Toward the end of the line in the millstream, if the flour is to be "bleached," the finished flour flows through a device that releases a bleaching-maturing agent in measured amounts. This duplicates the natural oxidation that occurs when flour is allowed to naturally age as in the old days when flour was stored for a few months. This whitened the flour and improved its baking characteristics. The modern bleaching process simply duplicates this natural oxidation process, but does so more quickly. In the bleaching process, flour is exposed to chlorine gas or benzoyl peroxide to whiten and brighten flour color.

The bleaching agents react and do not leave harmful residues or destroy nutrients. In soft wheat products chlorine gas is also used to control cookie diameter and cake height.

ENRICHMENT, MALT AND LEAVENING

The flour stream passes through a device that measures out and releases specified quantities of enrichment. Malt may be added to bread flours at this point to add loaf height as well for flavor.

Grains have been enriched since 1941 with iron and the B vitamins riboflavin, niacin and thiamine. As a result, the crippling diseases pellagra and beriberi have been eradicated from the U.S. population. In 1998, folic acid was added to the enrichment formula. Data from U.S. birth certificates indicate neural tube defects have decreased by 19 percent and spina bifida by 23 percent following folic acid fortification in the U.S. grain food supply. Enriched grain products have more than twice the amount of folic acid as whole wheat. A slice of enriched white bread has 37 mcg versus whole wheat at 17.5 mcg. Studies show folic acid may also help prevent heart disease, cancer, strokes and Alzheimer's disease.

FINISHED PRODUCT TESTING

After milling, lab tests are run to ensure that the flour meets specifications. Millers also conduct routine monitoring of indicator natural organisms. Although dry flour does not provide an environment that is conducive to microbial growth, it is important to understand that flour is a minimally processed agricultural ingredient and is not a ready-to-eat product. Flour is not intended to be consumed raw. The heat processes of baking, frying, boiling and cooking are adequate to destroy any pathogens that may be present in flour and reduce the potential risk of food borne illness.

The North American Millers' Association is the trade association representing the wheat, corn, oat and rye milling industry. NAMA's 46 member companies operate 170 mills in 38 states and Canada. Their aggregate production of more than 175 million pounds per day is approximately 95 percent of the total industry capacity.

FLOUR

Flour is a finely ground powder prepared from grain or other starchy plant foods and used in baking. Although flour can be made from a wide variety of plants, the vast majority is made from wheat. Dough made from wheat flour is particularly well suited to baking bread because it contains a large amount of gluten, a substance composed of strong, elastic proteins. The gluten forms a network throughout the dough, trapping the gases which are formed by yeast, baking powder, or other leavening agents. This causes the dough to rise, resulting in light, soft bread.

Flour has been made since prehistoric times. The earliest methods used for producing flour all involved grinding grain between stones. These methods included the mortar and pestle (a stone club striking grain held in a stone bowl), the saddlestone (a cylindrical stone rolling against grain held in a stone bowl), and the quern (a horizontal, disk-shaped stone spinning on top of grain held on another horizontal stone). These devices were all operated by hand.

The millstone, a later development, consisted of one vertical, disk-shaped stone rolling on grain sitting on a horizontal, disk-shaped stone. Millstones were first operated by human or animal power. The ancient Romans used waterwheels to power millstones. Windmills were also used to power millstones in Europe by the twelfth century.

The first mill in the North American colonies appeared in Boston in 1632 and was powered by wind. Most later mills in the region used water. The availability of water power and water transportation made Philadelphia, Pennsylvania, the center of milling in the newly independent United States. The first fully automatic mill was built near Philadelphia by Oliver Evans in 1784. During the next century, the center of milling moved as railroads developed, eventually settling in Minneapolis, Minnesota. During the nineteenth century numerous improvements were made in mill technology. In 1865, Edmund La Croix introduced the first middlings purifier in Hastings, Minnesota. This device consisted of a vibrating screen through which air was blown to remove bran from ground wheat. The resulting product, known as middlings or farina, could be further ground into high-quality flour. In 1878, the first important roller mill was used in Minneapolis, Minnesota. This new type of mill used metal rollers, rather than millstones, to grind wheat. Roller mills were less expensive, more efficient, more uniform, and cleaner than millstones. Modern versions of middlings purifiers and roller mills are still used to make flour today.

RAW MATERIALS

Although most flour is made from wheat, it can also be made from other starchy plant foods. These include barley, buckwheat, corn, lima beans, oats, peanuts, potatoes, soybeans, rice, and rye. Many varieties of wheat exist for use in making flour. In general, wheat is either hard (containing 11-18% protein) or soft (containing 8-11% protein). Flour intended to be used to bake bread is made from hard wheat. The high percentage of protein in hard wheat means the dough will have more gluten, allowing it to rise more than soft wheat flour. Flour intended to be used to bake cakes and pastry is made from soft wheat. All-purpose flour is made from a blend of soft and hard wheat. Durum wheat is a special variety of hard wheat, which is used to make a kind of flour called semolina. Semolina is most often used to make pasta. Flour usually contains a small amount of additives. Bleaching agents such as benzoyl peroxide are added to make the flour more white. Oxidizing agents (also known as improvers) such as potassium bromate, chlorine dioxide, and azodicarbonamide are added to enhance the baking quality of the flour. These agents are added in a few parts per million. Self-rising flour contains salt and a leavening agent such as calcium phosphate. It is used to make baked goods without the need to add yeast or baking powder. Most states require flour to contain added vitamins and minerals to replace those lost during milling. The most important of these are iron and the B vitamins, especially thiamin, riboflavin, and niacin.

THE MANUFACTURING

PROCESS

Grading the wheat

- 1 Wheat is received at the flour mill and inspected. Samples of wheat are taken for physical and chemical analysis. The wheat is graded based on several factors, the most important of which is the protein content. The wheat is stored in silos with wheat of the same grade until needed for milling.

Purifying the wheat

In 1795, an American engineer published a book called The Young Millwright and Miller's Guide. In the book, simple theories are transformed into a set of mechanical devices that form a flour mill. At the back of the book is a drawing, illustrating how these devices make a continuous production line in which the human hand is eliminated from the beginning of the process to the end of production. The author of this book was Oliver Evans, himself the son of a miller. He and his brothers ran their own mill, developed the systems, and perfected the operations that led to the automated grain mill.

Today, Evans is considered one of America's most ambitious mechanical innovators. He used his understanding of the way in which water turned a mill wheel and developed it into a viable grain-milling system.

Most important was the fact that his system contained the idea of the integrated and automated factory. When a machine substitutes human intervention, the problems of the fully automated assembly line are solved. This concept was not fully applied until the 1920s by Henry Ford, who was able to develop a successful, operational assembly line. Ford had the advantage of living at the end of the machine age, but Oliver Evans was the first to present the concept of automation before it was even possible.

Henry Prebys

- 2 Before wheat can be ground into flour it must be free of foreign matter. This requires several different cleaning processes. At each step of purification the wheat is inspected and purified again if necessary.

- 3 The first device used to purify wheat is known as a separator. This machine passes the wheat over a series of metal screens. The wheat and other small particles pass through the screen while large objects such as sticks and rocks are removed.
- 4 The wheat next passes through an aspirator. This device works like a vacuum cleaner. The aspirator sucks up foreign matter which is lighter than the wheat and removes it.
- 5 Other foreign objects are removed in various ways. One device, known as a disk separator, moves the wheat over a series of disks with indentations that collect objects the size of a grain of wheat. Smaller or larger objects pass over the disks and are removed.
- 6 Another device, known as a spiral seed separator, makes use of the fact that wheat grains are oval while most other plant seeds are round.
- The wheat moves down a rapidly spinning cylinder. The oval wheat grains tend to move toward the center of the cylinder while the round seeds tend to move to the sides of the cylinder, where they are removed.
- 7 Other methods used to purify wheat include magnets to remove small pieces of metal, scourers to scrape off dirt and hair, and electronic color sorting machines to remove material which is not the same color as wheat.

Preparing the wheat for grinding

- 8 The purified wheat is washed in warm water and placed in a centrifuge to be spun dry. During this process any remaining foreign matter is washed away.
- 9 The moisture content of the wheat must now be controlled to allow the outer layer of bran to be removed efficiently during grinding. This process is known as conditioning or tempering. Several methods exist of controlling the amount of water present within each grain of wheat. Usually this involves adding, rather than removing, moisture.
- 10 Cold conditioning involves soaking the wheat in cold water for one to three days. Warm conditioning involves soaking the wheat in water at a temperature of 115°F (46°C) for 60-90 minutes and letting it rest for one day. Hot conditioning involves soaking the wheat in water at a temperature of 140°F (60°C) for a short period of time. This method is difficult to control and is rarely used. Instead of water, wheat may also be conditioned with steam at various temperatures and pressures for various amounts of time. If conditioning results in too much moisture, or if the wheat happens to be too moist after

purification, water can be removed by vacuum dryers.

Grinding the wheat

- 11 Wheat of different grades and moistures is blended together to obtain a batch of wheat with the characteristics necessary to make the kind of flour being manufactured. At this point, the wheat may be processed in an Entoleter, a trade name for a device with rapidly spinning disks which hurl the grains of wheat against small metal pins.
- Those grains which crack are considered to be unsuitable for grinding and are removed.
- 12 The wheat moves between two large metal rollers known as breaker rolls. These rollers are of two different sizes and move at different speeds. They also contain spiral grooves which crack open the grains of wheat and begin to separate the interior of the wheat from the outer layer of bran. The product of the breaker rolls passes through metal sieves to separate it into three categories. The finest material resembles a coarse flour and is known as middlings or farina. Larger pieces of the interior are known as semolina. The third category consists of pieces of the interior which are still attached to the bran. The middlings move to the middlings purifier and the other materials move to another pair of breaker rolls. About four or five pairs of breaker rolls are needed to produce the necessary amount of middlings.
- 13 The middlings purifier moves the middlings over a vibrating screen. Air is blown up through the screen to remove the lighter pieces of bran which are mixed with the middlings. The middlings pass through the screen to be more finely ground.
- 14 Middlings are ground into flour by pairs of large, smooth metal rollers. Each time the flour is ground it passes through sieves to separate it into flours of different fineness. These sieves are made of metal wire when the flour is coarse, but are made ofnylon or silk when the flour is fine. By sifting, separating, and regrinding the flour, several different grades of flour are produced at the same time. These are combined as needed to produce the desired final products.

Processing the flour

- 15 Small amounts of bleaching agents and oxidizing agents are usually added to the flour after milling. Vitamins and minerals are added as required by law to produce enriched flour. Leavening agents and salt are added to produce self-rising flour. The flour is matured for one or two months.
- 16 The flour is packed into cloth bags which hold 2, 5, 10, 25, 50, or 100 lb (About 0.9, 2.3, 4.5, 11.3, 22.7, or 45.4 kg). For large-scale

consumers, it may be packed in metal tote bins which hold 3000 lb (1361 kg), truck bins which hold 45,000 lb (20,412 kg), or railroad bins which hold 100,000 lb (45,360 kg).

QUALITY CONTROL

The quality control of flour begins when the wheat is received at the flour mill. The wheat is tested for its protein content and for its ash content. The ash content is the portion which remains after burning and consists of various minerals. During each step of the purification process, several samples are taken to ensure that no foreign matter ends up in the flour. Since flour is intended for human consumption, all the equipment used in milling is thoroughly cleaned and sterilized by hot steam and ultraviolet light. The equipment is also treated with antibacterial agents and antifungal agents to kill any microscopic organisms which might contaminate it. Hot water is used to remove any remaining traces of these agents. The final product of milling is tested for baking in test kitchens to ensure that it is suitable for the uses for which it is intended. The vitamin and mineral content is measured in order to comply with government standards. The exact amount of additives present is measured to ensure accurate labeling.

BYPRODUCTS/WASTE

A kernel of wheat consists of three parts, two of which can be considered byproducts of the milling process. The bran is the outer covering of the kernel and is high in fiber. The germ is the innermost portion of the kernel and is high in fat. The endosperm makes up the bulk of the kernel and is high in proteins and carbohydrates. Whole wheat flour uses all parts of the kernel, but white flour uses only the endosperm.

Bran removed during milling is often added to breakfast cereals and baked goods as a source of fiber. It is also widely used in animal feeds. Wheat germ removed during milling is often used as a food supplement or as a source of edible vegetable oil. Like bran, it is also used in animal feeds.

FLOUR MILLING

Flour mills began to be established in the town of Minneapolis in the mid-1850s. Powered by St. Anthony Falls, the mills were supplied with rapidly increasing crops of wheat grown by new settlers in western and southern Minnesota and the Dakotas. Railroads began linking Minneapolis to the west in the late 1860s. The number of Minneapolis flour mills grew rapidly.

A few things kept the Minneapolis mills from competing successfully with flour mills in other parts of the country, however. When flour was made from the hard spring wheat of the Northern Plains using conventional milling techniques, it was discolored and speckled with particles of husk or bran, and it did not keep well. In addition, conventional mill stones destroyed much of the most nutritious part of the wheat kernel.

In the 1860s and 1870s, the millers solved these problems. They developed a process that made it possible to separate the nourishing "middlings" layer of the wheat kernel, process it, and return it to the flour. A second innovation replaced conventional millstones with large chilled porcelain or iron rollers that ran at a lower speed. This prevented discoloration due to heat and minimized the crushed husk and bran that speckled the flour. By the late 1870s Minneapolis flour was recognized as the best in the nation, and it quickly replaced winter-wheat flour in both national and international markets. The mills located on the west bank of the Mississippi made that area the nation's leading flour center.

The Pillsbury Company completed its gigantic A Mill on the east side of the river in 1880. Containing two identical units, it had a capacity of 4000 barrels of flour a day when it opened. By 1905 the mill had tripled its output. Its owners claimed that it was the largest flour mill in the world. Over the years numerous buildings were added to the complex, including a grain storage elevator built in 1910 and linked to the mill by conveyors, another elevator and annex built between 1914 and 1916, and a cleaning house and nine-story warehouse built in 1917. The Pillsbury A Mill is the only mill still operating in the St. Anthony Falls milling district.

Tremendous consolidation took place within the flour industry between 1880 and 1900, as numerous mergers occurred. In 1876, 17 firms operated 20 mills; in 1890, four large corporations produced almost all of the flour made in Minnesota. By the early 1900s, three corporations based in Minneapolis controlled 97 percent of the nation's flour production. They were Washburn-Crosby Company, which became General Mills; Pillsbury-Washburn Flour Mills Company, which became Pillsbury Flour Mills Company; and Northwestern Consolidated Milling Company, which became the Standard Milling Company. This Minneapolis "Flour Trust" dominated the national flour market until the 1930s.

As consolidation took place, the number of operating mills stabilized at about two dozen, but auxiliary buildings multiplied rapidly. Warehouses, grain elevators, boiler rooms, engine houses, packing facilities, and railroad tracks crowded the land along the river. Over the years, the labor of many men constructed canals, mills, and support buildings. Others unloaded newly arrived grain onto conveyor belts that carried it to the millers, who put it through the rollers and processed it into the final product. Still other workers packed the flour, first into barrels and later into bags. Under brand names like Gold Medal and Pillsbury's Best, the newly packaged flour found its way to markets all over the world.

WHEAT FLOUR

Wheat flour is a powder made from the grinding of wheat used for human consumption. More wheat flour is produced than any other flour. Wheat varieties are called "soft" or "weak" if gluten content is low, and are called "hard" or "strong" if they have high gluten content. Hard flour, or *bread flour*, is high in gluten, with 12% to 14% gluten content, its dough has elastic toughness that holds its shape well once baked. Soft flour is comparatively low in gluten and thus results in a loaf with a finer, crumbly texture. Soft flour is usually divided into cake flour, which is the lowest in gluten, and pastry flour, which has slightly more gluten than cake flour. In terms of the parts of the grain (the grass fruit) used in flour—the endosperm or protein/starchy part, the germ or protein/fat/vitamin-rich part, and the bran or fiber part—there are three general types of flour. White flour is made from the endosperm only. Brown flour includes some of the grain's germ and bran, while whole grain or *wholemeal flour* is made from the entire grain, including the bran, endosperm, and germ. Germ flour is made from the endosperm and germ, excluding the bran.

Types

- All-purpose or plain flour is a blended wheat with a protein content lower than bread flour, ranging between 9% and 12%. Depending on brand or the region where it is purchased, it may be composed of all hard or soft wheats, but is usually a blend of the two, and can range from low protein content to moderately high. It is marketed as an inexpensive alternative to bakers' flour which is acceptable for most household baking needs.
- Bleached flour or maida flour is a white flour treated with flour bleaching agents to whiten it (freshly milled flour is yellowish) and give it more gluten-producing potential. Oxidizing agents are usually employed, most commonly organic peroxides likeacetone peroxide or benzoyl peroxide, nitrogen dioxide, or chlorine. A similar effect can be achieved by letting the flour oxidize with oxygen in the air ("natural aging") for approximately 10 days; however, this process is more expensive due to the time required. Flour bleached with benzoyl peroxide has been prohibited in the UK since 1997.
- Bread flour or strong flour is always made from hard wheat, usually hard spring wheat. It has a very high protein content, between 10% and 13%, making it excellent for yeast bread baking. It can be white or whole wheat or in between.
- Bromated flour has a maturing agent added. The agent's role is to help with developing gluten, a role similar to the flour bleaching agents. Bromate is usually used. Other choices are phosphates, ascorbic acid, and malted barley. Bromated flour has been banned in much of the world, as bromate is classified as possibly carcinogenic in humans (Group 2B) by theInternational Agency for Research on

Cancer (IARC), but remains available in the United States.

- Cake flour is a finely milled white flour made from soft wheat. It has very low protein content, between 8% and 10%, making it suitable for soft-textured cakes and cookies. The higher protein content of other flours would make the cakes tough. Highly sifted cake flours may require different volume amounts in recipes than all-purpose flour.
- Using the scoop and level method, well-sifted flour usually produces 125 g per cup. However, most American recipes are written with 140 g of flour per cup, so weighing and experimentation can be helpful in baking unfamiliar recipes. Small weight differences can greatly affect the texture. American Cake flour is bleached; in countries where bleached flour is prohibited, plain flour can be treated in a domestic microwave to improve the texture of the end product. Related to cake flour are masa harina (from maize), maida flour (from wheat or tapioca), and pure starches.
- Durum flour flour made of Durum wheat which is suited for pasta making, traditional pizza and flatbread for doner kebab.
- Graham flour is a special type of whole wheat flour. The endosperm is finely ground, as in white flour, while the bran and germ are coarsely ground. Graham flour is uncommon outside of the US. Graham flour is the basis of true graham crackers. Many graham crackers on the market are actually imitation grahams because they do not contain graham flour or even whole-wheat flour.
- Instant flour is pregelatinized (precooked) for easier incorporation in gravies and sauces.
- Pastry flour or cookie flour or cracker flour has slightly higher protein content than cake flour but lower than all-purpose flour. Its protein content ranges between 9% and 10%. It is available as a white flour, a whole-wheat flour, or a white flour with the germ retained but not the bran. It is suitable for pie pastry and tarts, some cookies, muffins, biscuits and other quick breads. Flour is shaken through a sieve to reduce the amount of lumps for cooking pastry.
- Self-rising or self-raising flour is white flour that is sold premixed with chemical leavening agents. It was invented by Henry Jones. Self-rising flour is typically composed of the following ratio:
- 1 cup (100 g) flour
- 1 $^{1}D_{2}$ teaspoons (3 g) baking powder
- a pinch to $^{1}D_{2}$ teaspoon (1 g or less) salt
- Sharp flour is produced in Fiji and primarily used in Indian cuisine.
- Spelt flour is flour produced from the type of wheat called spelt. It is less commonly used in modern cooking than other wheat varieties.

It is still used for specialty baking.

- Tang flour or wheat starch is a type of wheat flour used primarily in Chinese cuisine for making the outer layer of dumplings and buns. It is also used in Vietnamese cuisine, where it is called *b□t l□c trong*.
- Atta flour is a type of flour used in Asia to make chapatis and other flat breads.

FLOUR STRENGTH – W INDEX

A device called Alveograph Chopin invented in 1921 by Marcel Chopin, provides an index called W that is now commonly used by professional bakers. W index measures the flour strength. The maximum of the curve, identified by P, represents the toughness of gluten, while L represents the extensibility, the higher the value of L the more elastic the dough will be.

Flours between 90 and 160 W are called "weak flours". They have a low protein content, usually 9%, used to produce biscuits or cakes.

Flours between 160 and 250 W have a medium force. They are used, for example, for Pugliese bread, pizza and focaccia.

Flours > 300 W Flours with a high W are called "strong flours" because they oppose a great resistance to the deformation of gluten. There are also flours with values exceeding 400 W, denominated Manitoba because originated from a region of Canada.

In general, the more a product requires long rising time, the more a flour will need a high W, because it better retains the carbon dioxide produced in the fermentation. Gluten is able to absorb water for one time and half its weight, then the stronger the flour is, the higher will be the hydration. It passes from an hydration less than 50% for weak flour up to values higher than 70% for strong flour

NATIONAL FLOUR IN THE UNITED KINGDOM

During World War II, the British government promoted "National Flour"; it was adopted in 1942 both for health reasons and those concerned about the import of wheat into the UK and losses during the war. The flour is described as being of 85% extraction, i.e. containing more of the whole wheat grain than refined flour, generally described as 70% extraction at the time. Parliamentary questions on the exact constitution of National Flour in 1943 reveal that it was "milled from a grist consisting of 90 per cent. wheat and 10 per cent. diluent grains. Authorised additions are calcium at the rate of 7 oz (200 g) per 280 lb (130 kg) of flour and dried milk at the rate of 2 lb (910 g) per 280 lb (130 kg) of flour and customary improvers in normal proportions." The diluent grains were barley, oats and rye and customary improvers were "certain oxidising agents which improve the quality of the bread baked from the flour, and their nature depends on the kind of grain used, whether hard or soft.". A survey of the composition of National Flour was conducted for the period 1946–1950 National Flour was discontinued in 1956 against the recommendations of the MRC as the government considered that the addition of nutritional supplements to refined flour removed the necessity for using National Flour on health grounds.

FLOUR PRODUCTION

Madagascar

Since mid-November 2010, Seaboard is operating in Madagascar under LMM Farine SA. The company is managing the industrial milling assets of a local company called KOBAMA SA; mainly consisting in a 288 MT Bühler flour mill, located in Antsirabe. The company is also under contract with SPAT, the State owned company managing the sea port of Toamasina/Tamatave, on the east coast, to manage the 26,000 MT storage capacity grain silos. Production of wheat flour is roughly half of Madagascar's consumption.

Kenya

National Flour was also a term for a flour introduced in Kenya by the colonial government which contained 70% wheat flour and 30% maize flour.

FLOUR ANALYSIS

The production of uniform bakery products require control over the raw materials used in their formation. Flour is a biological material and when obtained from different sources can vary considerably in its protein quality, protein quantity, ash, moisture, enzymatic activity, color, and physical properties. It is essential for the baker to be aware of any variations in these characteristics from one flour shipment to the next. The purpose of flour testing is to measure specific properties or characteristics of a flour. Ideally the results of these tests can be related to the flour's performance in the bakery. The American Association of Cereal Chemists (AACC) publishes approved methods for determining various properties of flour and bakery products.

Moisture

The simple air-oven method is sufficiently accurate for the routine analysis of flour moisture at the flour mill or bakery. The procedure involves heating a small sample of flour (~2g) for 1 hr at 266°F (130°C + 1°C) and taking the loss in weight as the moisture content.

The moisture content of the flour is important for two reasons. First, the higher the moisture content, the lower the amount of dry solids in the flour. Flour specifications usually limit the flour moisture to 14% or less. It is in the miller's interest to hold the moisture as close to 14% as possible. Secondly, flour with greater than 14% moisture is not stable at room temperature.

Organisms naturally present in the flour will start to grow at high moistures, producing off odors and flavors.

Ash

Ash is the mineral material in flour. The ash content of any given flour is affected primarily by the ash content of the wheat from which it was milled and its milling extraction. The test for determining the ash content involves incinerating a known weight of flour under controlled conditions, weighing the residue, and calculating the percentage of ash based upon the original sample weight. The ash content of wheat varies from about 1.50 to about 2.00%. The pure endosperm contains about 0.35% ash. Considering that the wheat kernel contains about 80% endosperm, it becomes clear that the non-endosperm parts of the kernel (pericarp, aleurone, and germ) are very high in ash when compared to the endosperm. Thus, the ash content is a sensitive measure of the amount of non-endosperm material that is in the flour.

The goal of milling is to separate the endosperm from the non-endosperm parts of the wheat kernel. This separating is difficult and never clean. Thus, there is always contamination of endosperm with non-endosperm and visa versa. As flour yield is increased, the amount of contamination with non-endosperm increases and the ash content increases. Thus, the ash content is a good and sensitive measure of the contamination of the endosperm.

Millers will often comment that the ash does not affect the baking performance of flour. This is probably true. However, the non-endosperm parts of the wheat kernel are known to decrease baking quality and as the ash content increases so does the level of non-endosperm material. The ash content of white pan bread flour has increased over the years from 0.45% in the 1950s to the current level of 0.50-0.55%. This has undoubtedly resulted from negotiations where the miller has agreed to the flour buyer's price but only if he can raise the ash content of the flour a couple of points (0.02%).

Protein

The amount of protein in a food material is usually determined by measuring the nitrogen content of the material and multiplying that value by a factor. The nitrogen content of a given protein varies depending on its source. For milk products a factor of 6.38 is used, for most cereal grains the factor is 6.25, and in wheat products the factor is 5.70. These factors depend on the percentage of nitrogen in the respective proteins.

The flour protein content is an important parameter for bread flour. Flours containing higher protein contents are more expensive than flours of lower protein content. Likewise, flours with very low proteins for cakes are also more expensive. There is usually, but not always, a good correlation between protein content and bakery performance of a flour.

The classic procedure to determine the nitrogen was the Kjeldahl procedure. This involved digesting the sample in concentrated sulfuric acid, then neutralizing the acid with concentrated sodium hydroxide, followed by distillation of the ammonia (derived from the nitrogen in the protein) into a standard acid. The procedure worked well, however it was an environmental nightmare. In addition to the strong acid and base, the catalysts used to speed the digestion included such materials as mercury and selenium. It should surprise no one that the procedure is seldom used today.

The Kjeldahl procedure has been replaced by the Dumas combustion procedure. In the original Dumas procedure the sample is mixed with cupric oxide and heated in a stream of carbon dioxide in a combustion tube packed with cupric oxide and copper metal. The organic material is converted to carbon dioxide, water and nitrogen. The gas stream is led into 50% potassium hydroxide. This absorbs the carbon dioxide and any oxides of sulfur, leaving only nitrogen as a gas. The volume of nitrogen is then determined. Various machines have been developed to carry out the analysis automatically. The percent nitrogen is then converted to protein using the appropriate factor. Both the Dumas combustion and the Kjeldahl procedures estimate the quantity (total amount) of protein and not the protein quality. As discussed elsewhere, the quantity of protein is extremely important in the baking performance of a flour.

Near Infrared Reflectance (NIR)

The rapid instrumental analysis of cereals and flours has considerable commercial appeal. Therefore, the near infrared reflectance (NIR) method of estimating protein and moisture contents has found ready acceptance in the milling and baking industries because it is capable of generating nearly instantaneous results. NIR instruments can be operated by non-technical personnel with good precision and reproducibility. The method's accuracy is dependent upon its calibration.

Near infrared (NIR) methodology has been developed for the determination of protein, moisture, and starch of cereals and their milled products. The range of the electromagnetic spectrum extends from the very long radio waves to the very short gamma rays. The near infrared region is between 0.75 and 2.5 microns (ìm).

The first commercial NIR instruments appeared in the 1970s and have been improved during the ensuing years by interfacing them with computers. This has led to the rapid evaluation of the spectral data whose numerical results are then shown on the readout screen.

In the NIR range, the absorption bands are broad and overlapping. Thus, measurements taken at any wavelength are affected by several components of the wheat or flour. Therefore, it is necessary to consider several bands of the spectrum to eliminate the interfering effects of other components. This approach necessitates measurements at several wavelengths and computations using multiple regression analysis, which requires computer facilities. The regression equations have to be developed for various cereal types and varieties to calibrate the instrument. They must be rechecked periodically with standard samples. While the equipment is expensive, it is also very efficient and worth the investment for laboratories that need rapid and accurate analyses.

The procedure for carrying out an analysis is quite simple. Essentially, it involves carefully filling a sample cup with the finely ground test material, e.g., flour or meal, and placing the cup in the drawer of the instrument. When the drawer is closed, the instrument automatically starts to analyze the sample by exposing its surface to radiation within a selected narrow band of wavelengths and measuring the reflectance. This reflectance is amplified and converted by the instrument's microcomputer into numerical results that are displayed on a readout screen. Some newer instruments are transmitted radiation rather than reflected. The entire operation takes approximately one minute. Some of the newer instruments are designed to analyze whole grain samples.

Free Fatty Acids

The level of free fatty acids in flour milled from sound wheat is very low. However, if either the wheat or the flour is subjected to poor storage conditions (high moisture and/or high temperature), enzymes will degrade the native grain lipids and produce free fatty acids. Thus, the level of free fatty acids is a good measure of the storage conditions of either the grain or the flour. Flours with high levels of free fatty acids will be more subjected to rancidity than will sound flours. This is of little importance in bread but quite important in dry products (cookies, crackers, croutons, pretzels, etc.).

The procedure for determining free fatty acids is quite simple. The lipids are extracted with a suitable solvent such as petroleum ether. The petroleum ether is then evaporated off and the lipid is dispersed in a toluene-alcohol mixture and titrated with standard potassium hydroxide.

Damaged Starch

The starch in wheat occurs as partially crystalline granules. When placed in excess water, the granules will absorb about 30% of their weight. The crystallinity of the granules restricts it from absorbing additional water. During milling some of the granules are damaged. The damage results from the shear on the granule during roller milling. The shear shatters/ruptures some of the crystals. The damage may include the entire granule or just a part of it. This loss of crystals allows the granule to take up more water and swell more. Damaged starch will absorb as much as 300X its weight in water. Hard wheat flour contains a much higher level of damaged starch than does soft wheat. This apparently is because the soft wheat crushes easily during milling and does not subject the starch to as much shear.

Damaged starch is positive factor in bread flour because it increases the water absorption. High water absorption increases the yield of dough and bread from a flour, which has obvious positive effects on bakery profits. Damaged starch is a strong negative in flours for cookies and other dry finished products.

The damaged starch is highly susceptible to α- amylase attack. Much of the damaged starch is degraded to maltose and small dextrins by the combination of α- and â- amylase. This is the major reason that bread flours are malted (α- amylase added) at the mill. If the damaged starch is not removed during fermentation it interacts with the gluten and reduces bread volume.

Damaged starch is generally measured by enzymatic methods. The amount of reducing sugar produced in a certain time with excess enzyme is measured. The flour sample is subdivided into 2 subsamples, one of which is treated directly with the enzyme. The second subsample is autoclaved to gelatinize all the starch and then treated with the same enzyme system. The value obtained for the non-autoclaved sample is divided by the value for the autoclaved sample and the result is multiplied by 100. This gives the percentage of damaged starch. Most hard wheat flours will have from 6-9% damaged starch by the AACC procedure.

A second procedure used in an instrument that uses an electrode system to measure iodine. The amount of iodine bound is related to the amount of damaged starch. The procedure is accurate by requires that the electrode be properly maintained.

Flour Color

Flour color is important because it affects the crumb color of the finished product. The color of the flour used for variety breads, that have a dark color because of non-wheat components in the formula, is not important. Unbleached flours have a creamy color because of the presence of carotenoid pigments in the endosperm. The level of these pigments and therefore the color of the flour will vary from one flour to another. The level of pigments is under genetic control. The pigments can be readily bleached with benzoyl peroxide (mixed with the dry flour at the mill) or by enzyme active soy flour in the bread formula.

Flour color can be judged by visual comparison with a standard patent flour. In the Pekar (slick test), the sample flour is slicked alongside the standard sample and their colors compared visually. This procedure is also useful to determine if the sample is contaminated with bran.

In the procedure, 10-15 grams of the flour to be tested is placed on a glass, plastic, or metal plate. The surface of the flour is smoothed with a clean flour slick to a wedge approximately one-fourth inch thick at the top end of the flour sample down to a thin film at the bottom edge of the plate. The sides of the flour sample are trimmed so they form a straight edge. Next, similarly slick a second flour beside the first making certain that the two flours join and a straight edge forms between the two samples. If addition flours are to be compared, they can be placed on the plate next to the other flours and "slicked" so that there is one continuous wedge of all the flours, with a distinct line of demarcation between them. Any color differences between the samples can then be readily evaluated.

Color difference attributable to bran can be further accentuated by submerging the same samples at an angle into fresh clean water until air bubbles cease to rise (1-2 minutes). The plate is then carefully removed and placed in a warm place for the surface to dry. The relative intensity of the sample colors can then be noted after the surface has dried. The above experiment can also be carried out by dripping the glass plate containing freshly prepared flour wedges into a solution containing pyrocatechin. The bran contains the enzyme polyphenol oxidase that will convert the pyrocatechin into brown pigments. After the surface has dried, the samples are inspected for the presence of bran specks. A number of instruments have been developed to measure the color of solids and foods. Although the may be useful with flour and baked products, they have not been readily accepted by the milling or baking industries.

Enzyme Activity

Although flour contains a large number of enzymes, only a few are measured and/or controlled. Clearly, the most important enzymes in bread flour are the amylases. Beta amylase is found in sufficient quantities in all flours. It has no action on native starch granules but does attack gelatinized and damaged starch. It acts from the non-reducing end of the gelatinized starch chain to produce maltose. It cannot go past a branch point so its action is stopped with a large part of the molecule still intact. This is called the beta limit dextrin. It will convert about 30% of the amylase and 45% of the amylopectin to maltose.

The other amylase of importance in wheat flour is α-amylase. Flour milled from sound wheat contains little or no α-amylase. Bread produced from flours with low levels of α-amylase will be low in volume and have a rough textured crumb. Thus, it is common to add malted barely or malted wheat flour to increase the α-amylase activity. Some millers will add fungal amylase preparations to increase the α-amylase activity. This requires a modified method of analysis.

Although sound grain contains low levels of α-amylase, the level of activity increases rapidly if the grain is sprouted. After the grain is mature, raising the moisture content (i.e. rain) may cause the grain to lose its dormancy and it may start to sprout while still in the field before harvest. This greatly increases the level of α-amylase and other enzymes.

α-Amylase Activity

α-Amylase breaks the α-1 4 bonds in starch in a more or less random attack.

It is not truly random as it does not break those bonds near an α-1 □6 branch point. Because of its attack pattern, each break dramatically reduces the size of the resulting dextrin. As a result the viscosity of the starch-water paste decreases rapidly. This is why α-amylase is sometimes referred to as the liquefying enzyme. Because of the rapid decrease in viscosity with each bond broken, measurement of viscosity is a sensitive measure of enzyme activity. The following three methods to measure α-amylase activity are all viscosity measuring procedures.

Falling Number. The falling number apparatus consists of a boiling water bath, matched test tubes (to conduct heat at the same rate), a stirrer, a stirring apparatus, and a timing mechanism. Flour plus a known amount of excess water is placed in a test tube and shaken to disperse the flour. The tube is placed in the apparatus that stirs the sample as if it is heated. At the end of stirring, the stirrer is dropped from the top position. The number of seconds required for the stirrer to fall through the flour-water paste is the falling number.

Sound flour will have a falling number of 400 seconds or greater. Increased enzyme activity will decrease the falling number. Flour milled from badly sprouted wheat may have falling numbers of 50 to 100 sec. Bakery flours are generally adjusted to 250-300 seconds. The procedure is rapid and reasonably reproducible. It can be used for either whole-wheat meal or flour.

Amylograph. In this procedure, flour and a buffer solution are stirred in a rotating bowl that is heated by an air bath. The sample is heated from room temperature to 95 minute. If one is only interested in the α-amylase activity, the test can be ended when the slurry reaches 95 . If the flour contains no α-amylase activity the viscosity (consistency) of the sample will continue to increase as the temperature rises to 95□. °Optimumly treated bread flours are in the range of 400-600 BU. If there is increased enzyme activity, the curve will peak at a lower viscosity (consistency) and at a lower temperature. The peak height is taken as the measure of enzyme activity. The amylograph procedure is relatively slow and requires a relatively are sample. The procedure is reproducible and still widely used to control the level of malt addition.

Rapid ViscoAnalyzer (RVA). The RVA was developed as a faster and more rugged version of the amylograph. Stimulating the amylograph, the temperature control can be programmed to heat at various rates. This viscosity is determined by the load on the stirring motor. As is the case with the amylograph, the height of the viscosity vs. temperature curve is related to the α-amylase activity of the sample. Because of the flexibility in controlling heating/cooling profile, the RVA has found many uses in cereal laboratories in addition to determining α-amylase activity. The RVA can also stimulate the falling number method when samples are heated at 95□ (203□) for three minutes. Stirring number is reported as the viscosity at the test's end.

Proteolytic Activity

Proteolytic enzymes hydrolyze proteins. Proteolytic activity can be divided into two basic types. Some enzymes hydrolyze an amino acid from the end of a protein molecule while other proteolytic enzymes attack the protein chain internally. The attack is not random but instead occurs between specific amino acids. The two types of enzyme are classified as exo- (which releases amino acids from the exterior) and endo- (which breaks the protein chain internally).

Soluble Nitrogen. In general the determination of proteolytic activity is difficult. The most popular method is to measure soluble nitrogen produced from a suitable substrate. The buffered enzyme is incubated with hemoglobin (substrate) for a suitable time. The protein is precipitated and the remaining soluble nitrogen determined. The results are reported as hemoglobin units (H.U.). This is a very popular method to measure proteolytic activity but it can be misleading. The test is biased to measure exo-enzyme activity. There can be considerable endo-activity with little or no soluble nitrogen produced. Additionally, flour proteins may be degraded differently than hemoglobin.

Rheological Measurement. The chemical determination of endo-proteolytic activity is complicated and difficult. Because the endo-proteolytic enzyme significantly reduces the size of the protein molecule by its activity, it changes the rheological properties (viscosity or consistency) of the system. Thus, a dough becomes more viscous and less elastic as the result of endo-proteolytic activity. The enzyme activity can then be estimated by following the change in rheological properties as a function of time. One of the advantages of using a rheological test is that it is not affected by exo-proteolytic activity. Reducing the size of the protein by one amino acid is insignificant from a rheological viewpoint. The other advantage is that the substrate used (native gluten) and the conditions of the test (dough) both apply directly to our area of concern.

GROWING APPETITE FOR WHEAT

Fig. Per-capita consumption of wheat flour roughly doubled over the past two decades, but at just a little more than 20 kg per year it is only a fraction of consumption in many more developed economies

Wheat consumption in Indonesia is growing rapidly, supported by an expanding middle class that has taken a liking to western cuisine. Indonesians still eat more rice than most other people in the world, but a fundamental change in the local diet is undeniable, as more and more consumers switch to toast for breakfast, pizza for lunch or doughnuts for dessert. Increasing demand for wheat-based foodstuffs in Indonesia presents exciting opportunities for investment in the wheat milling and food processing industries.

INSTANT NOODLES AND TALKING BREAD

The single main driver of rising wheat consumption in Indonesia is the growing popularity of instant noodles – particularly among young city-dwellers who appreciate the convenience of ready meals. More than half of Indonesia's wheat flour is turned into noodles. Indonesia is the second-biggest market for instant noodles and home to the world's largest instant noodle producer, Indofood Sukses Makmur. Trade policies aimed at protecting local farmers against rice imports have boosted domestic rice prices, ironically adding to the popularity of wheat-based instant noodles as a cheap alternative to traditional rice dishes. Meanwhile, retail chains such as Singapore-based BreadTalk and Indonesia's J.CO Donuts & Coffee are doing their part to expand the local bakery market, which consumes large amounts of wheat flour as well.

Growth potential far from exhausted

Wheat played an insignificant role in Indonesia until the late 1960s, but since then has been on a rapid ascent. Wheat imports grew from 170 thousand (MT) in 1967 to 6.5 million MT in marketing year 2011/2012, according to data from the United States Department of Agriculture. Per-capita consumption of wheat flour roughly doubled over the past two decades, but at just a little more than 20 kg per year it is only a fraction of consumption in many more developed economies, which highlights the market's growth potential.

There have been isolated attempts at cultivating wheat in Indonesia despite the tropical climate, but none of those efforts have progressed beyond the experimental stage. The industry will remain fully dependent on imports in the foreseeable future.

A market dependent on imports

The bulk of Indonesia's wheat supply comes from Australia, followed by Canada and the United States. The vast majority of shipments are in the form of grain delivered to mills in Indonesia. Wheat grain imports were valued at $2.3 billion in 2012, according to figures from the Central Statistics Agency (BPS). By contrast, Indonesia only bought $188 million worth of wheat flour from abroad in 2012. This still makes Indonesia one of the largest wheat flour importers of the world.

The government aims to limit imports of wheat flour to the necessary minimum. In December 2012 it imposed a 20% temporary emergency tariff to protect Indonesian millers and in the summer of 2013 officials were mulling more permanent measures. Its trade policies put the government at loggerheads with Turkey and Sri Lanka, the predominant exporters of wheat flour to Indonesia in 2012. Turkey has threatened to take WTO action against Indonesia's flour import policies.

Good news for wheat millers

Indonesia's protectionist stance on wheat flour imports is actually good news for the domestic milling industry, which will require substantial investment to meet future demand for flour. Tapping into this potential, FKS Indonesia, Malaysia's Malayan Flour Mills and Toyota Tsusho from Japan formed a joint venture, PT Bungasari Flour Mills Indonesia, with a first plant expected to commence operations in West Java in 2014.

At the beginning of 2013, Mitsubishi Corporation of Japan purchased of a 10% stake in Sriboga Raturaya, another leading player in the wheat flour sector in Indonesia, in order to tap into the growing market potential. Singapore-listed Wilmar International, for its part, announced the construction of two wheat mills in East Java.

New market entrants in the milling business need to take into account the fact that they are up against competition from well-integrated local players, including the giant Bogasari Flour Mills, a subsidiary of Indofood. On the bright side, the expanding market and the need for more modern and efficient mills should leave room for future growth. The spike in food prices in 2013 should also, in principle, compel the government to ensure a level playing field in the milling industry, which is currently characterized by a small number of companies.

Opportunities in food processing

Further downstream, appealing business opportunities await investors in food processing and retail. While they will hardly displace rice as the country's staple diet, bread, cereals, biscuits and cakes are carving out growing markets for themselves in Indonesia. The fact that per-capita consumption of these products is still very low means that their growth potential is all the higher. Government officials have been urging Indonesians to diversify their carbohydrate intake away from an over-reliance on rice, but the more powerful force behind changing culinary habits is likely a general westernization of Indonesian food. Foods that do not need cooking, such as breakfast cereals and bread, trump rice when it comes to accommodating the urban lifestyles of office workers.

Sales of bread and pastries rose by 12% to 30 trillion RP in 2012, according to the Indonesian Bakery Association (APEBI). While Jakarta and Surabaya are already well served with bakeries and patisseries, up-and-coming cities such as Medan and Makassar still harbour substantial growth potential. A number of highly successful franchises with strong brand identities point the way to success in Indonesia's emerging bakery market. Breakfast cereals appeal to Indonesians for their presumed health benefits over rice. Many cereals are still imported to Indonesia and sold at prices significantly higher than in their originating countries. The premium that a small but growing consumer segment is happy to spend on cereals suggests that in-country producers can achieve significant margins and market share.

Due to the fact that sales of wheat-based foods rely to a large extent on middle class consumers, they should prove quite resilient to economic downturns or rising inflation. The growth of the wheat product market in Indonesia, therefore, is a force to be reckoned with for years to come.

UNIFINE MILL

A Unifine mill is a single one-pass impact milling system which produces ultrafine-milled whole-grain wheat flour that requires no grain pre-treatment and no screening of the flour. Like the grist or stone mills that had dominated the flour industry for centuries, the bran, germ, and endosperm elements of grain are processed into a nutritious whole wheat flour in one step. Consumers had accepted whole wheat products produced by grist or stone mills. The flour produced by these mills was quite coarse as they included the bran and the germ elements of the grain.

As the nutritional value of vitamins, micronutrients, antioxidants, phytonutrients, amino acids, and fiber, were completely or relatively unknown in the late 19th century, removing the bran and the germ with the roller mill, invented at that time, was an attractive idea. With the elimination of the bran and the germ, the resulting "white" flour composed entirely of the endosperm produced an appealing product that research has since proven to be nutritionally deficient: The endosperm contains less than half of the total minerals and B-vitamins of the wheat kernel. Perhaps as significantly is the lost total food value since the bran and germ represent 17% of the whole grain, and the process of eliminating the bran and shorts in the roller mill typically yields only 70 to 75% of grain weight as flour product, thus significantly reducing the human food supply as well.

HISTORY

Development of the Unifine impact (one pass) milling system began in England in the late 1930s. The goal was to develop a simple, holistic system that would pulverize all the elements of the raw material into a fine powder by impacting a high speed flywheel. It was hoped that the resulting flour, made up of smaller particles, would have bakingqualities similar to the white, refined flours produced by the roller mills, yet retaining all of the bran, germ and endosperm of the whole grain. Following World War II, with England focused on rebuilding their shattered infrastructure, the Englishman John Wright eventually made his way to Pullman, Washington. There he succeeded in enlisting engineers at the Division of Industrial Research at Washington State College (now Washington State University) in the project. Following the development of a successful prototype, the milling, baking, and consumer acceptance of Unifine products was studied and funding of the first generation of commercial-grade mills came from a grant from the Washington State Grange. This grant was made possible by a donation by the Secretary of the Washington State Grange, Leonard Fulton, who ultimately went on to operate the first unifine flour mill.

Upon discovering that these mills could not be patented, the college opted to register the name *Unifine* and authorized Fulton and his *Fairfield Milling Company Inc.* to begin distribution of the first commercial flour milled by the machine under the brand name *Unifine* in 1962. A second Unifine Mill began operation under the label *Flour Girls* in the late 1970s directed and funded by individuals that participated in the research and development of the mills at the college.

The flour produced was used by home bakers to make light, whole wheat bread without the dense texture of breads made from traditional whole wheat flours. During that era of simmering consumer interest in the nutritional merits of whole wheat flour, these mills realized modest but ultimately unsustainable success. After roughly twenty years, these companies ceased operations and a new generation of unifine flour mills began producing flour under the *Azure Standard* brand. These flours are now marketed throughout the greater Pacific Northwestern section of the United States.

THE RISE OF WHOLE WHEAT FLOUR

Despite historical consumer preference for refined white flour, whole wheat flour products are ascendant largely due to changing consumer attitudes. The Whole Grains Councilindustry association reports an approximate doubling of the whole wheat flour production from 2003 to 2007. In another visible example, whole wheat bread has reached approximate parity with white bread as measured by slice volume in the United States; as of 2010, whole wheat bread narrowly surpasses white bread as measured by dollar volume. Fortification of white flour whole grains are more nutritious than refined products and wheat is no exception.

Whole wheat flour is more nutritious than refined white flour, although through food fortification, some micronutrients are added back to the white flour (required by law in some jurisdictions). Fortified white wheat flour does not, however, contain all of the macronutrients, fiber, antioxidants, phytonutrients, and much of the protein of the wheat's bran and germ. Whole wheat is a good source of calcium,iron, fiber, and other minerals like selenium.

INDUSTRY RESPONSE

Roller mills have adapted to the demand for whole grain products and most commercial whole wheat flour is currently produced using this milling system. In this case, the bran and the germ are further processed and then blended back into the endosperm (*white* flour) that it was separated from in the first place. While doing so enables the flour mills to use their existing equipment, it is a complex process.

The roller mill method usually requires *tempering* the grain before milling (raising the moisture content); in contrast, dry grain is milled in the case of the Unifine mill, which may account for the suggested decreased rancidity rates reported in Unifine flour.

Applications

The Unifine mill has not proven suitable for grinding harder materials such as gravel, or producing mineral powder for the mining industry or large scale powder-making that theroller mill system dominates. However, in the agricultural industry, where all the nutritional elements of the soft raw materials are desired in the end product, pulverizing it into powder in a single pass by the Unifine Mill has proven to be cost effective and less invasive. In addition to grains, a variety of agricultural products have been efficiently processed using this method including legumes and grapefruit rinds.

ROLLER MILL

Roller mills are mills that use cylindrical rollers, either in opposing pairs or against flat plates, to crush or grind various materials, such as grain, ore, gravel, plastic, and others. Roller grain mills are an alternative to traditional millstone arrangements in gristmills. Roller mills for rock complement other types of mills, such as ball mills and hammermills, in such industries as the mining and processing of ore and construction aggregate; cement milling; and recycling.

PRODUCING WHEAT FLOUR

To produce refined (*white*) wheat flour, grain is usually tempered, i.e. moisture added to the grain, before milling, to optimize milling efficiency. This softens the starchy "endosperm" portion of the wheat kernel, which will be separated out in the milling process to produce what is known to consumers as *white flour*. The addition of moisture also toughens the bran and ultimately reduces the energy input required to shatter the kernel, while at the same time avoiding the shattering of bran and germ particles to be separated out in this milling process by sieving or sifting.

The endosperm portion of the kernel makes up about 80% of the volume and is desirable because the products produced by this white flour are often considered to have milder flavor, smoother texture, and, in the case of bread, greater volume. The balance of the kernel is composed of the bran and the germ which tend to be coarser. With the invention of the roller milling system in the late 19th century, the bran and the germ were able to be removed, dramatically improving the appeal of baked products to the public.

The moistened grain is first passed through the series of break rollers, then sieved to separate out the fine particles that make up white flour. The balance are intermediate particles of endosperm (otherwise known as product *middling* or *farina*) and coarse particles of bran and germ. The middling then makes multiple passes through the reduction rolls, and is again sieved after each pass to maximize extraction of white flour from the endosperm, while removing coarser bran and germ particles.

To produce *whole wheat* flour, 100% of the bran and germ must be reintroduced to the white flour that the roller milling system was originally designed to separate it from.

Therefore, these elements are first ground on another mill (usually a pin mill). These finer bran and germ fractions are then reintroduced to the endosperm (*white flour*) to produce whole wheat flour made of 100% of the kernel of wheat.

GRISTMILL CONVERSION

In the 19th century roller mills were adapted to grist mills before replacing them. The mill used either steel or porcelain rollers. Between the years 1865 and 1872, the Hungarian milling industry upgraded and expanded the use of stone mills combined with roller mills in a process known as Hungarian high milling. Hungarian hard wheat so milled was claimed as integral to the "First in the world" success of the Vienna Bakery of the 1867 Paris Exposition.

Other applications

- Specialized for the high production of superfine pyrophyllite powder making in glass fiber industry
- Specialized for the high production of gangue powder making in coal industry
- Specialized for the high production of various of chemical raw material powder making in the chemical industry.

WORKING PRINCIPLE

While working, motor drives the hanger of the grinding roller to rotate through V pulley and centre bearing. The roller, which is hung by bearing and pendulum shaft, will roll along the inner circle of the roll ring while the hanger is rotating. A dust removal blower will generate negative pressure at the inlet and outlet of the grinder to prevent dust and radiating the heat in the machine.

WHEAT CULTIVATION IN INDIA: CONDITIONS, AND DISTRIBUTION

Next to rice, wheat is the most important food-grain of India and is the staple food of millions of Indians, particularly in the northern and north-western parts of the country.

It is rich in proteins, vitamins and carbohydrates and provides balanced food. India is the fourth largest producer of wheat in the world after Russia, the USA and China and accounts for 8.7 per cent of the world's total production of wheat.

CONDITIONS OF GROWTH:

Conditions of growth for wheat are more flexible than those of rice. In contrast to rice, wheat is a rabi crop which is sown in the beginning of winter and is harvested in the beginning of summer. The time of sowing and harvesting differs in different regions due to climatic variations.

The sowing of wheat crop normally begins in the September-October in Karnataka, Maharashtra, Andhra Pradesh, Madhya Pradesh and West Bengal; October-November in Bihar, Uttar Pradesh, Punjab, Haryana and Rajasthan and Nov.-Dee. In Himachal Pradesh and Jammu & Kashmir.

The harvesting is done in Jan.- Feb. in Karnataka, Andhra Pradesh, M.P., and in West Bengal; March-April in Punjab, Haryana, U.P. and Rajasthan and in April-May in Himachal Pradesh and J&K. The growing period is variable from one agro climatic zone to other that effects the vegetative and reproductive period leading to differences in potential yield. The important factors affecting the productivity are seeding time and methodology, crop establishment and climatic conditions during the growing season.

Wheat is primarily a crop of mid-latitude grasslands and requires a cool climate with moderate rainfall. The ideal wheat climate has winter temperature 10° to 15°C and summer temperature varying from 21°C to 26°C. The temperature should be low at the time of sowing but as the harvesting time approaches higher temperatures are required for proper ripening of the crop. But sudden rise in temperature at the time of maturity is harmful.

Wheat thrives well in areas receiving an annual rainfall of about 75 cm. Annual rainfall of 100 cm is the highest limit of wheat cultivation. The isohyet of 100 cm marks the boundary between wheat growing areas on one hand and rice growing areas on the other.

In areas of less than 50 cm annual rainfall, irrigation is necessary for its successful growth. In fact, wheat can be grown in areas with as little as 20-25 cm annual rainfall provided proper irrigation faculties are available.

About 5 to 7 watering are required in irrigated areas depending upon the amount of rainfall. While prolonged drought, especially in rainfed areas, at the time of maturity is harmful, light drizzles and cloudiness at the time of ripening help in increasing the yield. Frost at flowering time and hail storm at the time of ripening can cause heavy damage to the wheat crop.

Although wheat can be grown in a variety of soils, well drained fertile, friable loams and clay loams are the best suited soils for wheat cultivation. It also grows well in the black soil of the Deccan plateau. Wheat cultivation is an extensive type of farming which is highly mechanized and requires comparatively less labour. It is mainly grown in the flat alluvial plains of north India. To sum up wheat requires a combination of factors including cool climate with moderate rainfall, flat and well drained plain areas, fertile friable loam and heavy inputs in the form of irrigation, HYV seeds, fertilizers and mechanization.

Production:

Wheat is grown on 13 per cent of the cropped area of India. Table 24.5 shows the production trends of wheat in India.

It is clear from the table that all the three aspects of the crop i.e. production, area and yield have recorded rapid growth particularly after the introduction of the Green Revolution strategy in 1967. The production had more than doubled from 109.97 lakh tonnes in 1960-61 to 238.32 lakh tonnes in 1970- 71.

During the same period the area under wheat had increased by over 41 per cent and yield had increased by 53.6 per cent. The development of new varieties of seeds has brought about a real revolution in wheat production.

The phenomena of overall development in wheat farming is still continuing although the pace of progress has slowed down with Green Revolution reaching its mature stage Production, area and yield of wheat reached their zenith in 1999-2000 after which varying trends have been observed .

Table. Production, Area and Yield of Wheat in India:

Year	**1950-51**	**1960-61**	**1970-71**	**1980-81**	**1990-91**	**1997-98**	**1998-99**	**1999-00**	**2000-01**	**2001-02**	**2002-03**	**2003-04**
Production (Million tonnes)	6.5	11.0	23.8	36.3	55.1	66.3	71.3	16 A	69.7	72.8	65.1	72.1
Area (Million hectares)	9.7	12.9	18.2	22.3	24.2	26.7	27.5	27.5	25.7	26.4	24.9	26.6
Yield (kg/hectare)	663	851	1307	1630	2281	2285	2590	2778	2708	2761	2618	2707

Our yield of 2,707 kg/hectare (2003-04) is still very low as compared to that of some other wheat producing countries like in Russian Federation, the USA, Australia and China.

It is estimated that yield can be raised upto 4,000 kg/hectare in irrigated areas and upto 2,0 kg/hectare in unirrigated areas by using appropriate location specific technology including better quality seeds, proper fertilizers and control of weeds, pests and diseases.

Further, there is vast scope for extending wheat cultivation to non-traditional areas like Assam valley and in Orissa. This can be done by timely harvest of the kharif crops and by reducing the extent of fallow land. West Bengal has already started growing wheat in sufficient quantity. By adopting these and some other positive measures, we can hope to increase the production of wheat upto 85-90 million tonnes by the year 2010 A.D.

Distribution:

Wheat production is mainly confined to North-Western parts of the country. Table 24.6 gives the distribution pattern of wheat in India.

Uttar Pradesh, Punjab and Haryana are the three prominent wheat producing states.

These states account for about 60 per cent of the wheat area and produce about three-fourths of the total wheat production in India. In fact, Punjab, Haryana and the contiguous western parts of U.P. have earned the distinction of being called the 'Granary of India'. The other major wheat producing states are Rajasthan, Madhya Pradesh and Bihar.

Table. Distribution of Wheat in India (2002-03):

State	Production	Area	Yield (quintal/ hectare)		
	Lakh tonnes	% age of all India	Lakh hectares	%age of all India	
1. Uttar Pradesh	236.12	36.27	90.94	36.58	26.0
2. Punjab	141.75	21.77	33.75	13.58	42.0
3. Haryana	91.92	14.12	22.68	9.12	40.5
4. Rajasthan	48.78	7.49	18.01	7.24	27.1
5. Madhya pradesh	42.85	6.59	30.79	12.38	13.9
6. Bihar	41.23	6.34	21.66	8.72	19.0
Others	48.31	7.42	30.77	12.38	—
India	650.96	100.00	248.60	100.00	26.2

Uttar Pradesh:

Uttar Pradesh is the largest wheat producing state of India accounting for over 36 per cent of the production and 36 per cent of the wheat area of the country. In 2002-03, this state produced 236.12 lakh tonnes of wheat. Fine alluvial soil deposited by the mighty Ganga and its several big and small tributaries and a close network of canals, supplemented by large number of tube wells have helped U.P. to occupy the top position.

More than half of the wheat area lies in the Ganga-Ghagra doab. Next in importance is the Ganga-Yamuna doab. These two doabs account for about 75 per cent wheat of U.P. About 55 districts of Uttar Pradesh produce wheat out of which 43 are the leading producers. Saharanpur, Muzaffamagar, Meerut,

Moradabad, Rampur, Budaun, Etawah, Hardoi, Bahraich, Kheri, Gonda, Basti, etc. are the main producing districts. However, wheat production to the east of Varanasi declines due to high rainfall and heavy soils.

Punjab:

Although very small state as compared to Uttar Pradesh, Punjab has emerged as a very important producer of wheat in India. The Green Revolution strategy has helped Punjab in making rapid strides in wheat production. In fact, Punjab has drawn maximum benefit from Green Revolution and in Punjab too it is the wheat crop which has been benefited the most.

The excellent irrigation system provided by a close network of canals and the tube wells is supplemented by light rainfall associated with the western disturbances. The fertile alluvial soil brought by the rivers of the Indus system is ideal for wheat production. Over and above, the Punjab farmer is very enterprising and is always willing to adopt the new farm technologies. Punjab accounts for over 21.77 per cent of the wheat production and 13.58 per cent of wheat area of India and has the distinction of giving the highest yields of 42 quintal/hectare.

In 2002-03, Punjab produced 141.75 lakh tonnes of wheat, thus occupying second position among the major wheat producing states of India. Punjab has 12 leading wheat producing districts. Jalandhar, Ludhiana, Sangrur, Bhatinda, Amritsar, Firozepur, Faridkot, Mansa, Kapurthala, Fatehgarh Sahib, Rupnagar and Patiala are the main producing districts. The state has a large surplus and contributes a lot of wheat to the central pool.

Haryana:

The physical and human conditions for wheat cultivation in Haryana are the same as those prevailing in Punjab, although to a lesser degree. The impact of Green Revolution is clearly visible in Haryana also. Presently, Haryana accounts for a little over 9 per cent of the wheat area of India and produces over 14 per cent of the total wheat of the country.

The yield 40.5 quintals/hectare is the second highest in the country next only to that of Punjab. Karnal, Kurukshetra, Ambala, Kaithal, Panipat, Sonipat, Rohtak, Jind, Hisar, Sirsa and Gurgaon are important producing districts.

Rajasthan:

Vast stretches of sandy desert, scarcity of rainfall and paucity of irrigation facilities have been restricting wheat cultivation in Rajasthan since long. But some of the irrigation projects initiated after Independence, especially the Indira Gandhi Canal, have brought about considerable improvement in the cropping pattern of the state.

Currently, Rajasthan accounts for 7.49 per cent of the total wheat production and 7.24 per cent of wheat area of India. Over 20 districts are producing wheat and 11 are major producers. Ganganagar, Hanumangarh, Bharatpur, Kota, Alwar, Jaipur, Chittaurgarh, Tonk, Sawai Mandhopur, Udaipur and Pali are important wheat producing districts of Rajasthan.

Madhya Pradesh:

Madhya Pradesh is the fifth largest wheat producing state and accounts for over 6 per cent of the total production of India. The state has over 30 lakh hectares of land under wheat. This is an indication of low yield which is only 13.9 quintal/hectare; about half of the national average of 26.2 quintals/hectare. Steps have to be taken to increase the yield so that the state occupies a prestigious position among the wheat producing states of India. Sagar, Vidisha, Tikamgarh, Morena, Sehore, Gwalior, Guna, Satna, Bhind and Chhatarpur are important wheat producing districts.

Bihar:

Bihar accounts for 6.1 per cent of wheat production and about 8.7 per cent of wheat area of India with a low yield of 19 quintal/hectare. This means that there is need to improve the situation with respect to yields. Most of the wheat is produced in the North Bihar Plain. Rohtas, Bhojpur, Saran, Nalanda, Paschim and Purba Champaran, Siwan and Begusarai are the main districts.

Others: Gujarat, Maharashtra, West Bengal and Himachal Pradesh are the other important producers of wheat in India. In Gujarat, wheat is mainly produced in Mahi and Sabarmati valleys. Mahesana, Junagadh, Bhavnagar, Amreli, Bharuch, Rajkot and Kheda are important wheat producing districts.

In Maharashtra, wheat is produced in the valleys of the Wardha, Tapi, Godavari, Bhima, Puma and Krishna. West Bengal has made significant progress both in area and production of wheat with the introduction of new technology.

From a meagre 45.5 thousand tonnes of production and 55.4 thousand hectares of land in 1966-67, the state has reached the figures of 887 thousand tonnes and 405 thousand hectares in 2002-03. Most of the production comes from Birbhum, Burdwan, Murshidabad and Nadia districts.

In Himachal Pradesh wheat is produced mainly in Kangra, Mandi, Sirmaur and Una districts. Srinagar, Baramula, Doda Anantnag, Jammu and Punch are the main producers in Jammu and Kashmir. Some wheat is also produced in Bijapur, Raichur, Belgaum and Dharwar districts of Karnataka.

TRADE:

About one-third of the total production of wheat enters trade. Punjab, Haryana, Uttar Pradesh, Rajasthan and Madhya Pradesh are surplus states and supply wheat to deficit states like Maharashtra, West Bengal, Bihar and the Union Territory of Delhi.

India imported 29.23 lakh tonnes of wheat in 1970-71 and 70.94 lakh tonnes in 1975-76. Since then India has become self-sufficient in wheat production and does not have to import wheat. Rather India is in a position to export small quantities of wheat.

MAJOR WHEAT PRODUCING STATES IN INDIA

MAJOR WHEAT PRODUCING STATES

The major wheat producing states in India are

1. Uttar Pradesh,
2. Punjab,
3. Haryana, and
4. Madhya Pradesh.

Uttar Pradesh

The state of Uttar Pradesh is the largest producer of wheat, accounting for over 34 per cent of the wheat produced in India.

It has the largest area under wheat. It is grown in almost every part of the state; but the greatest concentration is in the western part.

The important wheat producing districts of the state of Uttar Pradesh are Meerut, Aligarh, Agra, Muzaffarnagar, Saharanpur, Bulandshahar, Kanpur and Mathura.

Punjab:

The Punjab ranks second (accounting of about. 20 per cent of the total) in wheat production in India. The important wheat pro-ducing districts in Punjab State are Ferozepur, Ludhiana, Patiala and Amritsar.

Haryana:

Haryana occupies the third place in wheat production among the states of India. The important districts of this state are Hissar, Ambala, Jind, Rohtak and Faridabad.

Madhya Pradesh:

Madhya Pradesh ranks the fourth position in wheat pro-duction. The main wheat producing districts of Madhya Pradesh are Sagar, Jabalpur, Sehare, Gwalior, Indore and Ujjain.

Other States:

The other wheat producing states of India are

- — Rajasthan (Ganganagar, Kota etc,),
- — Bihar (Saran, Champaran, Gaya, Patna),

— Maharashtra,
— Gujarat,
— West Bengal,
— Karnataka,
— Jammu and Kashmir,
— Himachal Pradesh and
— Jharkhand.

Production: The average wheat production of the country is more 1,2oo kg per hectare. The yield is higher on irrigated lands. Punjab and Haryana have the highest yields (above 1,520 kg per hectare). The production has been steadily raised due to the introduction of high yielding varieties, such as, Sonara, Hira, Moti, Sonalika and Kalyan Sona. These are selected from the original Mexican dwarf wheat and they give much higher yields.

5

Pulses Industry

The term "legume" refers to the plants whose fruit is enclosed in a pod. Legumes represent a vast family of plants including more than 600 genera and more than 13,000 species.) When growing, legumes fix nitrogen into the soil, which reduces the need for chemical fertilizers. Well-known legumes include alfalfa, clover, fresh peas, lupins, mesquite, soy and peanuts.

Pulse:

Pulses are part of the legume family, but the term "pulse" refers only to the dried seed. Dried peas, edible beans, lentils and chickpeas are the most common varieties of pulses. Pulses are very high in protein and fibre, and are low in fat. Like their cousins in the legume family, pulses are nitrogen-fixing crops that improve the environmental sustainability of annual cropping systems.

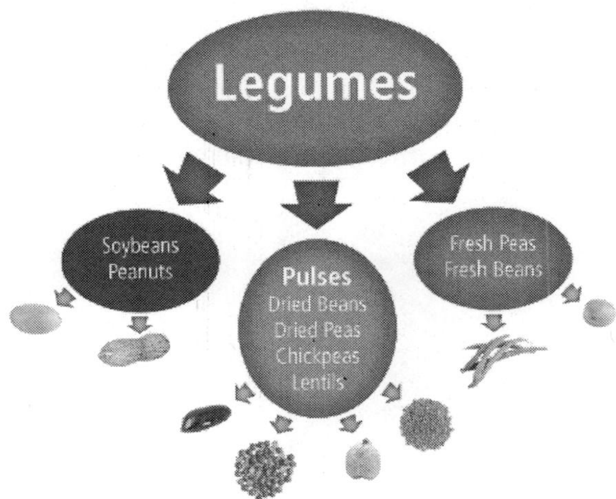

Pulses are a great tasting addition to any diet. They are rich in fibre and protein, and have high levels of minerals such as iron, zinc, and phosphorous as well as folate and other B-vitamins. In addition to their nutritional profile and links to improved health, pulses are unique foods in their ability to reduce the environmental footprint of our grocery carts. Put it all together and these sensational seeds are a powerful food ingredient that can be used to deliver the results of healthy people and a healthy planet.

Pulses come in a variety of shapes, sizes and colours and can be consumed in many forms including whole or split, ground in to flours or separated into fractions such as protein, fibre and starch.

Pulses do not include fresh beans or peas. Although they are related to pulses because they are also edible seeds of podded plants, soybeans and peanuts differ because they have a much higher fat content, whereas pulses contain virtually no fat.

PULSES MARKET: INDIA & WORLD

Pulses are seeds of annual legumes that include plants such as Bambara beans, dry beans, horse beans, dry chickpeas, cow peas, dry lentils, lupins, dry peas, pigeon peas, and vetches that are used for feeding humans as well as cattle. Pulses play an important and varying role in farming systems and in the diets of poor people worldwide.

They are ideal in achieving three developmental goals in developing countries—improving nutrition and health conditions, reducing poverty through higher food security, and enhancing ecosystem resilience. Besides their nutritional benefits and use as cattle feed, pulses production provides a number of agronomic advantages to the producers. The rotational benefit of pulses tends to raise the supply of soil nitrogen, reducing, as a result, the requirement of not only additional nitrogenous chemical fertilizers for the following crops, but also that of chemical pesticides and weedicide, disrupting thereby the periodical crop disease and insect cycles. A multi-layer planning horizon by farmers would capture such benefits through pulses cultivation for the crops grown the year after pulses, realizing their optimum yields, and lower, consequently, the cost for herbicides and fungicides.

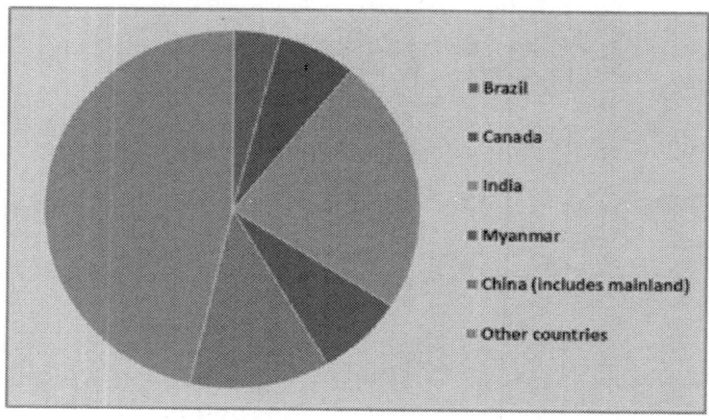

Fig. Share of major pulses producers in 2012

The world's major producers of pulses are India (23.1%), Canada (6.7%), China (12.08%), Myanmar (7.57%), and Brazil (4.03%), which together account for half of the global output.

The pulse industry in India generally refers to a number of crops like chickpeas (locally known as chana), tur, masur, urad, moong, and peas. According to 2012 statistics from the United Nation's Food and Agriculture Organization (FAO), the most important pulses by production are dry beans (29.4%), dry peas (24.5%), chickpeas (13.7%), dry cow peas (8.5%), pulses (nes) (7.2%), and broad beans (5.7%). These together contributed 89% to the total global output of 70 million tonnes in 2012. In world production, dry bean is the most important going by area and production, followed by chickpea and pea. Lentil, which constitutes 4.6% of the global pulses output, is mainly produced in India, Australia, and Canada.

This study provides global and regional trend analysis on the pulse crop production, price, trade, and consumption patterns observed in the developing world, developed countries, and globally from 1960s to 2011. Reviewing secondary data and published research and analysis reports, the study targets major pulse producers including both developing and developed countries.

MARKET FACTORS

Pulse crops lack futures market. This is possibly the major reason why prices are negotiated directly by the different market functionaries, including exporters and importers, through the supply chain of pulses, based on supply and demand factors for each type of pulse crop from year to year. The absence of a price-discovery mechanism due to the absence of futures market in pulses calls for forecasting practices that generate effective price predictions that will help in understanding the future pricing of pulse crops, enhancing the success in producing and improving the distribution mechanism. Because such forecasting practices are difficult to develop, all factors affecting such price predictions are not quantifiable.

Price being the major analyzable variable, the factors that influence the supply and demand side of the market need to be examined. The key supply-side determinants that affect prices are productivity and area used for cultivating pulses, globally. These factors are pragmatic in the long run, and cannot have considerable influence over short-run analysis carried over in this study. The demand-side determinants are consumption pattern, population, and income growth, urbanization, changes in food habits, and shifts in trade flows, and so on. Although each of these factors is not studied separately, the effects of these factors are captured through few measurable and quantitative variables like trade flows, per-capita consumption, stock variation, and so on. Also, this study doesn't get into many details to understand the influence of competing feed ingredients like soya bean meals on pulses demand.

PRODUCTION ISSUES

World supply is by far the most important factor affecting farm pulse price changes from year to year. For production, though much dependent on weather conditions, the long-run factors are area under cultivation and potential yields. Compared with markets in other commodities like cereals and oil seeds, the pulses market remains a relatively thin market owing to its small aggregate global output. Global cereal production grew nearly three times in the past half a century, but pulse output has risen at a slow pace of less than one and three-fourths through the same period.

In absolute terms, pulse production increased from 41 million tonnes in 1961 to 70 million tonnes in 2012, showing a net increase of only around 29 million tonnes, with a growth of barely 1.4% yearly . However, on the bright side, over the past 15 years, the overall pulse production has increased at a rate higher than the growth rate in population both in developing and developed countries, and there are significant improvements in production due to the increased consumption trends globally. Production of pulses increased from 56 million tonnes in 2001 to 70 million in 2012, representing a growth of 2.2 % yearly.

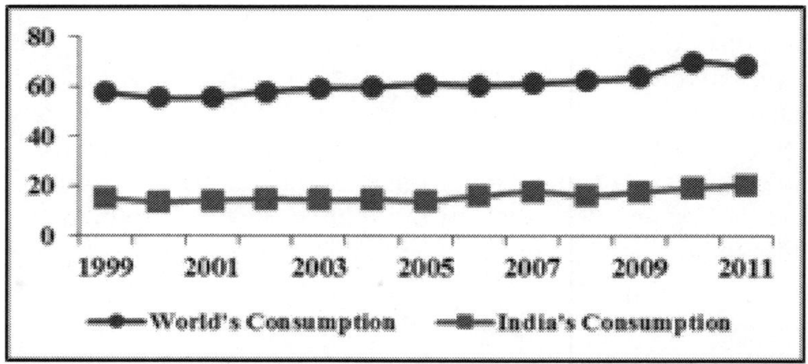

Fig. Pulse yield (kg/hectare) for major pulse producers, 1999 to 2012

While pulses markets have improved in recent years, the complexities of pulse production compared with other crops span from agronomic to other problems like policy matters. In major pulse-producing countries, due to the lack of policy attention by the government, investments attracted by pulses are much fewer than those in cereal and other crops. Other factors that have inhibited the productivity growth are lack of irrigation, low appli-cation of fertilizers, climatic conditions, and low remunerative prices to the farmers.

India, although being a major producer and consumer of pulses, due to restricted irrigation facilities and barren land areas, and poor policy initiatives to promote the pulse market, the productivity problems are much worse than those in other major pulse-producing countries. Pulse productivity is also much higher in most major pulse-producing countries than that of India. Thus, the pulse yield in Canada improved from 1141 kg/ha in 1961 to 1893 kg/ha in 2012. Other countries such as Brazil, China, and Myanmar showed similar trends through the same period . However, the yield in India hasn't improved much, and has always been hovering around 600 kg/ha since 1961.

Table. Pulses yield (kg/hectare), 1961 and 2012

Country/ Year	1961	2012
China	876	1431
Myanmar	442	1323
Canada	1141	1892
Brazil	668	1027
India	540	641

GLOBAL TRADE

The trend in cross-border trade across the world is a major factor that influences pulses prices. Global trade in pulses increased almost six fold over the past three decades, from 1.7 million tonnes in 1981 to 12.4 million in 2011. With the value of global exports increasing more than 11 times over the same period, the unit value of exports increased almost four times from $133.8 in 1961 to $654.6 in 2011, representing an annual average increase of 7.6%. On the other hand, the total production globally increased by just around 69% over the same half a century, from 40.35 million tonnes to 68.2 million tonnes. Evidently, prices of pulses traded in the international markets are rising more swiftly than their production, with demand for pulses running ahead of supply. It follows that the growing import demand for pulses is influencing the prices of pulses. That portends the future of pulse prices, as demand is destined to rise, with anticipated population growth and increasing incomes in developing economies of not only India, but across the nations in southeast Asia, as well as western Africa and South Africa.

Incidentally, the expansion of global trade of pulses has delivered a platform for many countries to be increasingly engaged in pulse cultivation and export trade. Canada, the U.S., and Australia amid developed countries, and China, Myanmar, and Argentina among developing countries, have emerged over the years as major exporters of pulses.

GLOBAL CONSUMPTION

Global consumption of pulses for food use differs from production, owing to stock variations from year to year, and the use of pulses for seeding, animal feeding, and other non-food utilization, besides wastages. Assuming little change in stocks from year to year, and for want of data on non-food uses of pulses, including seeding, which will be in any case a small fraction of the total production, one may tacitly assume that global consumption is equal to global production. This simplistic assumption does not in any way detract from the utility of thus derived global consumption, as more important than absolute consumption *per se* is the year-to-year variation in it. The year-to-year production will necessarily reflect the year-to-year variation in consumption, as non-food uses do not vary much from year to year, and may well be assumed to remain unchanged from year to year like year-beginning stocks, too.

*T*he trends in global and India's pulse consumption. With steady increase in production, consumption of pulses also has been rising gradually from year to year, both globally and in India. In fact, India accounts for nearly a third of the global pulses consumption. India's share in the global pulses consumption has been rising over the years. In 1999, its share was 26.38%, which rose to a little over 30% in 2011. Not surprisingly, India has emerged as a major importer of pulses in the world, with its share in global pulses imports swelling from just 3.8% in 1999 to 26.47% in 2011. In fact, in 2009 it contributed as much as 31.6% to the world trade. The share has fallen in recent years, owing mainly to increase in the country's production, following increase in minimum support prices (MSP) provided by the government.

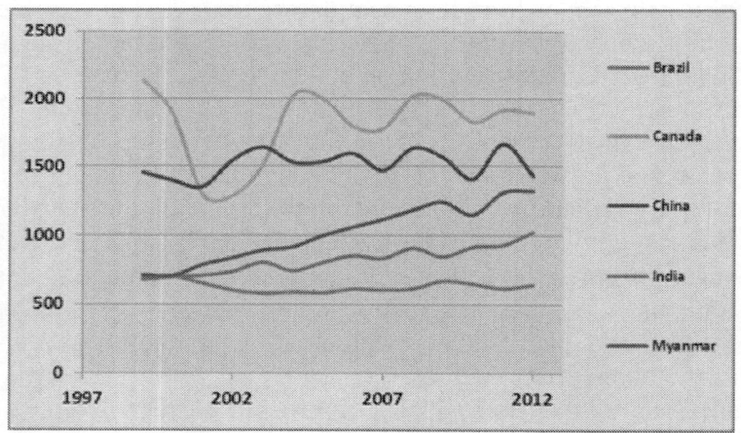

Fig. Global consumption of pulses vis-à-vis consumption of pulses in India, 1999–2011 *(in million tonnes)*

With a modest increase in the overall global production and consumption of pulses through a little over a decade, the per capita consumption of pulses, globally as well as in India, also showed a moderate positive rising trend since the beginning of this century . India's per capita consumption has been rising due not so much to increase in domestic production as to increasing imports, though some increase in production has, no doubt, taken place in the past few years. Although, the annual growth in pulse production in India has been, by and large, less than the growth in population, per capita consumption has improved, thanks to liberalization of pulses import policies since 1990s, and imposition of export curbs.

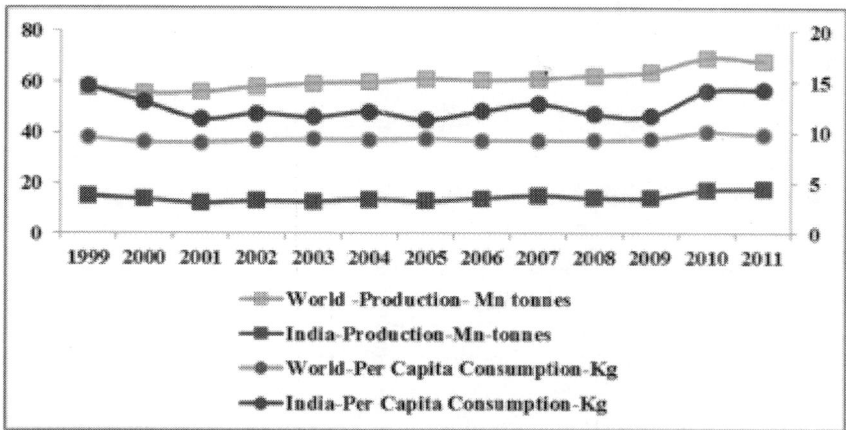

Fig. Trends in global and India's production (in million tonnes) and per capita consumption (in kg per annum), 1999–2011

PRICES OF PULSES

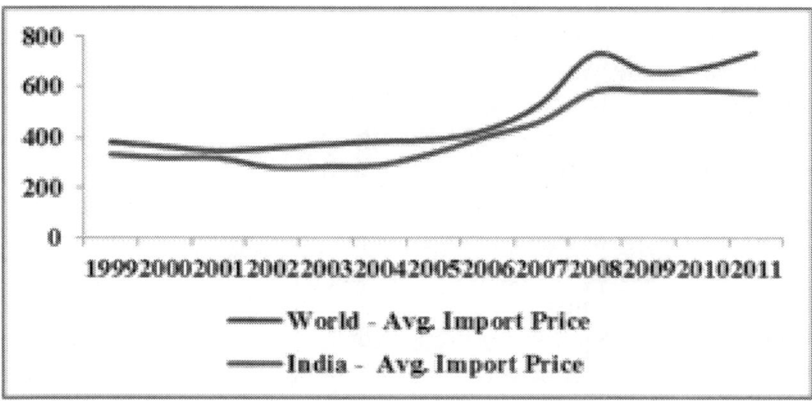

Fig. World and India's average import prices (in $ per tonne) of pulses, 1999–2011

For this study, import prices of pulses have been chosen, as these truly reflect the prices of pulses that are traded in the global market. *T*he average import prices of pulses for the world as a whole, and for India separately. As may be seen, the average prices of pulses, both globally and for India, have been rising, implying that the supply of pulses has been increasingly lagging behind demand.

But the world average import prices have generally been higher than those that India pays for its imports. This is probably due to India's strong bargaining position in the world market, as it is the largest importer of pulses. India also usually prefers to import low-priced pulse varieties. Over the years, India has been importing more from nearby countries like Myanmar in Asia, and West Africa, than from distant land like the U.S. and Canada. It has thus been saving on transport costs.

Conclusion

The pulse crop, an important source of nutrition and income for millions around the world, is cultivated over 58 million hectares in developing countries and another three million hectares in developed countries. Nearly 15% of the global crop enters world trade. Considering the anticipated increase in global demand in the future, owing to rising incomes, and growing population on the one hand, and the supply-side constraints like land availability for pulse cultivation, lack of technological breakthrough in pulse varieties and cultivation, resulting in low productivity, on the other, it seems that unless area under pulses expands significantly, or productivity improves appreciably, it would be difficult for the pulses market to see any appreciable growth in the coming years.

With no varietal breakthrough in cultivation seen anywhere on the horizon, and the expected growing competition for food and feed crops for the available cultivable land, it appears unlikely that either pulse cultivation will expand considerably, or pulse productivity will improve much, over the next two decades. Based on the estimated population in 2020 and 2030, and based on the last 10-year trend growth in global consumption, the demand for pulses for these two years would increase to 75.9 million tonnes in 2020, and 81.9 in 2030, from the current level of a little over 70 million. It follows that the supply–demand chasm will widen in the future, resulting in further inflation in pulse prices. India, being a major producer and consumer of pulses, will necessarily have to bear the brunt of such price inflation.

The authorities should therefore take appropriate steps to divert, to some extent, the demand for vegetable proteins from pulses, to proteins from oilmeals, if not to encourage consumption of milk and meat products among the Indian populace.

PRODUCTION TREND

Table. Area Production and Yield of Total Pulses in India

Year	Area (million hectares)	Production(million tonnes)	Yield (kg./ hectares)
1980-81	22.46	10.63	473
1990-91	24.66	14.26	578
2000-2001	20.35	11.08	544
2010-11	26.40	18.24	691
2011-12	24.46	17.09	699
2012-13	23.47	18.34	781

In India pulses are cultivated on marginal lands under rain fed conditions. Only 15% of the area under pulses has assured irrigation. Because of the high level of fluctuations in pulse production (due to biotic and abiotic stress) and prices (in the absence of an effective government price support mechanism) farmers are not very keen on taking up pulse cultivation despite high wholesale pulse prices in recent years. Farmers are getting attracted towards cash crops like Bt cotton, maize and oilseeds (mainly soybeans) because of better return and lower risk. Consequently area under these crops has increased over the years to the detriment of pulses .

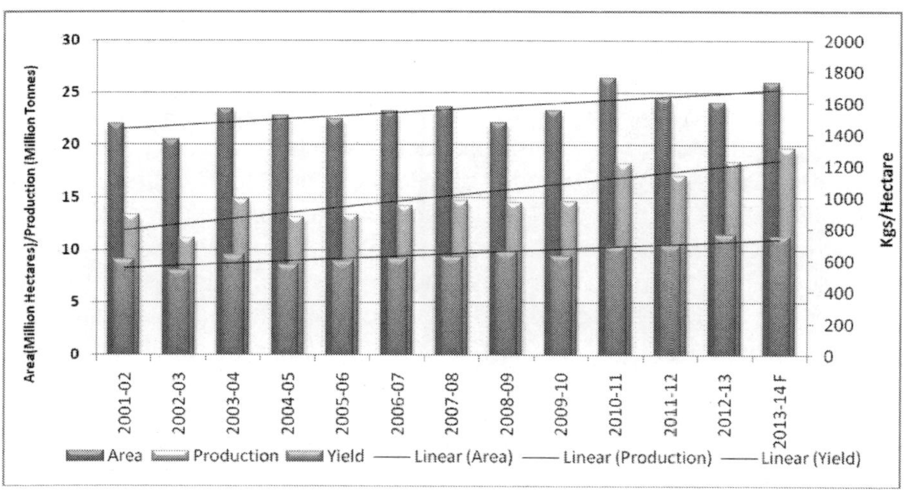

Fig. Trend in Area, Yield, and Production of Pulses

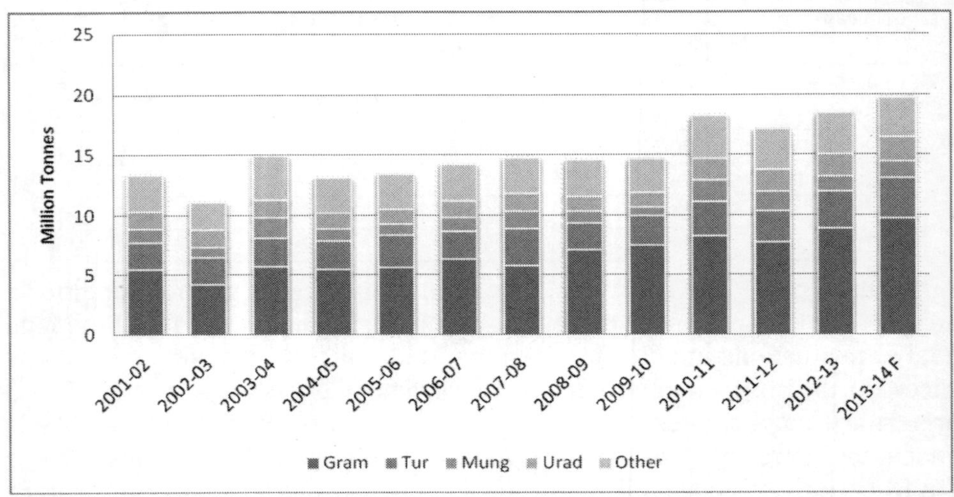

Fig. Trend in Pulse Production by Type

Nevertheless, improvement in yields, albeit modest, has contributed to higher pulse production in recent years . Most of the increase in pulse production in recent years has been in gram . Low pulse yield in India compared to other counties is attributed to poor spread of improved varieties and technologies, abrupt climatic changes, vulnerability to pests and diseases, and generally declining growth rate of total factor productivity

In order to give the much needed fillip to pulse production, the government has included pulses in the NFSM (along with wheat and rice) since the launch of NFSM in October 2007 and has been significantly increasing the MSP for most pulses. Over the past four years, the increase in MSP was a massive 87 percent for tur, 71 percent for urd, and 63 percent for mung. Among rabi pulses MSP for gram for MY 2014-15 was fixed at Rs. 3,100 per quintal and masur at Rs, 2,950 per quintal, although a modest increase over the MY 2013-14 level of Rs. 3,000 and Rs. 2,900 per quintal, nevertheless a massive increase of 76 percent and 58 percent, respectively, since 2010-11 .

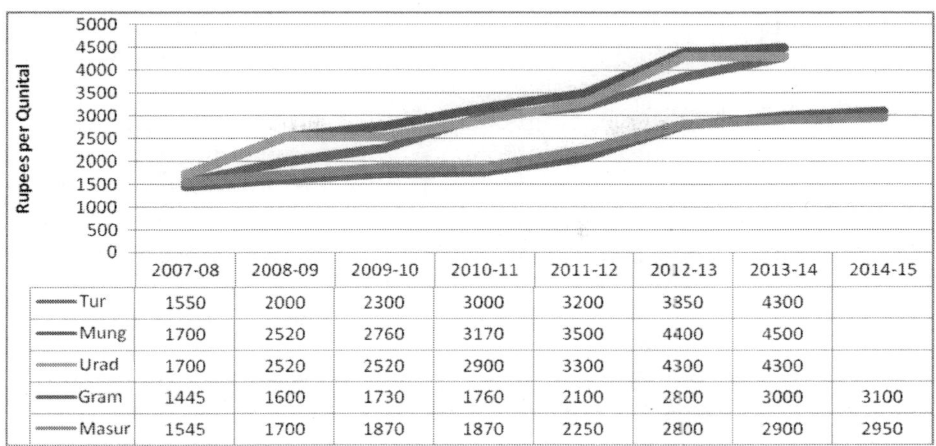

	2007-08	2008-09	2009-10	2010-11	2011-12	2012-13	2013-14	2014-15
Tur	1550	2000	2300	3000	3200	3850	4300	
Mung	1700	2520	2760	3170	3500	4400	4500	
Urad	1700	2520	2520	2900	3300	4300	4300	
Gram	1445	1600	1730	1760	2100	2800	3000	3100
Masur	1545	1700	1870	1870	2250	2800	2900	2950

Fig. Trend in Minimum Support Prices for Pulses

CONSUMPTION AND PRICES

Pulse production has recorded less than one percent annual growth during the past 40 years, which is less than half of the growth rate in Indian human population. Consequently per capita production and availability of pulses in the country has witnessed sharp decline. Per capita net pulse availability has declined from around 60 grams per day in the 1950s to 40 grams in the 1980s and further to around 35 grams per day in 2000s. However, in the past four years, there has been significant increase in consumption averaging around 50 grams due to somewhat higher production, thanks to the National Food Security Mission (NFSM) focus on pulses, and larger imports, mostly of dry peas from Canada and Australia .

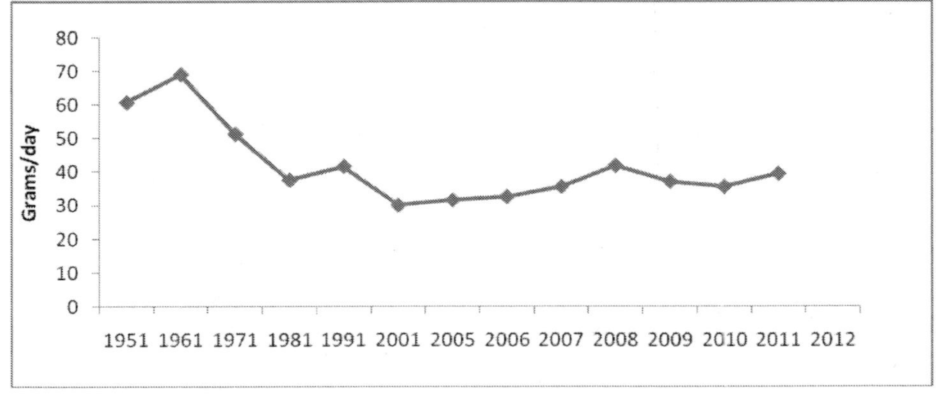

Fig. Per capita net availability of pulses

Higher production combined with larger imports has resulted in a marginal increase in pulse consumption estimated at around 50 grams per day in 2012-13 compared to less than 40 grams prior to 2012-13. This level of consumption is estimated to have been maintained in 2013-14. Lager imports of dry peas in recent years due its lower international prices have resulted in its increased share in the domestic pulse consumption. The increasing mismatch between production and consumption of pulses has resulted in larger imports of pulses in recent years. Imports of pulses in 2012-13 (Apr-Mar) were a record 4.0 million tonnes an increase of 500,000 tonnes over 2011-12.

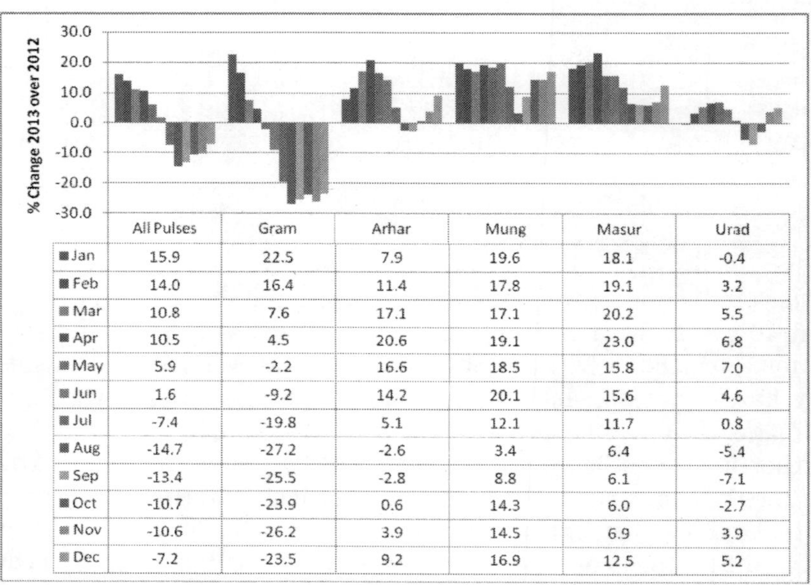

	All Pulses	Gram	Arhar	Mung	Masur	Urad
Jan	15.9	22.5	7.9	19.6	18.1	-0.4
Feb	14.0	16.4	11.4	17.8	19.1	3.2
Mar	10.8	7.6	17.1	17.1	20.2	5.5
Apr	10.5	4.5	20.6	19.1	23.0	6.8
May	5.9	-2.2	16.6	18.5	15.8	7.0
Jun	1.6	-9.2	14.2	20.1	15.6	4.6
Jul	-7.4	-19.8	5.1	12.1	11.7	0.8
Aug	-14.7	-27.2	-2.6	3.4	6.4	-5.4
Sep	-13.4	-25.5	-2.8	8.8	6.1	-7.1
Oct	-10.7	-23.9	0.6	14.3	6.0	-2.7
Nov	-10.6	-26.2	3.9	14.5	6.9	3.9
Dec	-7.2	-23.5	9.2	16.9	12.5	5.2

Fig. Wholesale Price Inflation Trend in Pulses (% change in 2013 over 2012)

2012-13 imports included 1.37 million tonnes of dry peas and dun peas (mattar), 506,000 tonnes of pigeon pea (tur), 642,000 tonnes of green pea (mung), 698,000 tonnes of chick peas, 506,000 tonnes of lentil (masur), 84,000 tonnes of kidney beans (rajma), 180,000 tonnes of other beans and 24,000 tonnes of other pulses. Imports in 2013-14 through November 2013 at 2 million tonnes were about 500,000

tonnes behind imports during the corresponding period of 2012-13 reflecting larger domestic production and higher cost of imported pulses due to the depreciation of Indian rupee against US$. Total imports in 2013-14 are projected at 3.5 million tonnes. Domestic price inflation for pulses as a group measured by Wholesale Price Index remained in the negative territory since June 2013, largely due a significant decline in gram prices, the major pulse in India. Price inflation in other pulses, mainly mung and masur, although showing some declining trend, remained high in 2013 .

Due to expected higher production of gram in 2014, price inflation of pulses as a group is likely to remain subdued in 2014-15, unless the 2014 kharif season pulse crop declines significantly.

TRADE

India imported about 4 million tonnes of pulses during 2012-13. Although based on current assessment kharif pulses production in 2013-14 has remained nearly the same as in 2012-13, due to a likely increase in *rabi* season pulse production, imports are expected to decline marginally during 2014-15. .

Is seen that import of pulses in 2013 has shown a decline in September. Gram imports were the highest in January, but became negligible thereafter as domestic production was at a record level. Dry pea imports are seen to be fluctuating while masur imports increased till July 2013. Overall, import requirements may be of the order of 3.8 million tonnes in the current year.

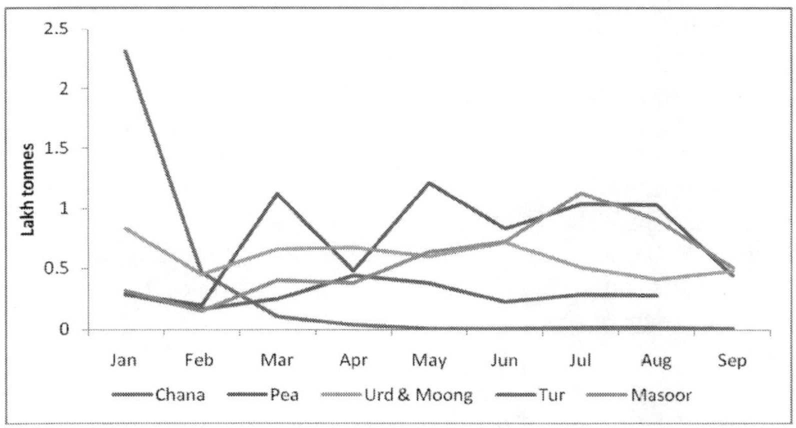

Fig. Month wise Pulse Import during 2013

Despite being world's largest producer of pulses, only small exports of pulses are taking place from India, both because of restrictions on exports and the high domestic demand. The supply- demand balance sheet for pulses is provided in Table 2.

Table. Demand and Supply Balance Sheet for Pulses (000 tonnes)

Total pulses	2010-11	2011-12	2012-13	2013-14
Production	18,240	17,090	18,340	19,770
Imports	2,780	3,500	4,010	3,500
Total supply	21,020	20,590	22,350	23,270
Total Export	209	175	200	200
Domestic Use	20,811	20,415	22,150	23,070
Total utilization	21,020	20,590	22,350	23,270
% imports to production	15.2	20.5	21.7	17.8

SUMMARY AND CONCLUSION

Because of the high level of fluctuations in pulse production (due to biotic and abiotic stress) and prices (in the absence of an effective government price support mechanism) farmers are not very keen on taking up pulse cultivation despite high wholesale pulse prices in recent years.

Nevertheless, improvement in yields, albeit modest, has contributed to higher pulse production in recent years, with most of the increase in pulse production in recent years in gram. Low pulse yield in India compared to other counties is attributed to poor spread of improved varieties and technologies, abrupt climatic changes, vulnerability to pests and diseases, and generally declining growth rate of total factor productivity. In order to give the much needed fillip to pulse production, the government has included pulses in the NFSM (along with wheat and rice) since the launch of NFSM in October 2007 and has been significantly increasing the MSP for most pulses. This has resulted in an above normal growth in pulse production in recent years. In the past four years, there has been significant increase in pulse consumption averaging around 50 grams due to somewhat higher production and larger imports, mostly of dry peas from Canada and Australia. The increasing mismatch between production and consumption of pulses has resulted in larger imports of pulses in recent year with imports in 2012-13 (Apr-Mar) reaching a record 4.0 million tonnes an increase of 500,000 tonnes over 2011-12. Despite being world's largest producer of pulses, only small exports of pulses are taking place from India, both because of restrictions on exports and the high domestic demand.

PULSES - LEGUMES

Pulses are seeds of plants belonging to the Leguminosae family. These are plants that house their seeds in double seemed pods or legumes (peas, beans, lentils, soya beans, peanuts, chickpeas etc.) They are grown for human consumption and have been eaten for centuries all over the world. There are approximately 13,000 species. Some pulses are completely edible, but normally only the seeds or beans are eaten, either fresh or dried.

THE FUNCTION OF PULSES

Pulses are included in the most important nutritional crops in the world. They are important ingredients for a great many different cold and hot dishes. Pulses are available in various forms and can be divided into race varieties. Take for example, two varieties of brown beans: the small, round bullet beans remain whole when cooked and are suitable for dishes where whole bones are required. The larger elongated beans, which break down during cooking are excellent for brown-bean soup.

Pulses can be used in the following ways:

1. In cold starters for example lentil salad

2. In soups, for example pea soup
3. In main course dishes such as cassoulet or chilli con carne
4. In vegetarian dishes
5. As a garnish

SPROUTING VEGETABLES FROM SEEDS

Sprouting vegetables are obtained by germinating seeds. The germination process takes place in a dark, humid and warm atmosphere.

Included in this group of vegetables are alfalfa, taugé, mustard cress or seed, bio cress, shiso purple or shiso green.

They are most commonly used in salads and as garnishes for sandwiches and cold dishes. Apart from alfalfa and taugé, they are all sold in the containers they are grown in. They are usually cut for use, half way down the stems. Germinated sprouting vegetables are richer in vitamin C and contain fewer calories than most seeds. They have higher protein content and contain more vitamin B and iron than most vegetables. They can be stored for a few days at a temperature of 0 - 1° C in a humid atmosphere

THE NUTRITIONAL VALUE OF PULSES

Pulses have a high nutritional value. They are rich in proteins (21 gram per 100 gram), carbohydrates (43 gram per 100 gram), fibre, the minerals phosphate, calcium and iron and the vitamins of the B-complex. The vegetable proteins in pulses can replace to a great extent animal proteins. This is important for vegetarians who use pulses as a substitute for meat.

They are low in sodium and saturated fats.

Carbohydrate is a starch, which provides energy in the human body. Unpeeled pulses contain many nutritious fibres or cellulose: Podded pulses (with the skins removed) lose a large amount of this indigestible cellulose, which stimulates digestion in the stomach and intestines. Soaking dried beans for several hours brings them back to life, activating enzymes, proteins, minerals and vitamins.

PURCHASING PULSES

When purchasing pulses, attention should be paid to the following:

1. The types of pulses available
2. The physical condition of the pulses
3. The quality of the various types of pulses
4. The price of the various types of pulses

1. The types of pulses available

Pulses can be divided into three main groups, which in turn can be subdivided according to their race.

- *Peas*, such as green or yellow peas, split peas, marrowfat peas or chickpeas
- *Beans,* such as brown beans, white and black beans, lima beans, kidney, mung or flageolet beans
- *Lentils,* such as peeled or unpeeled red, brown, yellow and green lentils

Young, fresh peas and beans are discussed in the section on vegetables.

WHY IT IS IMPORTANT TO PURCHASE PULSES FROM THE LAST HARVEST.

Pulses from the previous harvest should always be purchased. The longer pulses are stored, the more time is required to soak and cook them. Older pulses have a tougher skin. Beans that have been stored too long can be used for blind baking tart bases.

The physical condition of pulses

A division is made in pulses between:

a. Dried pulses
b. Pre-prepared pulses, which are sold as preserves, dried or frozen.

Dried pulses

Check when buying pulses that there are not too many broken seeds. When buying in bulk, a sample should be taken. From this sample a cooking trial should be done and the following points carefully noted:

- The flavour
- The toughness of the skin
- The cooking time

Pre-prepared pulses

By preserving pulses, the storage time and preparation time can be reduced. Examples of pre-prepared pulses are:

- In dried form: pureed soups, such as pea soup or brown-bean soup
- In tins or jars: tinned brown beans, marrowfat peas in jars, (pasteurised or un-pasteurised)
- Deep-frozen: loosely frozen peas or beans

PRODUCTS MADE FROM A BASIS OF PULSES

A distinction is made between:

- convenience products
- meat replacement products
- various other products

Convenience products

Since pulses are so suitable for preparation in advance, there are many convenience products on the market. Examples of these are: ready to heat and eat meals such as chilli con carne or marrowfat peas with bacon and onions.

Meat replacing products

Soya beans are the most versatile of all the pulses. From soya beans, the following meat replacement products are made: tempeh, tofu (also known as soya curds or tahoe) and soya meat

- *Tempeh* is a fermented product made by the controlled fermentation of cooked soya beans with a Rhizopus mould (tempeh starter). The tempeh fermentation by the Rhizopus mould binds the soya beans into a compact white cake. Tempeh fermentation also produces natural antibiotic agents, which are thought to increase the body's resistance to intestinal infections. This cake, where the beans are still visible, can be marinated, stewed, fried or boiled.

- *Tofu,* also known as soya bean curd, is a soft, cheese-like food made by curdling fresh hot soya milk with a coagulant. Traditionally the curdling agent used to make tofu is nigari, a compound found in natural ocean water, or calcium sulphate, a natural mineral. Curds can also be produced by acidic foods like lemon juice or vinegar. The curds are generally pressed into solid blocks. It is used in a similar way to tempeh.

- *Soya meat*: this looks similar to meat, has a similar consistency and a nutritional value similar to meat, but is cheaper to buy. It can be bought in tins and in a dried form. Dried soya meat must be soaked before use. It can be marinated, coated in breadcrumbs, fried, deep-fried or used in stews.

Various other products

There are other products made from soya beans:

- *Soya meal*. Soya meal is made from soya beans that have their skins removed and are flattened and roasted then milled. The oil in the beans is extracted with the aid of solutions during a chemical process. The colour of soya meal is yellow/white. It is used in bakery products, in sweet products, diet products, cooked meats, soups and sauces.
- *Soya milk*. Soya milk is made from boiled soya beans. It is available both in liquid and powder forms. Children who are allergic to cows milk, have often no reaction to soya milk.
- *Miso*. Miso is a brown paste that is used to improve the flavour of soups and sauces.
- *Toatjo*. Toatjo is similar to miso and is also a thick paste. It is sometimes mixed with sambal or used in combination with tempeh.

THE QUALITY OF THE VARIOUS PULSES

Pulses are judged on the following points:

- The shape and size must be identical
- The colour should be regular and characteristic of the type
- The fruits should not be mouldy or smell musty
- They should have an unblemished, soft and thin skin
- They should have a high purity ratio
- The fruit should not be contaminated by beetles

All pulses should be sorted by size, colour and quality. The legal demands for the correct naming and hallmarks is set out in the Pulses Decree of 1985.

The price of the various types of pulses

The price of the various types is dependent on the size and the harvest, the quality and the form they are sold in. It may be dried, tinned, potted or deep-frozen.

Normally the product is more expensive the larger the seeds become. The size has no influence on the flavour or the nutritional value.

THE TREATMENT OF PULSES IN THE KITCHEN

The handling of pulses in the kitchen is separated into three phases:

1. The delivery of pulses to the kitchen
2. The storage
3. The preparation

The delivery of pulses to the kitchen

Special attention should be paid to the following:

a. That the type of pulses delivered match the order form
b. That the correct amount has been delivered
c. That the quality is satisfactory

The storage of pulses

Dried pulses are best stored in good, airtight packaging in a cool, dry and dark storage area. They can be stored for maximal one year. Under the influence of light, moisture and heat, beans can germinate. Pulses discolour when stored in light. If they are stored in a damp or humid area, they can become mouldy. Airtight containers will protect them from coming into contact with insects or rodents. Pulses in tins or jars can be stored for a year or longer. In glass jars, they should be stored in a dark storage to avoid light discolouring the product through the glass. Deep frozen varieties should not be stored for more than a month at a temperature of - 18° C. Check the details on the packaging.

Storage of convenience, meat replacements and other products:

Convenience products are purchased deep-frozen. Take note of the use-by dates when storing and preparing.

Soya beans cannot be stored so long due to their high fat content and therefore the chance that they will become rancid. The storage time of soya products varies, depending on the composition and preparation techniques.

1. Tempeh can be stored for three days in the fridge and a month in the freezer.
2. Tofu, soya curds or tahoe can be stored three days in the fridge and one month in the freezer
3. Soya meat, which is dried or tinned, can be stored for a year in a cool and dry area.

Other products:

1. Fat soya flour can be stored for three months in a cool and dry area. Fatless soya flour can be stored in similar conditions for nine months
2. Liquid soya milk can be stored for three to six months in a cool and dry area. In powder form, it can be stored for six months in similar conditions.
3. Miso and toatjo can be stored in the fridge for a year.

Note: pay attention to the use-by dates on all products packaging.

The preparation of pulses

Pulses can be cooked in the water they are soaked in or fresh water. During soaking, a percentage of the vitamin B dissolves in the water, it is therefore better to use this water to cook beans and peas that are cooked for soup. Salt should not be added to the cooking water as this will encourage the pulses to burst open and break down during cooking.

Besides valuable nutrients, pulses also contain anti-nutritive agents. The most important anti-nutrients in unprocessed soya beans are protease inhibitors (trypsine and chymotrypsine) and haemaglutines-lectines. Sufficient cooking at high temperatures can destroy these poisonous toxins.

Incidents of food poisoning have been reported associated with the consumption of raw or undercooked red kidney beans. Symptoms may develop after eating only a few beans and include nausea, vomiting and abdominal pain followed by diarrhoea. A naturally occurring haemaglutin is responsible for the illness, but can be destroyed by high temperature cooking, making the beans completely safe to eat.

THE PRODUCTION OF PULSES

Pulses are a very important food source particularly in Middle and South America, the Middle East, China, Africa and Asia. They are grown practically over the whole world. Peas grow best in a slightly milder climate and are normally dried artificially. Beans and lentils require a warm and dry climate to develop properly and to dry well.

Peas are grown mainly in France, England, Belgium and Germany. Many types are also grown in Holland. Harvesting is normally in July and August.

Beans are grown mostly in Africa, The U.S.A., China, Canada, Argentine, Chilli, Bulgaria, Hungary and Italy. White beans are also grown in Holland and are also harvested in July and August.

Lentils are mainly grown in China, the U.S.A., Canada, Chilli and Argentine. A less common, specialised type of grey lentils, are also grown in Puy, in France (known as Puy lentils).

THE ROLE OF PULSES IN HUMAN NUTRITION: *A REVIEW*

Pulses belong to the family leguminosae . The family leguminosae is made up of many species which are cultivated all over the world (Rubatzky and Yamaguchi, 1997). Legumes have a wide range of usage, some are used as fodder or green manure, some are used as silage, while others are extracted for their oil, notably soyabean and groundnut . Such oil contributes a great deal to the energy intake of people all over the world. Majority of legumes are grown for their green pods, green seeds, or dried seeds . The term pulses cover all those grown for their dried seeds . Pulses have a variety of functions. The use of pulses range from their forming a staple diet to their being used as condiments, milk, cheese and snacks (Reddy *et al.*, 1986; Uzogara and Ofuya, 1992). They play a very important role in human nutrition. The present paper reviews the work that has been done on the nutritional value of pulses.

Table Production of Pulses by Continent in 10^3 Mt*

PLS	SCIENTIFIC NAME	N & C AMERICA	S. AMERICA	AFRICA	EUROPE	ASIA	USSR
[1]Dry Beans	Phaseolusvulgaris	2627	2839	1911	830	6366	170
Broad beans	Vicia faba	88	109	1124	551	2408	-
Peas (dry)	Pisum sativum	435	98	334	2727	2377	7800
Chickpeas	Ciser arietinum	180	26	290	90	7257	-
Lentils	Lens culinaris	288	-	136	74	1714	-
Cowpea	Vignaunguiculata	57	-	1003	6	27	-

Asia is the largest producer of the pulses listed above, followed by the USSR, where most of the pulses produced are in the form of dry Peas (Pisum sativum). The next largest producing continent for all pulses is Africa and the types of beans majorly produced are dry beans (Phaseolus vulgaris), broad beans (Vicia faba) and cowpeas (Vigna unguiculata). The continent that produces next to Africa is Europe, where most of the pulses produced are dry Peas (Pisum sativum). The least producing continents are North America, Central and South America. In these continents the dry beans (Phaseolus vulgaris) constitutes the pulse produced most.

Consumption of Pulses: Pulses are consumed all over the world. Consumption is higher in those parts of the world, where animal proteins are scarce and expensive for example, South East Asia and Africa . In this part of the world, they provide a large proportion of the protein required for adults and children. About 20% of the protein presently available to man, come from pulses in the developing countries .

The nutritional value of pulses: The nutritional importance of pulses are numerous, they can be a valuable source of energy. The energy content of most pulses have been found to be between 300 and 540 Kcal / 100g . Energy is required for all metabolic processes. The energy of Pulses come from the nutrient supply of protein, fat and carbohydrate.

Table. The Energy Content Of Some Pulses Commonly Consumed By Man

Pulses	Scientific name	Energy (kcal/100g)
Cowpeas	Vigna unguiculata	340
Chickpeas	Cicer arietinum	347
Broad bean	Vicia faba	320
Cluster bean		307
Lentil	Lens culinaris	302
Mung bean	Vigna radiata	310
Peanut	Arachis hypogea	570
Pigeon pea	Cajamis cajan	301
Soya bean	Glycine max	403

The carbohydrate supply: The carbohydrate content of pulses is high (Reddy *et al.*, 1985; Oke *et al.*, 1995). The high carbohydrate content contributes a great deal to the energy supply of pulses. A large percentage of pulses occurs as starch , about 1.8 - 18% occurs as oligossacharide while 4.3 - 25% occurs as dietary fibre . Although the oligossacharides, which are made up of raffinose, stachyose, verbascose, cause gas production in man, they are presently believed to have some beneficial effects.

They can shorten transit time and promote the growth of bifido bacteria in man. Infact researchers in Japan have actually suggested that oligossacharides from soyabeans could be used as substitute for common table sugar. They are also hypothesized to improve longevity and reduce colon cancer risk (Hayakawa *et al.*, 1990; Koo and Rao, 1991). The high dietary fibre content of pulses , are postulated to have some important physiological effects, such as reducing the transit time in the mammalian gut . This would help to relieve gastrointestinal conditions such as constipation and diverticular disease. It is also capable of lowering the blood cholesterol level due to its ability to bind with cholesterol in the human gut (Burkitt and Trowell, 1985). This feature is being suspected as being capable of reducing colonic cancer in man (Davis and Stewart, 1987; Hangen and Bennink, 2002). Pulses also have low glyceamic indices (Hatford, 1985; Björek*et al.*, 2000), which makes them valuable foods for diabetics. The cotyledon of legumes like locust bean and guar (guar gum) reduces postprandial glucose and insulin concentrations in man (Fairchild *et al.*, 1996; Gatenby, 1991; Feldman *et al.*, 1995).

PROTEIN SUPPLY

Pulses have a high protein content , the value is about twice that in cereal and several times that in root tuber , so they can help to improve the protein intake of meals in which cereals and root tubers in combination with pulses are eaten (Kushwah *et al.*, 2002). Pulse when eaten with cereals, can also help to increase the protein quality of the meal . In man, protein helps in the repair of body tissue, synthesis of enzymes and hormones and also in the supply of energy.

In children, the consumption of pulses should be encouraged, particularly where animal protein is scarce and expensive, as this would help to furnish the child with the necessary amino acids required for growth.

Table. Starch and Total Carbohydrate Content of Pulses

Common name	Scientific name	Total carbohydrates %	Starch %	Amylose content of starch %
Winged bean	Psophocarpustatragonubulus	24.0 – 42.2	–	–
Smooth peas	Pisum sativum	56.6	36.9 – 48.6	23.5 – 33.1
Wrinkled pea	Pisum sativum	–	24.0 – 36.6	62.8 –65.8
Great Northern beans		61.2 – 61.5	44.0	10.2 – 30.3
California small white beans		–	57.8	29.1 – 32.6
Broad beans	Vicia faba	57.3	41.2 – 52.7	20.7 – 45.5
Lentil	Lens culinaris	59.7	34.7 – 52.8	20.7 – 45.5
Cowpea	Vigna unguiculata	56.0 – 68.0	31.5 – 43.0	–
Lupine seed	Lupinus spp	–	0.3 – 3.5	–
Black gram	Vigna mungo	56.5 – 63.7	32.2 – 47.9	43.9
Common name	Scientific name	Total carbohydrates %	Starch %	Amylose content of starch %
Bengal gram	Cicer arietinum	60.1 – 61.2	37.0 – 50.	31.8 – 45.8
Mung gram	Vugna radiata	53.3 – 61.2	37.0 – 53.6	13.8 – 35.0
Red gram	Cajanus cajan	57.3 – 58.7	40.4 – 48.2	39.6
Red kidney bean	Phaseolus vulgaris	56.3 – 60.5	31.9 – 47.0	17.5 – 37.2
Navy bean	Phaseolus vulgaris	58.4	27.0 – 52.7	22.1 – 36.0
Pinto beans	Phaseolus vulgaris	54.6 – 63.7	51.0 – 56.5	25.8
Pink beans	Phaseolus vulgaris	–	42.3	14.9 – 35.3
Black eye beans	Vigna unguiculata	–	41.2	15.8 – 38.3
African yam bean	Strepnostylisstenocarpa	40.8	–	–

Table. Dietary Fibre Content of Pulses (Per 100g of Whole Mature Seeds)

Legume	Dietary fibre	References
Chickpea	25.6	1
Groundnut	6.1	2
Kidney bean	25.4	2
Mung bean	15.2	1
Pea	16.7	1
Soya bean	11.9	2
Cluster bean	4.3	2
Lentils	11.7	2
Pigeon pea	15.0	2

Table. Protein Content Of Pulses

Common name	Scientific name	Protein content g/100g DM	
		Mean	Range
Broad bean	Vicia faba	24.0	22.0 – 38.2
Chick pea	Cicer arietinum	22.2	19.1 – 31.2
Common bean	Phaseolus vulgaris	23.9	15.2 – 36.0
Common pea	Pistum sativum	23.1	14.2 – 36.1
Cowpea	Vigna unguiculata	24.0	20 – 34.2
Pigeon pea	Cajanus cajan	21.0	17.9 – 31.0
Groundnut	Arachis hypogaea	26.2	17.1 – 31.0
Soya bean	Glycine max	40.3	28.7 – 50.1
African yam bean	Streptpstylis stenocarpa	18.4	18 – 22

Table. Protein Quality of Cereal Grain and of Cereal Grain / Bean Diets Fed at Equal Levels of Dietary Protein

Protein source	Average weight gain (g)	PER
100% rice	43	2.15
90% rice + 10% beans	56	2.32
100% maize	13	0.87
90% maize + 10% beans	32	1.40
100% sorghum	12	0.88
90% sorghum + 10% beans	30	1.39
100% wheat	19	1.05
90% wheat + 10% beans	41	1.73
100% oats	34	1.60
90% oats + 10% beans	75	2.37
Casein	75	2.71

FAT SUPPLY: The fat content of pulse varies in different species. Most species contain about 1% fat, while groundnut and soyabean, have very high fat content, about 30% for soyabean and 49% for peanut . The fat content besides contributing to the energy needs, provides the needed essential fatty acids for man. A pulse like soyabean, contains linolenic acid, which is an omega–3–fatty acid. This fatty acid is currently being studied for its ability to reduce the risk of heart disease and cancer.

MICRONUTRIENT SUPPLY

VITAMIN SUPPLY: The vitamins present in appreciably quantities in pulses are thiamin, riboflavin, pyridoxine and folic acid; vitamin E and K are also found in pulses. The B-vitamins act as co-enzymes in biological processes Vitamin E is known to play a role as an antioxidant inhibiting the oxidation of vitamin A in the GIT and of polyunsaturates in the tissues. It is also believed to maintain the stability of cell membranes (Davies and Stewart, 1987). Vitamin K functions primarily in the liver where it is necessary for the formation of blood clothing factors.

Conclusion: Thus far, the many important functions of pulses have been highlighted. Their consumption should be encouraged in both adults and children. Because of their high dietary fibre content, I will advice more usage among the affluents who can afford lots of animal protein. Their use should also be encouraged among malnourished children because of their high protein content.

The use of pulses as components of weaning foods in combination with cereals is also recommended, as this would give cheaper cereals with more complete protein. Finally, the use of oil from pulses should be encouraged because of the high polyunsaturated fatty acid content. Polyunsaturated fatty acids are suspected of being capable of reducing the risk of heart diseases.

POST HARVEST TECHNOLOGY :: AGRICULTURE :: PULSES

Pulses constitute essential components of vegetarian diet. Pulses are major source of protein in Indian vegetarian diet. These are main source of protein providing most of the essential amino acids to a certain degree. Economically, pulses are cheapest source of protein. Pulses are Bengal gram, pigeon pea, black gram, green gram, lentil, etc. Pulses are mainly consumed in the form of dehusked split pulses, as these are rich in proteins. In vegetarian diet pulses are main source of protein.

Green gram, red gram, bengal gram, horse gram, cluster bean, field bean, cow pea are some of the common types of pulses.In general, their protein content is high and is commonly more than twice that of cereal grains, usually constituting about 20 per cent of the dry weight of seeds. The protein content of some legumes like soyabean is as high as 40 per cent.

NUTRITIVE VALUE OF PULSES

Pulse seeds are also sources of other nutritionally important materials, such as vitamins and minerals.

Carbohydrates: Food pulses contain about 55-60 per cent of total carbohydrates including starch, soluble sugars, fibre and unavailable carbohydrates. Minerals: Pulses are importantly sources of calcium, magnesium, zinc, iron, potassium and phosphorus.

Vitamins: Pulses contain small amounts of carotene, the provitamin A.

TOXIC CONSTITUENTS OF PULSES

The seeds of pulses include both edible and inedible types. Even amongst the edible legumes toxic principles occur and their elimination is important in order to exploit them for edible purposes. Two thermoliable factors are implicated in toxic effects. Inhibitors of the enzymes trypsin, chymotrypsin and amylase haemagglutinins, which impede the absorption of the products of digestion in the gut. In addition, legumes also contain a goitrogen, a toxic saponin, cyanogenic glycosides and alkaloids.

Elimination of Toxic Factors

It has already been indicated that soaking, heating and fermentation can reduce or eliminate most of the toxic factors of the pulses. Correct application of heat in cooking pulses can eliminate most toxic factors without impairment of nutritional value. Cooking also contributes towards pulse digestibility. Heat causes the denaturation of the proteins responsible for trypsin inhibition, haemagglutination and the enzyme responsible for the hydrolysis of cyanogenic glycosides. The mode of application of heat is important. Autoclaving and soaking followed by heating are effective. Another way of eliminating toxic factors is by fermentation, which yields products more digestible and of higher nutritive value than the raw pulses.

PROCESSING

Processing: Processing of pulses is of primary importance in improving their nutritive value. The processing methods used are soaking, germination decortications, cooking and fermentation.

Soaking: Soaking in water is the first step in most methods of preparing pulses for consumption. As indicated above, soaking reduces the oligosaccharides of the raffinose family. Soaking also reduces the amount of phytic acid in pulses.

Germination: Germination improves the nutritive value of food pulses. The ascorbic acid content of pulses increases manifold after 48 hours germination. Germinated and sprouted pulses have been used to prevent and cure scurvy. The riboflavin, niacin, choline and biotin contents of all pulses increase during germination. The germination process reduces and/or eliminates most of the antinutritional and toxic factors in several pulses.

Decortication: A simple method is to soak the seeds for a short time in water; the husk takes up more water than the seeds and may be easily separated by rubbing while still moist. In the alternative, the soaked grains may be dried and the husk removed by pounding and winnowing. Roasting also renders the husk easier to separate. Roasted legumes like those of Bengal gram and peas are widely used in India.

Cooking: Cooking destroys the enzyme inhibitors and thus improve the nutritional quality of food pulses. Cooking also improves the palatability.

Fermentation: The processing of food pulses by fermentation increases their digestibility, palatability and nutritive value. Fermentation process improves the availability of essential amino acids and, thus, the nutritional quality of protein of the blend. In general, the nutritive value of the legume based fermented foods has been shown to be higher than their raw counterparts.

Pulse milling

Pulses are usually converted into Dhal by decutilating and splitting. Both dry and wet milling processes are employed. By and large carborundum emery rollers are used for dehusking and burr grinders for splitting. Decuticling is seldom complete in single pass requiring multiple passes, each pass producing 1.5 to 2% fines reducing recovery of dal.

Basic processes in dhal milling are cleaning, dehusking, splitting, separation and bagging. Major variation is involved with dehusking process only. Dhals like Arahar, urad, moong and lentil are difficult to dehusk as a result repeated operations by dehusking rollers are required. Rewetting and drying is done to loosen portions of husk sticking after repeated rolling. Linseed oil is used to impart shine or better appeal to the milled dal.

The removal of the outer husk and splitting the grain into two equal halves is known as milling of pulses. To facilitate dehusking and splitting of pulses alternate wetting and drying method is used. In India trading milling methods produce dehusked split pulses. Loosening of husk by conditioning is insufficient in traditional methods. To obtain complete dehusking of the grains a large number of abrasive force is applied in this case as a result high losses occur in the form of brokens and powder. Yield of split & pulses in traditional mills are only 65 to 75% due to the above losses compared to 82 to 85% potential yield.

Milling of Pulses

In India, there are two conventional pulses milling methods ; wet milling method and dry milling method. The latter is more popular and used in commercial mills.

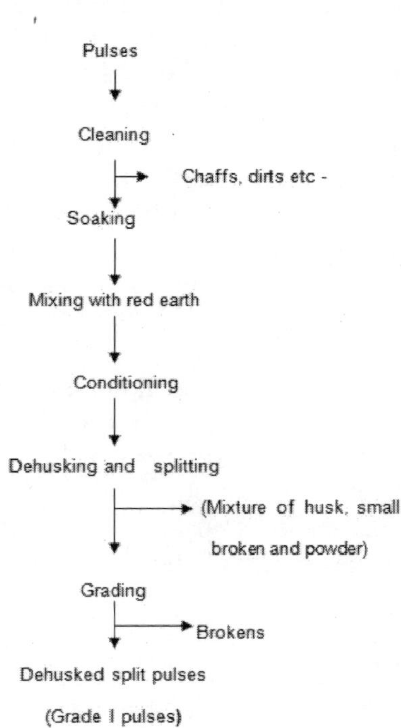

Traditional dry milling method ('DHAL' MILLING)

There is no common processing method for all types of pulses. However, some general operations of dry milling method such as cleaning and grading, rolling or pitting, oiling, moistening, drying and milling have been described in subsequent paragraphs.

Cleaning and grading

Pulses are cleaned from dust, chaff, grits, etc., and graded according to size by a reel type or rotating sieve type cleaner.

Pitting

The clean pulses are passed through an emery roller machine. In this unit, husk is cracked and scratched. This is to facilitate the subsequent oil penetration process for the loosening of husk. The clearance between the emery roller and cage (housing) gradually narrows from inlet to outlet. As the material is passed through the narrowing clearance mainly cracking and scratching of husk takes place by friction between pulses and emery. Some of the pulses are dehusked and split during this operations which are then separated by sieving.

Polishing

Polish is given to the dehusked and split pulses by treating them with a small quantity of oil and / or water.

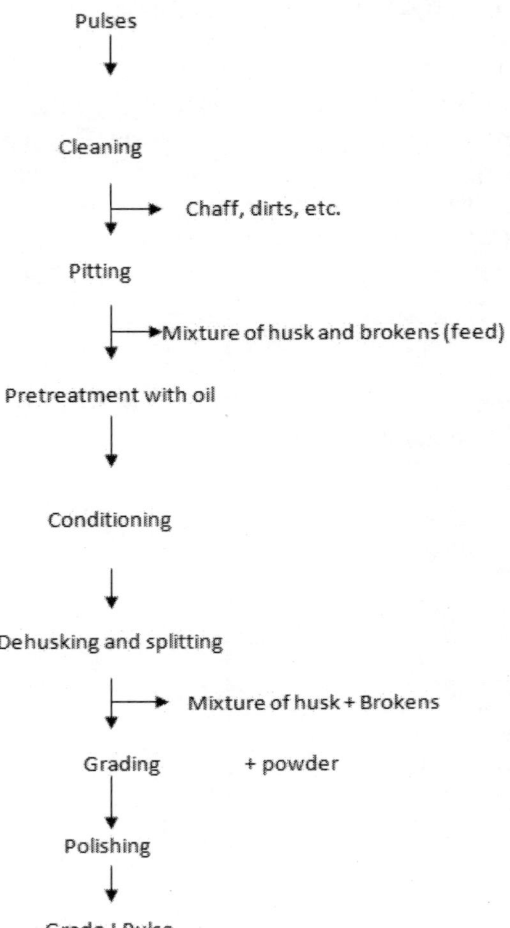

Pretreatments with oil

The scratched or pitted pulses are passed through a screw conveyor and mixed with some edible oil like linseed oil (1.5 to 2.5 kg/tonne of pulses). Then they are kept on the floor for about 12 hours for diffusion of the oil.

Conditioning of pulses

Conditioning of pulses is done by alternate wetting and drying. After sun drying for a certain period, 3-5 per cent moisture is added to the pulse and tempered for about eight flours and again dried in the sun. Addition of moisture to the pulses can be accomplished by allowing water to drop from an overhead tank on the pulses being passed through a screw con-veyor. The whole process of alternate wetting and drying is continued for two to four days until all pulses are sufficiently conditioned. Pulses are finally dried to about 10 to 12 per cent moisture content.

Dehusking and Splitting

Emery rollers, known as Gota machine are used for the dehusking of conditioned pulses About 50 per cent pulses are dehusked in a single operation (in one pass). Dehusked pulses are split into two parts also, the husk is aspirated off and dehusked, split pulses are separated by sieving. The tail pulses and unsplit dehusked pulses are again conditioned and milled as above The whole process is repeated two to three times until the remaining- pulses are dehusked and split.

COMMERCIAL MILLING OF PULSES BY TRADITIONAL METHODS

The traditional milling of pulses is divided into two heads, namely, dry milling and wet milling. But both the processes involved two basic steps : (i) Precon-ditioning of pulses by alternate wetting and sun drying for loosening husk and (ii) subsequent milling by dehusking and splitting of the grains into two cotyledons followed by aspira-tion and size separation using suitable machines. 100 per cent-dehusking and splitting of pulses are seldom achieved particularly in cases of certain pulses like Red gram, black gram and green gram. Of them Red gram is the most difficult pulses to dehusk and split. Only about 40 to 50 per cent Red gram grains are dehusked and split in the first pass of preconditioning and milling. As sun drying is practiced the traditional method is not only weather dependent but also it requires a large drying yard to match with the milling capacity. As a result it takes 3 to 7 days for complete processing of a batch of 20 to 30 tonnes of pulses into dhals. Moreover milling losses are also quite high in the traditional method of milling of pulses.

In general, simple reciprocating or rotary sieve cleaners are used for cleaning while bucket elevators are used for elevating pulses.

Pitting or scratching of pulses is done in a roller machine. A worm mixer is used for oiling as well as watering of the pitted pulses.

Blowers are used for aspiration of husk and powder from the products of the disc sheller or roller machine. Split dhals are separated from the unhusked and husked whole pulses with the help of sieve type separators.

Sieves are also employed for grading of dhals.

In general, the raw pulses may contain 2 to 5 per cent impurities (foreign materials), some insect infested grains and extra moisture. Though the clean pulses contain about 10-15 percent and 2-5 per cent germs, the yield of dhals commercial dhal mills varies from 68-75 per cent. It may be noted that the average potential yields of common dhals vary from 85 to 89 per cent. These milling losses in the commercial pulses mills can be attributed lo small brokens and fine powders found during scoring and simultaneous dehusking and splitting operations.

PULSE CONSUMPTION, SATIETY, AND WEIGHT MANAGEMENT

The worldwide prevalence of obesity has reached epidemic proportions . Because excess body fat is associated with the development of life-threatening chronic conditions such as heart disease, type 2 diabetes, and certain types of cancer , viable and sustainable solutions for sustainable weight loss and prevention of weight gain are urgently needed. Generally, selection of a diet high in fiber, low in energy density and glycemic load, and moderate in protein is thought to be particularly important for weight control . Such a diet may be achieved by regularly consuming food from certain food groups, including fruits, vegetables, and whole grains; some lean meats, nuts, and legumes; and limited consumption of food from other groups, including high-fat meats, sugar-sweetened beverages, bakery items, and highly processed foods. In this review, we will focus of the role of legumes, particularly the nonoilseed pulses, in energy regulation and successful weight control, highlighting the work that has been published in the past 10 y.

TERMINOLOGY: LEGUMES, PULSES, AND BEANS

The pods or fruits of plants in the botanical family Fabaceae, or Leguminosae, are commonly known as legumes. Legumes include alfalfa, clover, lupin, green beans and peas, peanuts, soybeans, dry beans, broad beans, dry peas, chickpeas, and lentils. According to the FAO , a pulse is a type of legume that is exclusively harvested for the dry grain and therefore excludes peanuts and soybeans, which are harvested for their oil. Pulses are also sometimes referred to as grain legumes or pulse grains. The published literature often refers to the *Phaseolus vulgaris*species; these include kidney beans, haricot beans, pinto beans, and navy beans. The health effects of soybeans and peanuts have been well studied. Although soybeans share some of the nutritional properties of pulses [e.g. high in fiber and protein, low glycemic index (GI)], they are thought to have unique health effects due to their high content of certain phytoestrogens such as isoflavones and other bioactive compounds . The effects of soybeans and soy protein and peanuts on body weight have been reviewed elsewhere and will not be covered here.

MACRONUTRIENT AND PHYTOCHEMICAL PROFILES OF PULSES AND ENERGY REGULATION

Pulses have a unique nutritional profile consistent with several dietary composition factors thought to assist with weight control. They also contain several antinutrients that have been suggested to play a role in energy regulation

. In particular, they are high in fiber, providing <“7 g/0.5 c (120 mL) serving. Pulses are also relatively low in energy density (1.3 kcal/g or 5.3 kJ/g) and a good source of digestible protein (average of 7.7 g of protein/0.5 c). Pulse carbohydrates are slowly digested , which allows some of the lowest GI among carbohydrate-containing foods.

Pulse GI typically range from <“29 to 48 (using glucose as the standard) compared with GI of 32–36 for dairy, 39–64 for fruit, 42–72 for grains, 49–80 for breakfast cereals, and 49–97 for root vegetables . The relatively slow digestibility and hence low GI of pulses has been attributed to several constituents, including carbohydrate composition, protein content and protein-starch matrix, and antinutrient factors such as enzyme inhibitors (e.g. amylase inhibitor, trypsin inhibitor), phytates, lectins, saponins, and tannins. The roles of fiber, energy density, carbohydrate type, GI and glycemic load, and protein in energy regulation and weight control in general have been reviewed in detail elsewhere .

PULSE CARBOHYDRATES

Starches account for 22–45% of pulse grain weight depending on the source, whereas starch content is low in the oilseeds . As is typical of other grains, pulse starches are composed of amylose, a linear □1,4-linked glucan with few branches in the molecular weight range of 10^5–10^6, and amylopectin, a highly branched and much larger molecule (molecular weight 10^7–10^9) composed of □1,4-linked glycosyl units of varying lengths connected by □1,6 branch points. Architecturally, amylopectin is divided into clusters containing the exterior branches and short linear chains, and an internal region containing longer linear chains linking clusters.

Both the amylose long linear chain and the amylopectin external linear chains reassociate or “retrograde” on cooling following gelatinization, although this retrogradation occurs much faster in amylose. Pulse starches generally have a higher content of amylose compared with cereal and tuber starches; this factor plus their associated high capacity for retrogradation may reduce the starch digestion rate, rendering them either slowly digestible and/or resistant to digestion.

SLOWLY DIGESTIBLE STARCH AND RESISTANT STARCH.

A number of reports infer a slowly digestible or resistant character of the starch in pulses . Slowly digestible starch is a term given to that fraction of starch that is not rapidly digested but digests and absorbs slowly throughout the course of the small intestines. The term resistant starch applies to the fraction that is not digested by the human □glucosidases, reaching the colon undigested with a general fate to be fermented by saccharolytic bacteria. These 2 nutritional classes of starch are perhaps best measured in vitro as described by Englyst et al. as starch digested by their system between 20 and 120 min and that undigested at 120 min, respectively.

The basis for the moderated digestion rate of pulse starches remains rather unclear. Reports generally implicate cellular and cotyledon tissue structures in impeding enzyme access to the starch or their comparably high amylose content, as discussed above . Certainly, processing the grains to disrupt native macrostructures increases the rate and extent of starch digestion, thus supporting the idea that slow digestion is at least partly related to digestive enzymes' poor access to starch .

DIETARY FIBER.

A recent thorough review of dietary fiber in pulses can be found in Tosh and Yada . In their raw state, pulses are high in fiber, with <“15–32% total dietary fiber; of this, approximately one-third to three-quarters is insoluble fiber and the remaining is soluble fiber. Insoluble fiber is associated with fecal bulking through its water-holding capacity, whereas soluble fiber ferments, positively affecting colon health through production of SCFA, lowered pH, and potential microbiota changes. Viscous soluble fiber may also increase gastric distention and help to slow gastric emptying rate .

OLIGOSACCHARIDES.

The oligosaccharides of pulses are often considered a negative attribute due to their high fermentability, with their associated rapid gas production and discomfort. Technically known as □galactosides, they are derived from sucrose and have 1–3 □1,6-linked galactosyl units attached. They are commonly known as raffinose (1 galactosyl unit), stachyose (2 galactosyl units), and verbascose (3 galactosyl units). Although generally considered a problem, and methods have been developed to partially remove them, the oligosaccharides may also be considered prebiotics , which are thought to be beneficial for health. □ Galactosidase, found in the product Beano, can be used to digest the galactosyl units from these oligosaccharides, leaving sucrose for further digestion.

PULSE PROTEINS

The 2010 review by Boye et al. provides comprehensive information on protein ranges in pulses, types of pulse proteins, their functional properties, and the effects of processing. Briefly, the amount of protein in pulses is <“17–35% on a dry weight basis. In terms of solubility in specific solvents, pulse proteins fall primarily into the albumin (water-soluble) and globulin (salt-soluble) classes. The storage proteins legumin and vicillin are globulins, and the albumins comprise the heterogeneous group of enzymes, amylase inhibitors, and lectins. In general, macronutrient studies have shown that protein is more satiating than carbohydrates or lipids . Moreover, the protein in pulses and soybeans has been implicated in providing satiety; however, little is known regarding whether it is a specific property or more than 1 property of these proteins that elicit this effect or simply the inherent high amounts. Sufian et al. found that pepsin-derived peptides from "country" beans (*Dolichos lablab*) stimulated secretion of cholecystokinin, a gut hormone related to satiety. Thus, pulse proteins as consumed may contain bioactive components that contribute to satiety.

PROTEASE AND AMYLASE INHIBITORS.

Protein-based protease inhibitors found in pulses act on either or both of the serine proteases trypsin and chymotrypsin . They are found in comparably high amounts in the pulses compared with other plant foods and negatively affect digestibility of food proteins if not processed (i.e. mainly cooked) properly . They do not appear to have an important role in weight management. On the other hand, □amylase inhibitors found in pulses, specifically dry beans (up to 2–4 g/kg), reduce starch digestibility and thus energy availability . Isolated □ amylase inhibitor lowers postprandial glycemic responses , although it may be inactivated through cooking or other processing methods . As discussed later in this review, several pulse extracts prepared with processing methods thought to retain amylase inhibitor activity have been tested in randomized, placebo-controlled trials for their potential to affect weight and fat loss.

PULSE PHYTOCHEMICALS

Phenolic compounds.

Pulses contain a range of phenolic compounds, with the darker grains such as black beans and red kidney beans generally having higher amounts. The phenolic compounds in pulses are generally polyphenols and include tannins, phenolic acids, and flavonoids . Antioxidant activity is related to total phenolic content . Their potential role in weight management is unclear, although studies indicate that certain phenolics interfere with enterocyte glucose absorption through interference with the glucose transporters .

PHYTATES.

Phytic acid, also known as myo-inositol hexaphosphate, is the major storage form of phosphate in plant cells . Pulses are one of the primary sources of phytate in the diet, the others being cereals, oilseeds, and nuts. Phytate has been shown to reduce the in vitro rate of starch digestion and delay postprandial glucose absorption in humans , which could contribute to satiety and delay the return of hunger, as discussed below.

PULSE CONSUMPTION AND ENERGY REGULATION

It is unknown which of the pulse components described above has the strongest influence on appetite regulation and potentially energy balance or whether multiple factors work in consort. Nonetheless, several lines of evidence exist that suggest that pulse consumption could potentially increase satiety and help with weight control when consumed regularly. These studies are reviewed below.

Pulse consumption, glycemic response, and satiety

Most studies , although not all , consistently show lower glucose and insulin responses to consumption of controlled amounts of pulses compared with other foods. The glycemic response (peak and area under the curve) to pulses is at least 45% lower than that of other carbohydrate-containing foods such as cereals, grains, pasta, biscuits, and tuberous vegetables . Whether a low glycemic response per se is mechanistically related to a reduction in satiety is a topic of much debate , although there are some data to support a slower return of hunger in response to low-GI meals in general .

Additionally, a second meal effect has been observed whereby a reduced glycemic response to a second meal occurs after consumption of a first meal low in GI . In those studies, a first meal containing barley and lentils improved glucose tolerance to a second meal compared with a first meal containing whole-meal bread.

The second meal effect is thought to be due primarily to an increase in colonic fermentation and only minimally to a reduction in gastric emptying rate . Fermentation in the colon produces SCFA, which can be oxidized and used for energy in preference to glucose. SCFA may also suppress hepatic glucose production . Both of these mechanisms could lead to more stable glucose patterns over time, which some have hypothesized may result in reduced appetite and energy intake . Furthermore, an increase in satiety has been linked with the consumption of bread prepared with the SCFA propionate . Colonic fermentation and its effects may be long-lasting, as it has been observed to occur up to 13 h after the previous meal .

Few studies have specifically measured the satiety and appetite responses to pulse consumption . In 2 different experiments, Leathwood and Pollet fed participants hachis parmentier (the French version of shepherd's pie) made with either potato puree or bean puree. Glycemic responses to the bean meals were significantly lower than with the potato meals.

In addition, participants reported significantly less hunger at 180 min, greater satiety at 240 min, and a lower desire to consume "something tasty" after consuming the bean meals. In this study, the meals were not matched for carbohydrate content, with the bean meals containing 7.5 g less carbohydrate than the potato meals. In another study, Holt et al. measured satiety responses over 2 h to 38 foods. All foods were served in 240-kcal portions (1 MJ). Of the protein-rich foods, ling fish led to greater satiety compared with lentils and baked beans. Also, baked beans and eggs led to greater satiety than did white bread.

Sparti et al. fed 14 healthy, normal-weight participants 3 meals that were either high or low in unavailable carbohydrate and measured metabolic and appetitive responses to the meals over 24 h in a metabolic chamber. The lunch and dinner meals from the high-unavailable carbohydrate regimen contained pulses (chickpea salad at lunch and red bean salad at dinner).

The diets were controlled for energy and macronutrient distribution but differed in fiber (60 vs. 3 g), slowly and rapidly digestible starch (63 vs. 24 g of slowly digestible starch), and resistant starch (18 vs. 4 g). Hunger was significantly greater and fullness significantly less after the low-unavailable carbohydrate lunch and dinner, but not breakfast, compared with the respective high-unavailable carbohydrate meals.

The diet high in unavailable carbohydrates also resulted in a significantly lower rapid rise in postprandial carbohydrate oxidation, and the difference in carbohydrate oxidation between diets was inversely correlated with hunger ratings. The investigators concluded that delayed carbohydrate oxidation associated with the diet high in unavailable carbohydrate resulted in less hunger. Because it is impossible to determine whether the different responses to the 2 diets were attributable to the difference in pulse content per se, it is recommended that more studies designed to better isolate the effects of pulses and incorporating the scope of measurements included in this study be conducted.

Wong et al. conducted a series of 3 preload experiments to study the effects of processing, recipe, and pulse variety on glycemic and appetitve responses and energy intake of pizza meals 2 h later. In the first 2 experiments, preload meals were matched for carbohydrate amount (50 g) and in the 3rd, they were matched for energy. In the first experiment, 2 types of canned navy beans (plain) were compared with navy beans that were soaked as one would prepare at home and made into a baked bean recipe. A glucose drink served as the control. The glycemic responses to the bean meals were not significantly different, and, not unexpectedly, all were significantly lower than the glucose drink. Appetite response was significantly lower only for the homemade beans compared with glucose, and the amount of pizza consumed in a test meal 2 h later was lower after the 2 canned beans but not the homemade beans.

In the second experiment, 3 different recipes made with canned navy beans (tomato sauce, maple style, pork, and molasses) and one made with homemade navy beans (pork and molasses) were compared with white bread as the control. Only 1 of the canned recipes (tomato sauce) and the homemade recipe led to a glycemic response that was significantly lower than that of white bread. The appetite responses tended to be lower for these same recipes, but these differences did not reach significance ($P = 0.09$) and pizza intake did not differ among treatments. Finally, in the 3rd experiment, which compared responses to different pulse varieties (chickpeas, lentils, navy beans, yellow peas), water and white bread, glycemic responses varied somewhat and tended to be lowest for lentils and chickpeas, but differences in appetite or subsequent pizza intake were not observed. This study provided only weak evidence and mixed findings for a satiety-promoting effect of pulses depending on how they are processed and prepared. Additional studies are needed comparing different recipes and processing methods of pulses to meals with alternative protein sources such as meat.

Glycemic and insulinemic responses and energy intake subsequent to consumption of breads made with normally processed chickpea flour, extruded chickpea flour, or white wheat flour were measured . The extrusion process involves higher temperatures and shear compared with those used during normal processing. Gelatinized starch during extrusion processing may fragment and align differently than when normally processed and, by retrogradation, potentially increase the resistant starch content of the chickpea flour. The results showed a significantly higher insulin response and a nonsignificant tendency toward a lower glycemic response after ingestion of the chickpea bread (normal process).

However, neither satiety nor energy intake differed among bread type at a buffet meal 2 h later, perhaps due to the variation in food form (chickpea flour) compared with other studies that have used whole pulses. In addition, the starch and fiber contents of the breads were not matched, which could have affected the results. Further studies on foods made with pulse flours may be of interest, given its potential as a functional ingredient and the expanding variety of products made with pulse flours now available, such as tortillas, pasta, and bakery products.

Even fewer studies have measured satiety responses to pulse consumption in studies lasting longer than 1 d. McCrory et al. recently completed a randomized intervention comparing 3 doses of pulse consumption on weight loss and adherence to 30% reduction in baseline energy intake over 6 wk. The doses were 1 Tbsp/d (15 mL), 0.5 c/d (120 mL), or 1.8–2.5 c/d for 6 d/wk. There was a significant time-pulse dose group interaction effect on average daily satiety ratings, where satiety ratings were highest in the group receiving 0.5 c/d, particularly over the first 3 wk.

In another recent study using a nonrandomized design in which participants served as their own controls , individuals were followed for a period of 4 wk on their usual diet, followed by 12 wk of chickpea supplementation (mean 104 g/d, which is just over 0.5 c/d), then another 4 wk on their usual diet. Participants reported a significant increase in feelings of satiation in the chickpea phase relative to the first habitual phase and a significant decrease in satiation in the second habitual phase relative to the chickpea phase. However, it is unclear when these ratings were collected during the study (i.e. daily, weekly, or at the end of each phase).

In summary, short-term studies (mostly single-meal studies) indicate reduced hunger and increased satiety 2–4 h after pulse consumption when meals were controlled for energy but not when controlled for available carbohydrate. This suggests that at least part of the effect of pulses on satiety may be mediated by available carbohydrate amount or composition. Across all of these studies, the control or comparison foods varied widely, from potato to cereal grains to glucose and white bread.

This raises the question of the optimal control food to use in determining whether pulse consumption helps to increase satiety in real-world situations. One possibility is to include a food that might otherwise be consumed in normal daily life instead of pulses, such as another protein source like meat, poultry, or fish, or an alternative carbohydrate source, such as whole grains. The effects of pulse consumption on subsequent energy intake are still largely uncertain, because very few of these studies measured subsequent energy intake. In addition, more studies are needed to identify whether regular daily pulse consumption can help to increase satiety on a regular basis relative to other foods and potentially help with weight control in the longer term.

PULSE CONSUMPTION AND BODY WEIGHT

Observational studies.

One way to determine whether longer term pulse consumption may affect body weight is to determine whether an association exists between pulse consumption and body weight cross-sectionally. Very few studies have examined this relationship. Papanikolaou and Fulgoni reported on the association of consumption of beans (a subgroup of pulses, as described above) with dietary quality and obesity risk in >8000 adult participants in the NHANES 1999–2002 using data from a single, multiple pass, 24-h dietary recall. They found that individuals who had consumed variety beans or baked beans had significantly lower body weights compared with those who had not consumed beans. In addition, the odds of being obese (BMI e" 30 kg/m^2) was significantly lower in variety bean consumers and baked bean consumers compared with nonconsumers (odds ratio = 0.78 and 0.77, respectively). Interestingly, when variety bean consumers were analyzed separately from baked bean consumers, the reduced risk of overweight or obesity was no longer observed in the baked bean consumers compared with nonconsumers.

There were several dietary differences associated with bean intake that could have mediated these relationships. Compared with bean nonconsumers, both baked bean consumers and variety bean consumers had significantly higher intakes of total legumes, fiber, and minerals and lower intakes of discretionary fat (trend toward significance in variety bean consumers). The variety bean consumers had lower intakes of meat and added sugars, whereas the baked bean consumers had lower intakes of total grains, whole grains, and vegetables and higher intakes of added sugars. These dietary confounders were not controlled for in analyses, so it is difficult to determine the degree to which the relative leanness in variety bean and baked bean consumers may be attributed specifically to bean consumption. Minimally, this study showed that bean consumption is associated with an overall dietary pattern and lifestyle that tends to be associated with relative leanness. This suggestion is also supported by other studies described below.

A few studies examined relationships between dietary patterns incorporating pulses but did not specifically isolate pulse consumption associations in their analyses. Most , although not all , showed an inverse association of the dietary pattern incorporating pulses with BMI or BMI increase over time. Other types of studies examined overall dietary patterns of high fruit and vegetable intake or a vegetarian lifestyle typically incorporating large amounts of pulses.

However, pulse intake was not quantified in those studies. As reviewed , most studies show that vegetarians weigh less than nonvegetarians. In addition, vegans and those on macrobiotic diets generally weigh less than lacto-ovo vegetarians. Others reviewing studies on fruit and vegetable consumption note that despite methodological inconsistencies among different studies leading to somewhat mixed findings, a pattern of higher fruit and vegetable intake has generally been associated with lower body weight.

In summary, studies examining the potential associations between pulse consumption and weight status consistently show that individuals with lower BMI consume a greater amount of pulses as part of their usual diet. However, very few studies have been conducted and only 1 considers beans separately from other pulses or legumes or from other food groups. Finally, these studies should be interpreted with caution, because confounding may exist, as is usually the case with cross-sectional associations. Cause and effect cannot be assumed, because pulse consumption may be part of an overall lifestyle that confers maintenance of healthy weight. Experimental study designs are necessary to determine whether pulses can be implicated as having independent effects on body weight.

EXPERIMENTAL STUDIES IN HUMANS

Pulse consumption and weight loss during intentional energy restriction.

Very few interventions testing effectiveness of whole pulses for weight loss during intentional caloric restriction have been published . The earliest study was conducted in 1987 in 15 type 2 diabetics with a mean BMI of 24.8 kg/m^2; about one-half of the participants were normal weight (BMI > 25 kg/m^2) and one-half were overweight or obese (BMI e” 25 kg/m^2). A 3-wk crossover design was used. Seven participants began with the control diet and 8 began with a legume-based diet. It is not stated whether the order of the diets was randomized; however, each participant switched to the other diet after 3 wk and there was no wash-out period.

Diets were designed to provide <“1600 kcal/d (6.7 MJ/d). Because of the wide BMI range in this study, a 1600-kcal/d intake would likely be anywhere from a 15–40% energy deficit, depending on initial energy requirement . Both diets were 20/34/56% of energy from protein/carbohydrate/fat, and the legume-based diet contained <“21% of energy from legumes. Based on 115 kcal (481 kJ) per 0.5 cup of pulses , the legume dose was probably about 1.5 c/d (21% of 1600 kcal = 336 kcal/d or 1.4 MJ/d of legumes).

The legume-based diet contained mostly pulses (green peas, brown beans, white beans, chickpeas, lentils, and yellow peas), but there was also a small amount of soybeans and green beans included. After 3 wk of consuming each diet, there was a small but significant weight loss after consuming the control diet but not the legume-based diet (no values given). Compliance monitoring was not mentioned in the publication.

The study by Sichieri et al. was originally published in Portuguese but was summarized in English in a subsequent paper . They conducted a randomized controlled trial in which 40 overweight or obese women (BMI e” 27 kg/m^2) were provided with an 1800-kcal/d (7.5 MJ/d) diet incorporating either rice and beans twice a day (with no meat) or lean meat twice a day. Diets had protein/carbohydrate/fat distributions of 14/15/71% of energy (beans and rice) or 18/25/57% of energy (lean meat). The rice and beans diet resulted in greater weight loss after 1 mo (2.4 vs. 0.9 kg; $P = 0.04$); however, the difference was not significant after 2 mo (3.8 vs. 1.5 kg; $P = 0.10$). The lack of a difference at 2 mo was likely due to loss of follow-up, which was 35% in the rice and beans group and 45% in the lean meat group. Potential reasons for the high drop-out rate were not discussed. However, the results of that study strongly suggest that pulses could aid weight loss during intentional caloric restriction if drop-out could be prevented or substantially reduced.

In the 6-wk intervention trial by McCrory et al. described above, 49 overweight and obese participants (BMI 25–35 kg/m^2) were randomized to consume either 1 Tbsp/d (low), 0.5 c/d (medium), or 1.8–2.5 c/d (high) of pulses for 6 d/wk while reducing their energy intake by 30% of baseline energy requirements daily. Foods with the requisite amount of pulses were provided as 4 servings/d [250 kcal (1.0 MJ) and 300 kcal (1.3 MJ) for women and men, respectively].

The foods were familiar foods such as casseroles and pasta dishes, and a variety of pulses were used including (but not limited to) chickpeas, lentils, black beans, pinto beans, navy beans, and split peas. Thus, 1000 (4.2 MJ/d) kcal/d were provided to women and 1200 kcal/d (5.0 MJ/d) were provided to men. Participants were counseled about how to choose the remainder of their energy intake (to meet the target intake) by following an exchange list. In addition to weight loss, adherence to the energy intake target was an outcome of interest. Seven participants dropped out of the study (2 from each group and 1 prior to randomization). Interestingly, the results showed there was no dose-response effect of pulse consumption on weight loss, with the weight loss being 1.8 ± 1.9 kg, 3.9 ± 2.2 kg, and 2.3 ± 2.3 kg in the low-, medium-, and high-pulse groups, respectively, and differing significantly only between the low- and medium-pulse groups.

Energy intake from the multiple pass 24-h recall dietary intake assessments also reflected a higher energy intake in the high-pulse group. The reasons for the lack of a greater weight loss in the high-pulse group are several and could be due to a "halo" effect of the high pulse provision on energy intake, an adaptation to the high pulse intake that disrupted appetite regulation mechanisms or lack of compliance with the high pulse intake. However, "flatulence and intestinal gas" ratings assessed by a 9-point rating scale were highest in the high-pulse group, suggesting that the group as a whole compliant with their intake of provided pulses.

In an 8-wk trial , 35 overweight or obese men were randomized to consume a control diet, a legume diet, a fatty fish diet, or a high-protein diet. The control, legume, and fatty fish diets were designed to provide 17/30/53% of energy as protein/carbohydrate/fat, whereas the high-protein diet was designed to provide 30/30/40% of energy from protein/carbohydrate/fat. Protein sources in the high-protein diet were primarily meat, eggs, and lean dairy products. For the legume diet, neither legume dose nor type was mentioned, but legumes were required 4 d/wk, fish was not allowed, and other animal protein intake was decreased. All diets were designed to produce a 30% energy deficit. Compliance was monitored weekly by interview with a dietitian and 3-d weighed food intake records at the week prior to the intervention and at wk 7. Based on reported intakes, compliance with the prescribed diets appeared to be quite good. Results showed significant weight loss in all 4 groups, but the legume group ("8.3% of initial weight) and high-protein group ("8.4% of initial weight) lost significantly more than the control group ("5.5% of initial weight). Absolute changes in body weight were not reported.

In the most recently published trial , 30 overweight and obese participants consumed a reduced energy intake diet for 8-wk prescribed at 30% energy restriction based on initial energy requirements. Participants were randomized to a treatment group that consumed 4 servings/wk of pulses or to a control group that restricted pulses during this time period. One serving was defined as 160–235 g of cooked pulses, depending on the prescribed energy intake. Because pulses average 90 g/0.5 c (120 mL) , 1 serving in this study ranged from <“0.9 to 1.3 c (216-312 mL). Therefore, the total dose ranged from 3.6 to 5.2 c (756-1092 mL) of pulses/wk.

The prescribed macronutrient distribution was the same for both groups, which was a protein/carbohydrate/fat distribution of 17/53/30 percent of energy. Compliance with the assigned pulse consumption and macronutrient distribution was good, as indicated by weekly monitoring by a dietitian and by 3-d weighed food records during the week prior to the intervention and during wk 7. Results showed significantly greater decreases in BMI and body weight expressed as percent of initial value in the pulse-consuming group compared with the control group (“2.0 vs. “0.9 kg/m^2 and “7.8 vs. “5.3%, respectively). Percentage body fat and waist circumference decreases, however, did not differ significantly between groups. Group values for reported energy intake or diet composition during the intervention were not reported; therefore, it is uncertain whether the differences in weight loss between groups could be ascribed to differences in energy intake or other metabolic effects of pulses on energy expenditure.

PULSE CONSUMPTION AND BODY WEIGHT WITHOUT ENERGY RESTRICTION

The effects of pulse consumption on body weight can also be explored by examining the results of pulse intervention studies in which chronic disease risk factors were the primary outcomes yet body weight was measured. Most of these studies were designed to provide energy in an amount necessary to maintain body weight.

Hence, no significant effects of pulse consumption on body weight were observed over 3- to 7-wk periods . Pulse consumption under less rigorous feeding conditions (e.g. ad libitum dietary intake, except for the provided pulses and control foods, with advice given to maintain usual dietary and exercise habits) over 2–16 wk also did not affect body weight . Similarly, body weight was not affected when pulses were added to a prescribed low-fat diet (28–32% of energy) . The lack of an effect of pulses on body weight under all of these study conditions is consistent with the suggestion that an increase in fruit and vegetable intake is likely to have only very small or modest effects on body weight loss unless advice on reducing energy intake is provided simultaneously . This may not be the case, however, if the fruit and vegetable load is very high or if multiple dietary changes are made at once. In support of this idea, and as Berkow and Barnard reviewed , controlled interventions that place participants on a vegetarian or vegan diet for several weeks have resulted in weight changes of 2.5–7.2 kg, with maintenance of these changes shown in a few uncontrolled studies.

STUDIES USING PULSE EXTRACTS

A few human clinical trials have examined the effects of pulse "extracts" taken as a dietary supplement on body weight and related parameters. During normal starch digestion, amylases break α1,4 bonds to allow it to be broken into more easily digested and absorbable units. The main ingredient in these extracts is thought to be αamylase inhibitor; thus, the extracts are often referred to as starch blockers.

Depending on the method of preparation, other components may also be present in the extracts. The effectiveness of pulse extracts were recently reviewed by Preuss . Briefly, extract preparations in the early 1980s were crude and not very effective at blocking starch digestion due at least in part to low amylase inhibitor activity . However, extract preparations in the later 1980s and beyond showed greater αamylase inhibitor activity and, hence, effectiveness at blocking starch digestion in short-term human studies [e.g.]. Also, initially there was some concern that the extract preparations contained lectins, which may be harmful to health; however, in animal studies, the extracts have been shown to be safe and the current preparation method is thought to result in the destruction of lectins . As with all dietary supplements, however, the commercially available preparations are not monitored regularly by the FDA for safety or content.

Several human trials testing the effectiveness of these extracts have been conducted in the last several years . All but 1 used a randomized, double-blind, placebo-controlled design and all included only initially overweight or obese participants. Intervention length ranged from 4 to 12 wk. Extract doses varied from pills to powders mixed in water taken with 1 or 2 carbohydrate-rich meals a day. In all studies, there was greater weight loss in the treatment group compared with the placebo group, but this difference was significant in only 3 studies. Overall, the mean weight loss among the 6 randomized controlled trials was 0.4 ± 0.2 kg/wk (0.5 ± 0.1% of initial weight/wk) in the treatment groups compared with 0.2 ± 0.2 kg/wk (0.2 ± 0.2% of initial weight/wk) in the placebo groups. Variable results among these studies could be due to factors such as differences in dietary composition, degree of energy deficit, compliance with the prescribed dietary regimens, and extract preparation/composition. Therefore, results look promising, but more research is needed to determine the effectiveness of pulse extract preparations. In addition, the relevance of these trials to consumption of whole pulses is uncertain. As mentioned earlier in this review, the activity of αamylase inhibitor is thought to be destroyed during cooking and/or processing , although low levels of activity may remain . Few studies have been conducted on the effects of repeated consumption of processed/cooked pulses and other legumes, which may contain some low level of [illegible]amylase inhibitor activity; therefore, this is an area that could be further researched.

PULSES IN THE U.S. DIET

Based on recent analyses of dietary intake data from the NHANES, few U.S. adults consume pulses in their usual diet. The proportion of U.S. adults estimated to consume pulses or legumes over 1–2 d varies from 8–30%, depending on the data set used, the number of days of intake available (1 in NHANES 1999–2002 and 2 in NHANES 2003–4), and the type of legume analyzed, i.e. dried beans , nonsoy legumes , or legumes including soy beans and green beans . None of the estimates appear to have included food products that may contain pulse fractions such as pea fiber in baked goods and pasta.

The USDA-recommended amount of legume consumption for most adults aged 19 y and older is 3 c/wk, with the exception of women aged 51 y and older for which the recommendation is 2.5 c/wk . Perhaps not surprisingly, pulse consumption in the US is markedly below the recommendation . The weighted average intake of legumes based on the available studies is <“0.15 c/d (36 mL), which is <“58–65% lower than the recommended amount. Kimmons et al. estimated that of the 30% of adults who do consume legumes, only about 40–45% of them achieved at least the recommended intake.

There are numerous factors that determine food choices, including, taste, cost, convenience, and nutrition . In the case of pulses and soybeans, there are likely additional factors, including purported physiological effects (digestibility issues), cultural factors, habits (e.g. vegetarianism/veganism), and knowledge about how to incorporate them into everyday diets. A strong incentive to increase pulse consumption may be their low cost, particularly for a high nutrient-dense food.

Drewnowski recently reported that beans were among the top 5 classes of food having the highest micronutrient to price ratio. Indeed, according to U.S. national surveys, pulse consumption is highest among low-income populations. Households in the lowest quartile of income (<130% of poverty level) represent 19% of the U.S. population but consume 27% of all cooked, dried beans . Furthermore, there are differences in the type of bean consumed by income level, with lower-income individuals consuming primarily pinto and lima beans and high-income individuals consuming more black beans and garbanzos. Some of these differences may relate to cultural preference for certain beans among minority populations, who tend to have lower average income levels than Caucasians.

Palatability or taste preferences could be another factor determining the choice to incorporate pulses as a major part of one's diet. Several studies have been conducted recently showing a general acceptability of foods incorporating pulses or pulse flours , although depending on the specific pulse and the population, the range of acceptability could vary widely . Simply increasing familiarity with pulses could also help to increase the likelihood they may be incorporated into a diet more regularly .

Digestibility issues and potentially adverse gastrointestinal effects of pulse consumption may also be of concern to many individuals. Few studies have included formal measures of gastrointestinal tolerance to pulse consumption. As reviewed by Veenstra et al. , moderate consumption tends to be well tolerated but tolerance decreases when pulse consumption reaches very high levels.

6

The Indian Feed Industry

Feed manufacturing on a commercial and scientific basis started around 1965 with the setting up of medium-sized feed plants in northern and western India. Feed was produced mainly to cater to the needs of dairy cattle. The poultry sector was not developed at that time and was restricted to backyard production, with the *desi* (or native bird) kept mainly for the production of eggs. The poultry industry is now growing in importance.

Today, the Indian feed industry is worth approximately Rs 45 billion, that is about US$1 billion.

THE LIVESTOCK INDUSTRY OF INDIA

India's animal wealth is quite large in terms of its populations of cattle, poultry, sheep and goats, camels, horses and pets . Recently, aquaculture has also been growing in importance in India.

Table. Livestock population in India

Table : Livestock population in India	
Livestock type	**Population**
	(millions)
Cattle	204.5
Buffaloes	84.2
Sheep	50.8
Goats	115.3
Pigs	12.8
Horses/ponies	0.8
Mules	0.2
Donkeys	0.9
Camels	1.0
Yaks	0.06
Mithuns	0.15
Total livestock	**470.86**

DAIRY CATTLE

Worldwide, India is number one in milk production, at 78.0 million tonnes *per annum*, and the dairy industry is spread across the whole country. India has one of the largest populations of cattle and buffalo in the world. In a total of 288 million head, there are 10 million cross-bred cows, 15 million good milch cows of local varieties and 36 million buffaloes of good milch varieties . The remainder of the cattle population is of a non-descript variety and a sizeable proportion consists of bullocks.

Table. Cattle and poultry indicators

Table : Cattle and poultry indicators	
Dairy	
Cross-bred cows *(millions)*	10.0
Improved cows *(millions)*	15.0
Improved buffaloes *(millions)*	36.0
Milk production *(million tonnes)*	78.0
Per capita consumption *(g/day)*	240
Poultry	
Commercial layers *(millions)*	150
Commercial broilers *(millions)*	650
Stock breeders *(millions)*	6.5
Egg production *(10^9)*	40
Per capita availability *(eggs/year)*	40
Poultry meat production *(million tonnes)*	1.0
Per capita availability *(g/year)*	1 000
Poultry feed production *(million tonnes)*	9.0
Annual growth	
Dairy industry	5%
Layer industry	6-7%
Broiler industry	10%

The cross-bred population is either Jersey or Holstein-Friesian, crossed with local cows. Cross-breeding was a natural solution to upgrading the milk yield in the absence of high-value imported varieties of pure-bred animals. The buffalo breeds are unique to India, and produce milk with a fat content of 7 to 8 percent.

Milk is seen as a health drink and a variety of Indian sweets are prepared from milk. The ice-cream market is growing.

Farms are located on the outskirts of cities and within cities. Almost all villages have a number of cattle, but there are only a few organized dairy farms. In India, dairy is not so much an industry as a smallholder farming activity.

Growth in the milk sector has occurred mainly through cooperative efforts. Cooperatives started by supplying milk collection centres, where milk was collected from villagers in quantities as small as 1 litre, and gradually started to provide other services to farmers, including education, artificial insemination, veterinary health support and feeding. The small farmers became prosperous, loan facilities were made available through banks, and member farmers started to share the profits from cooperatives. Cooperatives also set up their own modern computerized feed plants. They have modern milk processing plants from which they produce and market pasteurized milk, butter, butter oil, chocolate, ice-cream and milk sweets, which are very popular with Indian consumers. Today, the feed production from cooperatives is about 0.6 million tonnes per year.

The National Dairy Development Board (NDDB), which has excellent facilities for research on breeding, nutrition and health care, has played a pivotal role in setting up cooperatives. Without NDDB and several of the existing dairy cooperatives, the milk sector in India would have suffered.

The dairy industry in India is expected to grow, but growth will be restricted to individual small farmers. It is unlikely that India will see the advent of large, organized dairy farming in the near future.

POULTRY

Compared with the rest of the livestock sector, the poultry industry in India is more scientific, better organized and continuously progressing towards modernization. Breeding and feeding management has improved through education, training, competition, expansion and survival instincts. India is the world's fifth largest egg producer, with a total production of 40 billion eggs per year. The broiler industry is growing at the rate of 10 percent *per annum*.

India has 150 million layers and 650 million broilers. Annual per capita consumption of eggs is 40, and that of broiler meat is 1 000 g. Although these figures are low in comparison with those for developed countries, the industry has great potential to expand because 30 percent of the country's population (about 300 million people) is developing economically and the demand for poultry products is therefore likely to grow.

The poultry industry has witnessed several ups and downs in the last 25 years as a result of unplanned growth and a lack of government regulation. Currently, it is growing at the rate of 10 percent in broilers and 6 to 7 percent in layers and is going through a phase of integration in broilers which is likely to change the face of the industry. Although the phenomenon is new, it is expected that there will be very rapid changes towards integration as more farmers find it increasingly difficult to run farms with marginal profits or negative margins. The poultry industry is very modern, with pure-line breeding, the latest vaccines and medicines, environmentally controlled poultry houses, up-to-date processing units, the latest management practices, chicken processing, exports of hatching eggs and excellent feed quality.

SHEEP, GOATS AND CAMELS

The sheep and goat sector is mostly in the hands of nomadic tribes and no significant scientific husbandry, rearing and management practices are implemented. Research on breeding and nutrition is being conducted at research institutes and agricultural universities.

Most of the country's camels are located in the desert area of the western part of India, in the states of Rajasthan and Gujarat, bordering Pakistan. Camels are reared by individuals who feed them local ingredients. There is a lack of scientific management practices, genetic studies and scientific feeding practices in camel rearing and the industry survives mostly on the basis of local, long-established knowledge of feeding and breeding. There is, however, a fairly good disease diagnosis and treatment system, with modern medicines and vaccines.

SWINE

India is a multilingual, multiracial country whose people hold various religious beliefs. Although the majority of the population is Hindu, there are sizeable minorities of Muslims, Christians, Sikhs, Buddhists, Jains, Parsees and others. India also has a large tribal population and is a plural society in which the sentiments of each social and religious group need to be respected for harmony and peaceful coexistence. Thus, most states in India have banned cow slaughter and the beef industry is therefore non-existent. The majority of people disapprove of pork consumption, maybe because of the lack of scientific management on swine farms. Swine reared on the streets are very unhygienic and buyers are always suspicious about the source of pork, so there is no organized pork industry.

AQUACULTURE

The aquaculture industry is relatively young. Prawns and fish are grown in both fresh and brackish water, the latter being located mostly in the southeast and southwest coasts. Aquaculture feed is manufactured with highly scientific methods and modern plants that use new technologies and are highly efficient. Multinational companies from Thailand and Taiwan Province of China have invested in this business. India exports most of its aquaculture products.

HORSES AND PETS

The Indian equine industry goes back more than 50 years and is considered modern, scientific and very well equipped in terms of every aspect of animal husbandry practices. The equine industry is spread across India and is restricted to horse racing. Imports of good genetic material are quite common in this industry. The feeding of these valuable animals is mostly at the farm level under the supervision of experienced people following traditional practices. What innovation there is tends to be closely guarded by the companies concerned.

The Indian pet industry is in a nascent stage, with the main focus being on dogs rather than cats and the emphasis on breeding and training. Regular dog shows are held by enthusiastic dog owners to increase awareness of the rearing of good-quality pure-breds; dogs are a source of pride for households. In many cities, animal health care systems are run by qualified vets with well-equipped facilities such as X-ray machines, surgical facilities, imported vaccines and the latest drugs.

The feeding of pets is however, left to the household. Some commercial preparations are available in the form of dog biscuits, chews, etc., but dogs are fed mostly on home-cooked food. One of the reasons for this could be the high cost of commercial pet food.

FEEDSTUFFS AND INGREDIENTS IN ANIMAL FEEDS

India is currently self-sufficient in livestock feeds and does not depend on imports. Instead, the country exports large quantities of solvent extracted meals, which are a major source of foreign exchange earning.

CEREALS AND GRAINS

Maize, sorghum and *bajra* (a type of millet) are commonly used in animal feeds. Wheat and rice are mainly retained for human consumption.

CAKES AND MEALS

Commonly used commodities of this kind are soybean, groundnut, rapeseed, sesame and sunflower meals in poultry feed. In cattle feed, in addition to these meals, others such as cottonseed and copra are used as premium ingredients.

FEEDS OF ANIMAL ORIGIN

Meat-meal, fishmeal, bone-meal and dicalcium phosphate of bone origin are the common raw materials available for animal feeding. It is interesting to note that, with the exception of some bone-based dicalcium phosphate, the Indian feed industry does not use materials of animal origin in dairy cattle feed. This was not out of fear of any zoonotic problems but the result of deep-rooted beliefs that the cow is sacred and must therefore be vegetarian. Now even the use of bone-based dicalcium phosphate has been banned and mineral-based dicalcium phosphate is used instead.

Fishmeal and meat-meal were popularly used in poultry feed, but the increased production, improved availability and better awareness of soybean meal has led to its replacing fishmeal and meat-meal in most poultry rations. It should be mentioned that farmers have faced production problems owing to the bacterial contamination of fishmeal and meat-meal. The quality of fishmeal is also very poor.

POPULAR BY-PRODUCTS

Some by-products are very nutritious and palatable to cattle, and these products form the bulk of cattle feed. They include wheat bran, rice bran and oil-extracted rice bran, tapioca, guar meal, safflower meal, maize gluten and molasses. A special mention should be made of Indian cattle feed's unique use of hulls or shells, popularly known as *chunis* in the local language. These shells come from pulses: horse gram, black gram, mung bean and pigeon pea.

MINERALS AND VITAMINS

Cattle feed is necessarily enriched with vitamins A and D3, and trace minerals such as iron, zinc, manganese, copper, cobalt and iodine. Calcium and phosphorus are also included. Poultry feed is enriched with all of these and all of the B complex vitamins.

FEED ADDITIVES AND SUPPLEMENTS

Feed additives and supplements have played a very important role in enhancing the performance of dairy animals and, even more so, poultry. Today they are necessary in any feed formulation and essential for the formulation of a balanced diet. The additives and supplements used are antibiotic growth promoters (their usage is not banned in India), prebiotics, probiotics, enzymes, mould inhibitors, toxin binders, anti-coccidial supplements, acidifiers, amino acids, by-pass fat, by-pass protein, non-antibiotic growth promoters, milk boosters, antioxidants, feed flavours and herbal preparations of Indian origin. A number of these products are imported from developed countries.

ANIMAL FEED COMMODITY PRODUCTION

MAIZE AND SORGHUM

Maize is one of the most important cereals used in animal feed. The annual production of maize is about 10.5 million tonnes; about 4 million tonnes of which are used in the starch industry, 4.5 million tonnes in animal feeds and 2.5 million tonnes in human consumption and seed production. Maize production has remained almost static in the past three years while demand is increasing. The major crop is during the Kharif season (June to October), which accounts for 90 percent of the total. The remaining 10 percent is harvested in the Rabi season (November to February).

The import of maize used to be restricted but, since April 2000, imports have been approved under open general licence (OGL). There are, however, 15 percent duty and a grain inspection fee to be paid, so there is no price parity between imported and domestically produced maize. There is no subsidy or minimum price index for maize, and the price varies with the market demand. Maize cannot be exported.

Sorghum and *bajra* are very sturdy varieties of millet that can grow under limited rainfall conditions and are popularly used in animal feeds. Production of sorghum has remained static. There is no export of sorghum and *bajra* (millet).

Table. Production of feed ingredients and solvent meals, 1998-1999

Table : Production of feed ingredients and solvent meals, 1998-1999		
Commodity	**Production**	**Export**
	(million tonnes)	*(million tonnes)*
Maize	10.2	0
Jowar	9.3	0
Soybean meal	2.7	2.73[1]
Groundnut meal	0.59	0.09
Rapeseed meal	1.05	0.92
Sunflower meal	0.52	0.03
Cottonseed cake	1.12	0
Rice bran (deoiled)	2.95	0.005

RICE BRAN AND SOLVENT-EXTRACTED RICE BRAN

Rice bran and solvent-extracted rice bran are by-products. India is one of the world's largest producers of rice, producing 87 million tonnes during 1998/99 (1.7 percent more than in the previous year), and India produces approximately 2.95 million tonnes of solvent-extracted rice bran, which is regularly exported.

OILSEED MEALS

India produces soybean, groundnut, rapeseed, sunflower, sesame and cotton meals and these are used as major ingredients in animal feeds. The production of solvent meals is shown in Table 3.

For animal feeds, soybean is the most frequently used oilseed meal and has completely replaced fishmeal in poultry feeds. Cottonseed cake and meal are often used in cattle feed throughout the country. Groundnut meal is less popular because of the aflatoxin problem. Rapeseed meal is second to soybean meal in production and second to cottonseed cake and meal for cattle feed. Sunflower meal is commonly used in both cattle and poultry feed.

India regularly imports edible oil and imported 4.4 million tonnes in 1998-1999. These imports have created problems for the country's crushers and, although India has about 600 solvent extraction units, they are running at only 50 percent of capacity.

India's economy is agro-based but the yield per hectare is a cause of major concern to the country's farmers and agriculture. The government recognizes this and there are subsidies on fertilizers and power tariffs. The government also assures base prices for many agro-based commodities. India's average yields per hectare of major commodities compared with the highest yields realized worldwide are given in Table 4.

Table. Average yield per hectare of selected agricultural seeds (in tonnes)

Seed	Highest yield worldwide	Indian yield
Soybean	2.62 (United States)	1.0
Rapeseed	3.52 (France)	1.0
Sunflower	1.78 (Argentina)	1.0
Groundnut	2.82 (United States)	1.5
Sesame	0.78 (China)	0.6
Maize	7.9 (United States)	1.6

With a population of 1 billion people, the demand for agroproducts is great and India will have to augment its agricultural production by several hundred percent if the country is to remain self-sufficient.

FEED STANDARDS AND SPECIFICATIONS

For cattle and poultry, nutritional standards have been prepared with respect to the genotype, environment, quality of available raw materials, maintenance methods, production and reproduction requirements, production capacity and phase of production.

Table. BIS standards, dairy feed requirements

Characteristic	Type I (IS: 2052, 1979, reaffirmed 1990)	Type II (IS: 2052, 1979, reaffirmed 1990)
Moisture *(maximum %)*	11	11
Crude protein *(maximum %)*	22	20
Crude fat *(minimum %)*	3	2.5
Crude fibre *(maximum %)*	7	12
Acid-insoluble ash *(maximum %)*	3	4

Table. BIS standards, poultry feed requirements

Characteristic	Broiler starter feed	Broiler finisher feed	Chick feed	Growing chicken feed	Laying chicken feed	Breeder layer feed
Moisture*(maximum %)*	11	11	11	11	11	11
Crude protein (N x 6.25)*(maximum %)*	23	20	20	16	18	18
Crude fibre*(maximum %)*	6	6	7	8	8	8
Acid-insoluble ash *(maximum %)*	3.0	3.0	4.0	4.0	4.0	4.0
Salt (as NaCl)*(maximum %)*	0.6	0.6	0.6	0.6	0.6	0.6

The Bureau of Indian Standards (BIS) is a central government organization that facilitates discussion between scientists and industry and prepares guidelines and specifications. Table 5 shows the BIS specifications for dairy cattle and Tables 6a, 6b and 6c those for poultry.

Table. BIS standards, poultry feed declaration requirements

Characteristic	Broiler starter feed	Broiler finisher feed	Chick feed	Growing chicken feed	Laying chicken feed	Breeder layer feed
Calcium (Ca)*(maximum %)*	1.2	1.2	1.0	1.0	3.0	3.0
Available phosphorus*(minimum %)*	0.5	0.5	0.5	0.5	0.5	0.5
Lysine *(maximum %)*	1.2	1.0	0.9	0.6	0.65	0.65
Methionine*(maximum %)*	0.50	0.35	0.3	0.25	0.30	0.30
Metabolizable energy *(minimum cal/kg)*	2 800	2 900	2 600	2 500	2 600	2 600

The specifications of both BIS and CLFMA are only guidelines and their use as standards is not compulsory. The animal feed business is competitive and feed manufacturers therefore endeavour to produce feed of the highest possible quality.

FEEDING PRACTICES AND THE USE OF COMPOUND FEED

In India, the term "compound feed" refers to feed that is nutritionally balanced and has been manufactured using the facilities of an analytical laboratory and under the supervision of nutritionists. There are also a large number of small-scale feed mixers who produce feed for local consumption. Such feed is termed "self-mixed feed" or "home-mixed feed".

CATTLE FEED

Cattle feeding practices are very traditional. Farmers choose their own ingredients and prepare their own formulations, believing that by these means they are able to pay more individual attention to their cattle. The productivity of the cattle is limited because of their poor genetic make-up, so high-quality compound feed (industry feed) may not necessarily generate a significant improvement in productivity and this has hampered growth of the cattle feed industry because most farmers are reluctant to use compound feed fully. Instead they compromise by using such feed in proportions of 5 to 60 percent, making up the balance with their own formulations. It is only in the case of highly productive animals that compound feed has been able to show its real potential and the importance of technology has been demonstrated.

The share of compound cattle feed manufactured by the industry, in relation to the overall potential, is low for the following reasons:

- The cattle population is fragmented and spread over large parts of the country. Farmers' low level of education and strong traditional beliefs mean that there is generally little awareness of compound cattle feed.
- More than 50 percent of the country's total milk production comes from a very large number of low-yielding cows and buffaloes. A further 25 percent of milk production comes from buffaloes and only the

remaining 25 percent of the total is produced by cross-bred and improved cows.

- Industrially manufactured compound cattle feed has proved its value for cross-bred cows and buffaloes but not for low-yielding cattle because of their genetic limitations. Home-mixed feed is very frequently used for buffaloes and low-yielding cattle.

POULTRY FEED

Poultry feed is divided into layer and broiler feed. In the case of layer feed, cost is the main constraint in using compound feed. An innovative, high-value compound feed can result in increased numbers of eggs, but the risks are too high because of the birds' long life cycle.

Compound feed has, however, made a major contribution to broiler feeding. This is an example of excellent coordination among instrument technology, formulations and use of feed additives and supplements. Cost is a less important factor because the performance improvements are greater than the cost increases and the birds' life cycle is short.

Two types of poultry feed are prepared. One is ready-made and in the form of mash or pellets. The second is in concentrated form for mixing with an energy source. Concentrates are protein sources, balanced in amino acids and containing vitamins, minerals and feed additives. They are mixed with energy sources such as maize, sorghum or bajra to prepare poultry rations.

THE QUALITY ASSURANCE OF COMPOUND FEED

The Indian feed industry employs the services of qualified nutritionists. Members of the industry have their own analytical laboratories and either have their own research and development facilities or have access to the research laboratories of agricultural universities or government institutions. The industry is fully committed to quality and its technical staff are knowledgeable about the nutrition of cattle, buffaloes, layers and broilers.

As well as the normal proximate principles, other analyses are regularly carried out, such as amino acids, aflatoxin, ochratoxin, castor, tannins and urease activity. There is a high degree of awareness of feed microbiology among the millers of feed. Feed raw materials and finished products are subjected to microbial counts, *Salmonella* and *Escherichia coli* testing and mould count, and contaminated materials are rejected and sometimes destroyed. Insurance cover is available.

The feed millers have acquired the latest technologies and modern equipment such as high-pressure liquid chromatography (HPLC) and near-infrared (NIR) analysers. All vitamins, minerals and other feed additives are regularly analysed using modern analytical techniques.

Regular seminars are conducted, short-term courses are arranged and

Indian scientists are constantly working to upgrade the quality of Indian feed and make it completely safe for animal feeding.

The quality of Indian feed can be compared with that of any Western feed. Today it is common to achieve a chicken house average of 310 eggs in 52 weeks, in layers, and body weights of 2.0 kg in less than six weeks, with a feed conversion ratio of between 1.8 and 1.9, in broilers. Dairy feed can use the genetic potential of Indian cattle at its maximum. The quality of Indian feed is satisfactory and innovation will continue.

RESEARCH AND DEVELOPMENT IN ANIMAL FEED

Given the importance of feed ingredients, Indian scientists have worked on various aspects of research and development in the field of animal feeds and feeding. In the 1960s, all Indian raw materials were analysed for their proximate composition, metabolizable energy values and deleterious factors. During the 1970s, the government sanctioned special projects to study the use of by-products in animal feeds. Various by-products were considered and their nutritional parameters studied (a list of the various by-products available in animal feeds is given in Table 9). Indian scientists analysed ingredients for their chemical values and studied their biological values, and this information was useful to the industry in the initial stages of growth. In the 1970s and 1980s subsequent research was conducted on the energy-protein and energy-amino acid ratios and the vitamin and mineral requirements of animals. During the next phase of research, the main focus was on bypass fat and bypass protein utilization in ruminants, and on the role of various feed additives in enhancing milk, egg and broiler meat production. Research and development work has been conducted on least-cost formulations and usage of synthetic amino acids.

THE FEED INDUSTRY AND CLFMA

CLFMA was formed in June 1967 as an association of feed manufacturers and associated industries such as ingredient suppliers, importers, feed additive manufacturers, consultants, hatcheries and milk cooperatives and feed machinery manufacturers. The objectives of CLFMA are to promote the concept of nutritionally balanced compound feed; to promote, assist, organize and coordinate scientific research in the field of animal nutrition; to conduct, assign, sponsor or co-sponsor surveys and studies; to collect, classify and circulate information related to animal feed to its members and government; to offer suggestions to government in formulating policies; and to impart training to livestock farmers, feed mill personnel, veterinarians, students and others. The office-bearers of CLFMA are elected and operate for a maximum of two years at one level. Over the years, CLFMA has been able to solve many problems of the industry, but many others still remain unsolved. CLFMA is gradually becoming a representative of the entire livestock industry. The feed production of its members is described in Table 10, while the industry's production of feed *vis-α-vis* potential is described in Table 11.

ISSUES IN THE ANIMAL FEED INDUSTRY

STANDARDIZATION AND REGULATION OF ANIMAL FEED MANUFACTURERS

As already mentioned, BIS has produced guideline feed standards and the industry also has its own guidelines. Currently there is no compulsion to use BIS standards, but the central government has been advising states to introduce their own regulatory standards. The industry, however, is resisting this move. One of the major reasons for opposition is that the government wants to legislate regulation under the Essential Commodities Act 1955 which is considered draconian and totally inappropriate in this context. There is no shortage of compound animal feeds anywhere in the country. In fact, the organized sector of the compound feed industry is facing serious problems resulting from a huge idle capacity, to the extent of 50 percent or more. New capacities are being added by global players in the feed business and by national as well as multinational integrators. The nature of animal feeds and the animal feed industry has completely changed. Increasingly, products, including new products, are being excluded from the purview of the Essential Commodities Act 1955. Major raw materials for compound animal feeds, such as groundnut, soybean, rapeseed and sunflower meals and cottonseed and rice bran extract, which are exported, are not covered by the Act. There is therefore no reason for it to cover the animal feed manufactured with these raw materials. Furthermore, the industry has several reservations about implementing BIS standards. There is a lack of flexibility in these standards and they are lagging far behind the industry's products. For cattle, they have not been revised for 30 years, while the BIS standards for poultry are obsolete.

Another feed standards issue that worries both the government and industry is that any changes to existing standards will be slow and difficult to arrive at because of participative conflicts and various lobbying groups. However, the industry's principal concern about compulsory standards is that they will disturb efforts to innovate and upgrade feed production in order to improve the productivity of the animals. This is because all innovations would have to be passed by BIS, and such a process is likely to take several years to complete.

CLASSIFICATIONS OF ANIMAL FEED SUPPLEMENTS/ADDITIVES FOR IMPORT

The classification of feed additives is a major hindrance to the Indian feed industry. Worldwide, animal feed supplements and additives are covered under chapter 23.09 of the Harmonized System of Nomenclature (HSN), to which

India is a signatory. In the HSN, all feed ingredients are listed under the "free" category for import, but the Indian Government put them into the "restricted" category in October 1995. Since then, there have been continuous discussions among the drug control authorities, the Director-General of Foreign Trade and the Central Excise Department, all of which want to bring feed additives under their administration so as to increase their own revenues. The industry, represented by CLFMA, has made several representations to the government, but these have been round various government departments, appellate tribunals, the High Court and the Supreme Court without providing any useful results for the industry.

COUNTERVAILING DUTY ON AMINO ACIDS

The essential amino acids, such as DL-methionine, L-lysine and L-threonine, are not manufactured in India. These products are vital ingredients of compound animal feed for improving the quality of the final feed and making it conversion-efficient. With a view to bringing about the rapid development of animal husbandry in India, the government reduced the import duty on essential amino acids to the present level of 10 percent customs duty, so that the feed price to livestock farmers would be economic. However, with the imposition of countervailing duty (CVD) and other duties, the objective of helping to promote animal husbandry has been defeated. Table 12 shows the import duty on amino acids in different countries.

LOCAL SALES TAX

Another threat to the industry is posed by local sales taxes. It must be noted that the feed industry is mainly commodity-oriented and, although it is value-added, it cannot support the burden of any kind of taxation. The industry has made several representations to the government and some state governments have accepted its point of view and refrained from levying any tax on animal feeds.

IMPORT AND EXPORT

Indian feed was exported to the Near East during the 1980s, but the export demand was reduced when feed mills were set up in the Near East. At present, India exports about 25 000 tonnes of feed to the Near East as general animal feed. There is no import of animal feed as such into India. However, the country does import certain chemicals, feed additives, amino acids and essentials for aquaculture feed.

THE FUTURE OF THE INDIAN FEED INDUSTRY - WINDS OF CHANGE

At the beginning of the twenty-first century, India has a population of 1 billion people. Although the annual growth rate has slowed from 2 to 1.8 percent, the base is so broad that changes in population dynamics are not perceptible. The population may stabilize by sometime between 2030 and 2040 if all sections of society support family planning wholeheartedly. The purchasing power of the middle class is growing (the middle class accounts for approximately 300 million people) and food habits are also changing.

The Indian economy is growing at the rate of 6 to 8 percent per annum. The livestock industry in India is the second largest contributor to gross domestic product (GDP), after agriculture, and accounts for 9 percent of the total. Consumption is likely to increase as follows: *per capita* milk from 240 to 450 g per year; *per capita* eggs from 40 to 100 per year; and *per capita*broiler meat from 1 000 to 2 000 g per year.

A major change is occurring in India on the economic front. The country has adopted a model that lies midway between liberal and public sector production, but growth has been affected by the poor performance of most of the public sector units, rising government costs and fiscal deficit, and the economy has suffered. A process of liberalization was set in motion by the government and has been implemented for the last eight to ten years. This has caused India to open up and invite investment from multinationals, liberalize imports, reduce government expenditure and remove public sector businesses. It also means that the days of nationalization, unnecessary government controls and restrictions will soon be over thanks to progress in the country's economy.

India has entered into an agreement with its trade partners under the World Trade Organization (WTO). The changes brought about by the liberalization process will be slow but certain. The government is opening up imports in a phased manner, and it is expected that this process will be completed by April 2003. In the meantime, about 930 items, including agricultural products, will be open for import under open general licence from April 2001, making it possible to import dressed chicken, milk and milk products.

Various livestock industry associations have taken issue with such imports in an attempt to protect their members. If the livestock industry is affected, the feed industry will also be affected. The Government of India has raised the tariff on all poultry and poultry products from 35 *percent* to the WTO boundary level of 100 *percent*. It therefore appears that there will be a level playing field.

In view of the expected rise in *per capita* consumption of chicken meat, eggs and milk, livestock production and productivity will grow. The dairy industry, which is cooperative-based, is growing with the increased capacities of milk processing units. The population of cross-bred cattle and buffaloes is also growing. Milk is very popular in India. The poultry industry is developing towards vertical integration and a few multinational companies have already entered the Indian poultry business. Although the live bird market currently accounts for about 90 percent of the total market, it is expected that the consumption of dressed chicken will grow in the next five years, from the existing 10 percent to 25 percent or more. This would mean establishing very hygienic and scientific processing units. Cold chains, branded chicken, chicken cuts, etc. will be introduced and, depending on the success and consistent quality, consumer preference for dressed meat will grow.

The next decade will see significant changes in restructuring, mergers, acquisitions, amalgamations, joint ventures, diversification, integration and efficient service chains, e-commerce and use of the latest information technology in global tenders, trading, export/import and other commercial activities. At the root of all these developments will be the scientific development of feed manufacturing technology. The Indian feed industry will increasingly use biotechnology, more scientific formulations, new molecules and natural and herbal products to improve animal productivity. Indian agriculture will also use biotechnology and genetically modified organisms (GMOs) to support the feed industry, which is entering a very exciting phase of growth for the next decade.

OPTIMIZING DAIRY FEEDING PROGRAMMES

Dairy cattle require specific amounts of nutrients to support various levels of performance, so changes in feed intake can have a dramatic impact on the formulation of rations and nutrient intake. Dietary nutrient densities are minimized when feed consumption is maximized, making it easier to formulate rations that are adequate in nutrients. The amount of feed that a dairy cow consumes is highly correlated to its nutrient intake. Every effort should be made to maximize feed consumption when feeding dairy cattle. As feed consumption declines, dietary nutrient densities are increased. The higher the intake, the more forage that can be included in a dairy ration and the fewer concentrates that will be required.

The most cost-effective feeding programmes can be implemented when feed consumption is maximized. Maximized feed consumption minimizes the cost of providing required nutrients because higher levels of forages and by-product feeds can be incorporated into the ration. When feed consumption is maximized there is more flexibility in the type of feeds that can be used in formulating the ration.

The quality of forage has a dramatic effect on feed consumption. Feeding the highest-quality forage will maximize feed consumption and nutrient intake and minimize dietary nutrient densities, ration cost and the quantities of concentrates that need to be incorporated into a ration. The feeding of roughages containing high fibre and low digestible energy levels is the primary cause of many dairy farms' failure to realize maximum dry matter intake. Higher forage levels also help to maintain a more stable and healthier rumen and reduce the animal's consumption of grain, which can then be put to other uses, including human consumption. As forage quality declines, the digestive passage rate becomes slower, resulting in a greater fill factor and causing a reduction in feed intake. When low-quality forages have to be fed, they should be chopped to minimize their depressing effect on feed consumption. Care needs to be taken not to chop forage so fine that milk butterfat is depressed by the resulting low effective fibre level.

Every effort should be taken to minimize heat stress so that feed consumption is not depressed. Shade is very important in areas where cows are exposed to high levels of solar radiation. In hot dry climates, applying water or using misters or evaporative coolers can be effective ways of lowering ambient temperatures, cooling cows and reducing heat stress. Circulating air with fans increases evapotranspiration and increases the dissipation of a cow's body heat load. Opening housing facilities to increase air circulation during times of heat stress increases air movement, which will increase cooling and reduce heat stress. Providing a cool water supply can also help to reduce heat stress.

Adequate consumption of water is critical for maintaining feed consumption; there is a high correlation between feed and water consumption in dairy cattle. When dairy cattle are required to consume poor-quality water, water and feed consumption will be depressed. Maximum performance will only be achieved when cattle have ad libitum access to a good-quality water source.

Poor-quality water or an inadequate supply of water will depress an animal's performance more quickly and more dramatically than any other nutrient deficiency. Adequacy of watering space must also be considered. When cows have to wait too long to drink, their water and dry matter consumption are decreased. If water sources of variable qualities are available, the highest-producing cows should be given the best-quality water.

When developing feeding programmes for dairy cattle, the goal should be to maximize feed consumption by trying to minimize the various factors that depress it. When feed consumption is maximized, performance is optimized, and this should be the primary goal of a dairy feeding programme.

VERSATILITY OF DAIRY CATTLE

Dairy cattle are unique in having the ability to convert cellulytic feed resources (forages, by-products, etc.) that are not suitable for human and monogastric animal (swine, poultry, etc.) consumption into a highly nutritious product, which is milk. Milk is high in nutritive value which can be used directly by the people who own the cows, or be sold as a means of generating income. In some parts of the world, as few as one or two cows can provide a substantial source of daily income for a family for an extended period of time, if adequate feed resources are available and the cows are fed and managed properly. Dairy cattle are very adaptable since they have the ability to convert a wide range of feed resources into milk. They can be grazed on a wide range of forages (improved and unimproved pastures, roadside forage, forage trees, etc.) or be maintained in partial or full confinement where they can be fed a wide range of harvested feeds (concentrates [such as cereal grains or oilseed meals]; ensiled crops [such as maize, sorghum or barley and various forage haylages/silages]; wet brewers' grains; agricultural processing wastes; various types of hays; and various by-product feeds [such as rice hulls, wheat bran and brewers' grains]); or crop residues (straw, maize stover, etc.). The manure produced by dairy cattle can also be a valuable resource and is used as either a fuel or a fertilizer in various parts of the world.

The versatility of dairy cattle makes them unique among livestock species. They can be maintained in highly productive systems, where feeding and management inputs are very high, and in subsistence-type systems, where inputs are very low. Dairy farming provides a nutritious marketable product without sacrificing the animals.

CONSIDERATIONS FOR DEVELOPING A DAIRY FEEDING PROGRAMME

The ideal dairy feeding programme is one that optimizes the use of available feed resources, so that profitability associated with milk production can be maximized. It has often been thought that one ideal feeding programme could be universally applied all over the world, and an example of such a supposedly universal programme would be the maize-soybean feeding programmes that have been developed and used extensively for swine. When maize and soybean meal are the most economic feed resources available, the maize-soybean programme would most likely be the feeding programme of choice but, for various reasons, it has often been used where maize and soybean meal are not the most economic feeds available. Dairy cattle do not have a standard feeding programme that can or should be universally applied. In fact, dairy feeding programmes need to be customized for individual farms, and ideally for individual animals, so that they can take advantage of the feed resource that are available to individual producers. The feed resources available even to neighbours can vary dramatically: one farmer might have pasture to graze, while the neighbouring farmer does not; another farmer might have hay to feed, while the next farm has only straw. In areas or regions where feed resources are available at similar prices, similar feeding programmes can be used, but even then, if the production levels of individual cows vary, different amounts of forage and concentrate will need to be fed. This means that feeding programmes should be customized to individual producers or regions based on the prices of feeds, the availability of feed resources, the feeds' nutrient content and availability and the milk producing ability of the cows.

Fortunately, some basic nutritional principles can be applied to the development of dairy cattle feeding programmes that allow for a wide range of feed resources to be effectively utilized in the production of milk. The reason dairy cattle are so versatile is that they are ruminant animals and have the ability to convert a wide range of carbohydrate substrates (cellulose, starch, etc.) in their rumen into nutrient sources (volatile fatty acids, microbial proteins, vitamins, etc.) that the cow can then absorb and use to produce milk. A wide variety of feed resources can therefore be fed to dairy cattle, including forages, crop residues (straws), by-products (rice hulls, wheat bran, beet pulp, etc.), silages and concentrate feeds (cereal grains and oilseed meals). In developing countries where traditional feed resources such as forages (alfalfa, ryegrass, etc.) and concentrates (maize, sorghum, soybean meal, cottonseed meal, etc.) are not readily available or not economically feasible for feeding, a wide range of other feedstuffs can be used to provided the nutrients required to produce milk. The challenge in both developed and developing countries is to optimize milk production while using available feeds to provide the required nutrients in the most economic way possible.

When formulating rations, nutritionists have often aimed at increasing the efficiency of production. Simply stated, they have tried to formulate feeding programmes that would convert the highest amount of nutrients consumed by the dairy cow into milk components (butterfat, protein, etc.). Using this approach they have always tried to maximize production, because the higher the production the more efficiently the cow converts the nutrients that it consumes into milk components. As an example of efficient dietary nutrient conversion, three feeding programmes were developed for three milk production levels (40, 20 and 10 kg per day) for a healthy 600 kg cow that is maintained under ideal conditions and has the genetic potential to produce 40 kg of milk (containing 3.5 percent butterfat and 3.2 percent milk protein) a day. Table 1 shows the amounts of nutrients (in terms of total digestible nutrients, net energy of lactation and crude protein) required to support each of the three different levels of milk production, the milk's nutrient content and the percentage of the dietary nutrients consumed by the cow that are recovered in the milk produced.

shows that a cow producing 40 kg/day of milk converts an average of 38 percent of the dietary nutrients it consumes into milk components, compared with an average of only 23 percent for a cow of the same weight producing 10 kg/day of milk. There is an improvement of approximately 40 percent in feed nutrient utilization efficiency between the 40 kg and the 10 kg milk production levels. It is often assumed that maximizing a dairy cow's milk production is always desirable (and this would be correct if feed resources were not a limiting factor), and the terms "maximizing" and "optimizing" milk production are sometimes used interchangeably when talking about formulating feeding programmes for lactating dairy cattle. A ration that maximizes milk production is one that maximizes the expression of the genetic milk producing ability of the cow, while maintaining the health of the animal's digestive system. However, the feed resources available are often not suitable for maximizing milk production because they do not contain the necessary nutrients, contain factors that limit nutrient availability or contain substances that cause nutrient intake to be depressed.

When the economics of milking production are being considered, maximizing performance does not always equate to optimizing profitability. In many situations, available feed resources are not suitable for maximizing milk production. This is especially true in developing countries, where it is often not economically feasible to feed concentrates (cereal grains and supplemental protein sources) to dairy cattle and, therefore, it is not normally possible to provide the adequate levels of dietary nutrients for cows to express their full genetic milk producing ability. Under these conditions it becomes necessary to formulate feeding programmes that will produce milk in the most economic way and optimize milk production (produce the most milk possible from the available resources and at the least cost), but not maximize it.

The first question to ask when formulating a feeding programme is whether milk production should be maximized or optimized. If feed quality and price are not limiting, the objective should be to maximize production, while maintaining proper digestive tract health, but when feed quality or price are limiting, the goal should be to optimize milk production. Optimizing production means producing the most milk for the least cost using the available feed resources.

This article focuses on one of the most important aspects of feeding dairy cattle - factors that influence feed intake. Dairy cattle require specific amounts of nutrients to support various levels of performance, so changes in feed intake have a dramatic impact on the formulation of rations and nutrient intake. Table 2 shows the effect that changes in feed intake have on the nutrient specifications for a ration.

Specific amounts of a nutrient (total digestible nutrients, net energy of lactation, crude protein, etc.) are required to support a specific level of performance. The requirements for producing 40 kg of milk are shown in Table 2a. When feed intake declines from 3.7 to 3.3 percent a significant increase in nutrient concentrations is required in the rations to provide the same amount of nutrients. In the Table 2 example, dry matter consumption declined by 2.4 kg (22.2 - 19.8 = 2.4 kg), which means that the required nutrients have to be provided by 2.4 kg less feed. The levels of dietary crude protein (CP) required to provide the same amount of CP increase from 16.96 to 19.02 percent, and total digestible nutrients from 73.3 to 82.2 percent. Changes in nutrient density of this magnitude can cause dramatic changes in the composition and amounts of concentrate feeds that need to be incorporated into a ration. Table 2b shows how the composition of the ration changes as the amount of dry matter being consumed changes. As intake declines nutrient density increases.

At the 3.7 percent (DM basis) level of intake the composition of the ration would be 55.7 percent alfalfa hay and 44.7 percent maize grain.

At the 3.3 percent (dry matter basis) level of intake the composition of the ration would be 26 percent alfalfa hay and 74 percent maize grain.

In terms of nutrient specifications only, both the rations shown in Table 2b would be satisfactory. They both provide the same amount of nutrients, but are dramatically different with respect to the amounts of forage and concentrate that they contain. The alfalfa level ranges from 55.7 to only 26 percent, and the maize content increases from 44.3 to 74 percent. The forage content of the ration decreases by approximately 50 percent (55.7 - 26/55.7 x 100 = 53.3 percent) and the concentrate content increases by approximately 40 percent (74 - 44.3/ 74 x 100 = 40.1 percent). Unfortunately, however, in order to maintain the health of the digestive tract, when formulating rations for dairy cattle factors other than nutrient specifications need to be considered, such as roughage level. The minimum level of roughage in a lactating dairy cow ration is considered to be 40 percent, so only the ration that is consumed at the 3.7 percent of body weight level would be considered feasible. The other ration would cause digestive problems and would therefore not be suitable for feeding to lactating dairy cattle. This means that it would not be possible to maintain the production level if feed consumption were reduced to 3.3 percent of body weight.

Another factor that should be considered is the difference in the cost of the rations. Typical costs for alfalfa hay and maize grain might be US$60 and US$120 per tonne, respectively. Based on these costs the two rations would have the following costs:

- *Ration 1*
  - Alfalfa $60 x 0.557 = $33.42
  - Maize $120 x 0.443 = $53.16
  - Total $86.58/tonne
- *Ration 2*
  - Alfalfa $60 x 0.26 = $15.60
  - Maize $120 x 0.74 = $88.80
  - Total $104.40/tonne

Based on alfalfa hay and maize grain prices the relative cost of each of the rations is computed ($104.40 - $86.58 = $17.82/$104.40 x 100 = 17.07 percent) so the ration cost for the higher intake level would be approximately 17 percent cheaper than that for the lower intake level. Since dry matter intake is different between the rations, actual costs based on different levels of feed consumption are computed: 22.2 kg x $0.0866/kg = $1.92/head/day, compared with 19.8 kg x $0.1044/kg = $2.07/head/day. So in this example, there would be a saving of 7.8 percent ($2.07 - $1.92 = $0.15/1.92 x 100 = 7.8 percent) for the higher intake level. Typically, the cost of the forage component of the diet is approximately 50 percent or less of the concentrate (cereal grain, etc.) cost, so similar savings could be expected to occur. When the price of the forage increases to approximately two-thirds of that of cereal grain there would be no difference in the feed cost. The higher the dry matter intake level, the higher the amount of forage that can be used in the ration. Higher forage levels also aid in maintaining a more stable and healthier rumen and reduce the animals' grain need; the surplus grain could then be put to other uses, including human consumption. As feed consumption declines, the proportion of concentrate required increases, and this is a major cause of concern as regards the health of the digestive tract and in countries where the cereal grain supply is limited.

When least-cost rations are being formulated the first computation that is done is the relative cost of the nutrients provided by the available feedstuffs. Table 2b is an example of what the prices of various nutrients that are provided by feeds would be, based on typical prices.

In most situations, dietary energy and CP cost the least when they are provided by forages, so maximizing the amount of forage in a ration, while still providing the other required nutrients, will usually minimize the cost. Typically, least-cost computerized ration formulation systems rank feedstuffs in terms of costs to provide a certain amount (1 kg, 100 kg, etc.) of a specific nutrient (total digestible nutrients, CP, calcium, phosphorus, etc.). Feeds are incorporated into the formulation on the basis of this ranking and starting with the least expensive source of a given nutrient. When the nutrient costs of forages and concentrates are similar, the cost of providing nutrients will not change as much as when feed intake is reduced and the ration needs to be reformulated.

In many developed and developing countries, energy often becomes cheaper when cereal grains are used. If the supply of cereal grains is limited and has to be used for human consumption (as is the case in some developing countries), such price considerations become irrelevant and the use of forages and locally available by-products will need to be maximized in dairy feeding programmes. The higher the feed intake, the more the forage that can be included in a dairy ration and the less the cereal grain that is required. This article discusses feed consumption and its regulation, as well as three of the factors (forage quality, environmental stress and water quality) that have the greatest impact on feed consumption and milk production in dairy cattle.

REGULATION OF FEED CONSUMPTION

The mechanisms involved in feed consumption and appetite regulation are complex. The following summaries briefly describe the factors that are involved in the regulation of feed consumption in dairy cattle. The two most important factors for dairy cattle that are not under any type of stress are the physiological and the chemostatic regulatory mechanisms of feed comsumption. Physiological regulation normally occurs when less digestible feeds, such as low-quality forages or bulky feeds (hulls, etc.) are being fed. Chemostatic regulation occurs when less bulky feeds that contain higher digestible nutrient contents are used.

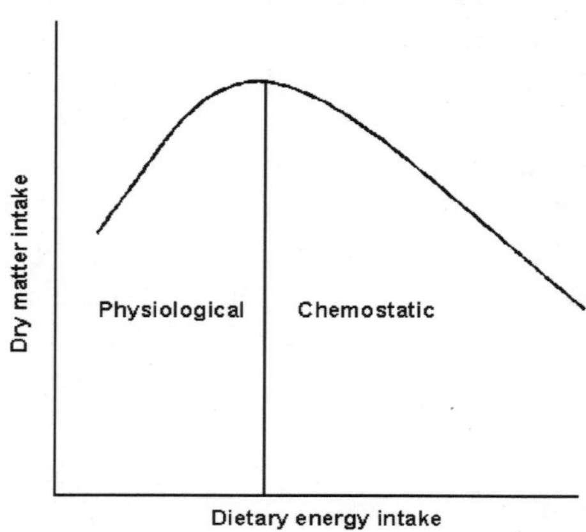

Fig. Regulation of feed consumption

PHYSIOLOGICAL REGULATION

Physiological regulation is based on the volumetric capacity of the digestive tract, in dairy cattle this specifically relates to the capacity of the rumen. Sensors located in the rumen of the dairy cow sense when the rumen is distended (full), at which time a signal is sent that causes the animal to stop consuming feed. This type of regulation occurs with feeds that contain low digestible nutrient densities and are bulky (low weight per unit volume), such as straws and other low-quality forages. Dramatic reductions in consumption occur when these types of feeds are fed. These feeds normally have low digestibilities because they are high in lignin, silica and acid detergent fibre, which depress the digestibility of the nutrients that they contain. Table 3 shows the impact that forage quality can have on dry matter consumption in cattle.

Table. Expected dry matter intakes of various forage qualities

Table : Expected dry matter intakes of various forage qualities	
	Dry matter intake
	(% of body weight)
High-quality hay	2.5 to 3.3
Medium-quality hay	1.5 to 2.5
Low-quality hay	1.25 to 1.75
Straw	1.0 to 1.5

As forage quality declines, the digestive passage rate becomes slower, resulting in a greater fill factor and causing a reduction in feed intake. This same type of reduction in feed intake also occurs when low-bulk density feedstuffs are mixed into complete rations (Kellems and Church, 1981). In most cases, physiological fill is a factor only when dairy cattle are being fed very low-quality feeds.

CHEMOSTATIC REGULATION

This mechanism functions when blood levels of specific metabolites rise, sending a signal that causes the animal's appetite to be depressed. In the case of dairy cattle, volatile fatty acids are the metabolites that cause the signal to be sent; a few hours after a cow has consumed a meal, the volatile fatty acid levels in the rumen start to rise as a result of rumen fermentation of the ingested substrates. The dietary digestible energy levels are directly related to the amounts of the metabolites that are produced. Peak volatile fatty acid production normally occurs in the rumen two to three hours after a high-concentrate (high in readily available carbohydrates) ration has been consumed and four to five hours after a high-forage (high in cellulose) ration has been fed. The volatile fatty acids that are produced in the rumen are then absorbed and the levels in the blood rise. Once a certain level of volatile fatty acids in the blood has been reached, the appetite of the animal will be depressed. The volatile fatty acids are continuously absorbed and metabolized by the cells, so when the blood volatile fatty acid level declines the animal's appetite will increase again.

Many other factors have been shown to have an influence on feed consumption, including health, parasite load and digestive disorders. The following sections discuss the effects that forage quality, environmental stress and water quality have on feed consumption in dairy cattle.

RELATIONSHIP BETWEEN NUTRIENT CONSUMPTION AND MILK PRODUCTION

The amount of feed that a dairy cow consumes is highly correlated to its nutrient intake. The level of available nutrients determines how much milk a dairy cow is able to produce. The available nutrients can either come from what the cow is consuming in its feed or be taken from its body reserves. If dietary nutrient consumption is not enough to satisfy the nutrient requirements for the animal's level of milk production, the animal will have to mobilize its body nutrient reserves in order to provide the missing nutrients. The nutrient reserves that an animal normally mobilizes are energy (fat) and protein (tissue). When this happens, the animal loses body weight, which is normal in high-producing dairy cattle. The combination of nutrients provided by the diet and derived from body reserves must be sufficient to supply the required nutrients for the amount of milk being produced. If adequate nutrients cannot be derived from these two sources, the cow will reduce its milk production to match the available level of nutrients: nutrient input (diet + body reserves) = output (milk + body composition). When cows are being fed at a high nutrition level but do not have the genetic ability to produce the amount of milk that their feed would allow them to produce, they will deposit the excess energy that they consume as body fat, thus gaining weight. Care therefore should be taken to ensure that the proper amounts of nutrients are provided to support the level of milk production that a cow is genetically capable of producing.

The feed consumption of dairy cattle changes as their productive status changes. They consume different amounts of feed during different stages of their lactation cycles, and different amounts when they are dry and not lactating. For example, dry matter consumption for a 600 kg dry cow that is 40 to 60 days from calving is 9 to 12 kg; when the same cow is ten to 15 days from calving, it will consume 11 to 13 kg of dry matter; rising to 24 to 27 kg when it is producing 45 kg of milk. When the milk production of a dairy cow increases, its feed consumption also increases. Table 4 shows how dry matter consumption increases as body weight and milk production increase. If this did not occur, it would be extremely difficult to formulate feeding programmes that would satisfy the nutrient needs of high-producing dairy cows.

Table. Dry matter intake in dairy cattle of different weights and milk production rates

Table : Dry matter intake in dairy cattle of different weights and milk production rates					
Milk production	Dry matter intake as percentage of body weight for:				
(4% FCM)[1]	400 kg cow	500 kg cow	600 kg cow	700 kg cow	800 kg cow
(kg/cow/day)					
10	2.7 (10.8)	2.4 (12.0)	2.2 (13.2)	2.0(14.0)	1.9(15.2)
15	3.2 (12.8)	3.0 (15.0)	2.6 (15.6)	2.3 (16.1)	2.2 (17.6)
20	3.6 (14.4)	3.2 (16.0)	2.9 (17.4)	2.6 (18.2)	2.4 (19.2)
25	4.0 (16.0)	3.5 (17.5)	3.2 (19.2)	2.9 (20.3)	2.7 (21.6)
30	4.4 (17.6)	3.9 (19.5)	3.5 (21.0)	3.2 (22.4)	2.9 (23.2)
35	5.0 (20.0)	4.2 (21.0)	3.7 (22.2)	3.4 (23.8)	3.1 (24.8)
40	5.5 (22.0)	4.6 (23.0)	4.0 (24.0)	3.6 (25.2)	3.3 (26.4)
45	---	5.0 (25.0)	4.3 (25.8)	3.8 (26.5)	3.5 (28.0)
50	---	5.4 (27.0)	4.7 (28.2)	4.1 (28.7)	3.7 (29.6)
55	---	---	5.0 (30.0)	4.4 (30.8)	4.0 (32.0)
60	---	---	5.4 (32.4)	4.8 (33.6)	4.3 (34.4)

IMPORTANCE OF FORAGE QUALITY

Forage is the most important component in the diet of dairy cattle because of the dramatic impact it has on dry matter and nutrient consumption. The quality and form of forage are two of the factors that have been shown to influence dry matter consumption and milk production in dairy cattle (Varhegyi, Szentmihalyi and Varhegyi, 1986).

FORAGE QUALITY

Forage quality can be defined simply as the ability of the dairy cow to digest and utilize the nutrient components provided by the forage source (Fahey and Hussein, 1999). The higher the content and digestibility of the nutrients, the higher the quality of the forage. The highest-quality and most digestible forage is young herbage, because it contains the lowest amount of structural carbohydrates (cellulose, hemicellulose) and lignin (Traxler et al., 1998). As a forage matures, its digestibility, rate of digestion and CP content decline, causing the cow to derive fewer nutrients from the forage . A decline in the quality of forage has an impact on the amount of other feedstuffs that the animal is able to consume. The slower passage time of the forage results in a reduction in intake of not only the forage but also other feeds that the animal is consuming (Groen and Korver, 1989).

The quality of a forage declines as it matures. The primary reason for this arises from reduced digestibility, which is related to increases in acid detergent fibre and lignin (Weston, 1996; Akin and Chesson, 1989).

Table 5 shows that, as alfalfa matures, its digestibility and CP content decline, reducing the amounts of nutrients that the cow can obtain from the alfalfa and, thus, also reducing intake. Forage quality has also been shown to have an effect on dry matter consumption , especially when low-quality forages are being fed.

Table. Effect of maturity of alfalfa on its digestibility

Table : Effect of maturity of alfalfa on its digestibility				
Milk production	Dry matter intake as percentage of body weight for:			
	Digestibility	Crude protein	Acid detergent fibre	Lignin
	(%)	(%)	(%)	(%)
Prebud	66.8	24	23	4
Bud	65.0	22	25	5
Early bloom	63.1	20	28	6)
Mid-bloom	61.3	19	31	7
Full bloom	59.4	17	33	8
Late bloom	57.5	15	35	9
Mature	55.8	13	38	10

The quality of the forage being fed to dairy cattle has a dramatic impact on not only dry matter consumption but also the proportion of nutrients that are being provided by other feedstuffs. Table 6 gives an example of the effect that changing forage quality has on nutrient consumption.

In the Table 6 example, the amount of concentrate (in this case wheat bran) required to maintain the same energy intake increases from 5.35 kg when good-quality alfalfa is fed, to 12.59 kg when straw is fed. Whenever the quality of the forage declines, the amount of concentrate required to be fed increases, if the same dietary energy level is to be maintained. In Table 6 the amount of dry matter consumption remains constant, but as forage quality declines, dry matter consumption also declines, so even greater quantities of concentrate will have to be fed.

In Table 6, the CP intake ranges from 2.87 kg down to 2.28 kg, which is still above the 2.09 kg minimum required to produce 20 kg of milk. As forage quality declines, the quantity declines and the amount of CP it provides decreases. Lower CP intakes also have a tendency to reduce feed intake because CP stimulates rumen fermentation, which increases dry matter intake.

Table. Effects of different qualities of forage on forage and concentrate consumption[1]

Table : Effects of different qualities of forage on forage and concentrate consumption[1]		
Total digestible nutrients (TDN) = 10.26 kg		
Crude protein (CP) = 2.086 kg		
Dry matter (DM) intake = 16.2 kg		
Specifications for feedstuffs	**TDN**	**CP**
Good-quality alfalfa hay	60 %	18.0 %
Poor-alfalfa quality hay	50 %	13.0 %
Wheat straw	40 %	3.6 %
Wheat bran	70 %	17.1 %
Good-quality alfalfa hay	10.85 kg	
Wheat bran	5.35 kg	
(CP content	2.87 kg)	
Poor-quality alfalfa hay	5.35 kg	
Wheat bran	10.85 kg	
(CP content	2.55 kg)	
Wheat straw	3.61 kg	
Wheat bran	12.59 kg	
(CP content	2.28 kg)	

Normally, 40 percent of roughage is considered the minimum level required when formulating ratios for lactating dairy cattle. The length of the dietary roughage component must also be considered. An inadequate amount of roughage or reducing the length of the roughage, so that there is not enough effective fibre, will cause butterfat depression and, often, digestive problems.

VISUAL APPRAISAL OF FORAGE QUALITY

Visual appraisal of forage can be useful in assessing its quality. The maturity of a forage can be estimated quite accurately by the number of buds, blossoms or seed heads that are present. Proper curing during the haymaking process can be assessed by the colour of the hay. Colour can also be used to assess the extent of nutrient losses associated with leaching resulting from exposure to rain and weather.

Bleached forages will have lower vitamin and CP contents. With legume-type forages, the leaf-stem ratio can provide a fairly accurate estimate of the nutrient content of the forage. When there are many leaves, the CP content is high; when there is more stem, the structural carbohydrates content will be higher and the digestible nutrients content lower. The CP content of a forage is closely correlated to its digestibility - the higher the CP content of a forage, the higher its digestibility will be.

PALATABILITY OF FORAGE

The palatability of a forage is affected by its taste (sweet, salty, bitter, acidic), olfactory and textural characteristics. Taste is normally the major factor affecting palatability. Dairy cattle are non-selective consumers and readily consume a wide range of feeds. Almost all livestock show a preference for sweet, so feed consumption can often be increased by adding molasses to a ration. Salt can also be used to increase the palatability of a feed but, once it reaches a certain level, increasing the salt content will depress feed consumption. Palatability can play a role in feed consumption when the animals have a choice, but dairy cattle do not usually have a choice, so palatability is not a major factor in feeding dairy cattle. Palatability normally becomes a factor only when attempts are made to feed spoiled feeds to dairy cattle.

PROCESSING OF FORAGE

The decrease in intake that occurs as a forage matures can be counteracted to some extent by reducing the physical size of the forage (through chopping or grinding), which will allow it to pass through the rumen at a faster rate. The passage rate out of the rumen is based on particle size and density. Small, dense particles are passed out of the rumen more quickly than larger forage particles (most of which are less dense and float), which are retained in the rumen. As the ruminal passage rate increases, exposure to the digestive processes decreases and the overall digestibility of the forage declines but, because more can pass through the digestive tract, the animal will increase its dry matter consumption and the net result is usually that the cow's digestible nutrient intake increases slightly. This is one of the reasons for chopping forages prior to feeding. Chopping is most beneficial when low-quality forages are fed, but forages should not be chopped into pieces that are too small, as this can result in a depression of milk butterfat.

INFLUENCES OF HEAT STRESS ON FEED CONSUMPTION

Heat stress is another factor that has been shown to have a major impact on the feed consumption of a dairy cow. Feed consumption decreases during hot weather and increases during cold weather . Several other factors have been found to be associated with, and have an influence on, heat stress, including humidity, air movement, shade and availability of water (Chastain, 1998).

TEMPERATURE AND HUMIDITY

Factors that influence the body temperature of dairy cattle can cause stress and have been shown to have dramatic effects on feed consumption. Both low and high temperatures can cause temperature stress and both can have impacts on nutrient consumption and nutrient utilization. As the core body temperature of an animal increases, the hypothalamus causes the cow's appetite to be depressed. This results in a depression of dry matter intake and can have a dramatic impact on nutrient intake and milk production. The effect that temperature has on feeding consumption is shown in Table 7.

Table : Intake adjustments for different environmental temperatures

Temperature	**Intake adjustment**
	(%)
> 35 °C, no night cooling	- 35
> 35 °C, with night cooling	- 10
25 to 35 °C	- 10
15 to 25 °C	None
5 to 15 °C	3
-5 to 5 °C	5
-15 to -5 °C	7
< -15 °C	16

Heat stress has a more dramatic impact than cool stress on feed consumption and milk production. It is not only related to ambient temperature, but also associated with humidity and air movement.

When the humidity increases, the cow's evapotranspiration is reduced and the animal cannot cool itself, which increases its core body temperature and depresses feed intake. Temperature alone is not a good way of measuring heat stress, so various heat indexes have been developed which take into account such factors as temperature, humidity and evaporation rate. The rectal temperature of dairy cattle has been found to be one of the best indicators of heat stress.

The duration of heat stress also influences feed consumption. High daytime temperatures can be tolerated if cooling occurs at night and the cows are able to dissipate the body heat that has built up during the day. The most severe heat stress occurs when both humidity and temperature are high and the night-time temperature does not decrease, so the cows cannot dissipate their body heat. In addition to depressing feed consumption, heat stress has also been shown to have an effect on milk composition. Milk protein percentages have been shown to decrease during periods of heat stress, and some reduction in milk butterfat has also be observed in dairy cattle.

WAYS TO MINIMIZE HEAT STRESS

During periods of heat stress cows will consume more water, so an adequate supply of water needs to be provided. Providing a cool water supply can help to reduce heat stress. Cows will consume more cool water during periods of heat stress; although it is not the temperature of the water but rather the additional evapotranspiration that helps the cows to cool. Providing adequate shade will help reduce the cows' uptake of solar heat, and shade is particularly important in areas where cows are exposed to high levels of solar radiation. Cooling the cows with misters and evaporative coolers can also be an effective means of lowering ambient temperatures and reducing heat stress in hot, dry climates. Circulating air with fans will increase evapotranspiration and increase the dissipation of a cow's body heat load (Mena et al., 1993; Chalong-Wichiraphakorn, 1995). Opening housing facilities during times of heat stress will increase air movement which will increase cooling and reduce heat stress.

WATER QUALITY

Water is one of the most important nutrients that an animal consumes. Numerous important biological processes require water, such as digestion, absorption, transport and excretion of nutrients and metabolites, components of milk, body temperature regulation and cellular metabolism. Death occurs about nine to ten times more quickly as a result of water deprivation than because of feed deprivation. Poor-quality water or the lack of an adequate supply will depresses an animal's performance more quickly and more dramatically than any other nutrient deficiency.

The amount of available water and the water quality are often overlooked when developing feeding programmes for dairy cattle. When the amount or quality of water becomes restrictive, an animal will not perform at the maximum of its genetic potential. If cows are only able to drink once or twice a day, they will produce less milk; and if adequate water is not available or the quality of the water is low, feed consumption will be reduced and performance will be depressed. Dry matter intake has been found to be highly correlated (at a ratio of 0.91) with water consumption (Dado and Allen, 1994).

FACTORS INFLUENCING WATER INTAKE

Water requirements vary considerably and are related to the type of diet being consumed and the environmental conditions under which the animal is being maintained. At 4 oC, a 545 kg non-lactating cow requires 30 kg/day of water, but at 32 oC the same cow will require 57 to 72 kg of water, depending on the humidity, because of increases in body water losses (Kellems and Church, 1998).

The water content of the ration being fed can also have a dramatic effect on the amount of drinking-water that is required. For example, 20 kg of maize silage will provide 13.4 litres of water. In areas where water quality or supply is low, the use of feeds that contain water, such as wet brewers' grains or silage, can be an effective way of increasing milk production. Environmental conditions such as temperature, humidity, wind movement and exposure to sun all alter the water requirements of an animal, as shown in Table 8.

Table. Relationship between environmental temperature and water requirements of livestock

Table : Relationship between environmental temperature and water requirements of livestock	
Environmental temperature Water requirements	
(kg/kg DM consumed)	
> 35 °C	8 to 15 kg
25 to 35 °C	4 to 10 kg
15 to 25 °C	3 to 5 kg
-5 to 15 °C	2 to 4 kg water
< -5 °C	2 to 3 kg[1]

Performance will only be maximized when good-quality water is freely available. It is important to have an adequate supply of acceptable-quality water available to the animals at all times. Non-lactating cattle consume approximately two-and-a-half to three times as much water as dry matter, and lactating cattle consume 4.5 to 5 kg of water for each additional kilogram of milk produced (Kellems and Church, 1998). When water intake is reduced, dry matter intake will also be reduced, resulting in reduced milk production . Diets that are high in CP or salt increase water requirements further.

Water intake in lactating dairy cattle is influenced by milk production, ambient temperature, humidity, salt intake, dry matter intake and other factors. Elevated environmental temperatures increase the consumption of water because of the increased losses that the cow undergoes as a result of increased evapotranspiration (Cecchini, 1998).

More water should therefore be provided during periods of elevated temperatures, or feed intake will be depressed. If water quality is marginal, the increase in water consumption can become problematic and consuming more water can put additional physiological stresses on the animals. Animals that do not have access to an adequate supply of water will consume less feed and produce less milk.

FACTORS INFLUENCING WATER QUALITY

The following factors can effect the quality of the water: alkalinity, total dissolved solids, specific minerals (nitrates, sulphates, etc.), and bacterial or algae content. Alkalinity is a measure of how much acid is required to neutralize the pH of a water supply. "Total dissolved solids" refers to the dissolved inorganic salts that are present in the water supply. Nitrates can be found in water supplies at levels that are toxic to dairy cattle because they are converted to nitrites in the rumen. Sulphates can cause diarrhoea, which will reduce the efficiency of nutrient absorption. A water supply that is too alkaline can cause physiological and digestive problems. Bacterial and algae contamination do not usually affect performance, except when they cause water palatability problems which lead to reduced water consumption. Some algae contain compounds that are toxic to animals if consumed in large quantities. Tables 9 and 10 show the recommended guidelines for water for use with livestock and poultry.

Table. Guidelines for total dissolved solids in water for livestock and poultry Total dissolved solids

Table : Guidelines for total dissolved solids in water for livestock and poultry	
Total dissolved solids	**Quality of water source**
(ppm)	
< 1 000	Excellent water source that can be used with all classes and types of livestock.
1 000 to 2 999	Water should be acceptable for all classes and types of livestock. Water approaching the upper limits may cause watery droppings in poultry, but performance should not be affected.
3 000 to 4 999	Water should be satisfactory to marginal for most livestock. Animals that are not used to drinking it might take a few days to adjust. If sulphate levels are high, animals might have diarrhoea. Performance will be only slightly depressed. Poor source of water for poultry, which would have increases in faecal water output; at the upper limits this water decreases growth and increases mortality, especially in turkeys.
5 000 to 6 999	Can be used for livestock, but some depression in productivity and physiological condition is likely to occur. There will be higher refusal rates and the water is likely to have a laxative affect. Should not be used for poultry.
7 000 to 10 000	Poor-quality water that will affect performance. Can be used for mature ruminant animals that are just being maintained. Should not be used with pregnant or lactating animals. Is not suitable for poultry or swine.
> 10 000	Unsatisfactory for all types and classes of livestock.

The most common minerals present in water include chlorine (Cl), sodium (Na), calcium (Ca), magnesium (Mg), sulphate (SO_4) and bicarbonate ($HC0_3$). The specific minerals that are present in the water depend on soil type and the source of the water. The tolerance of animals to alkaline (dissolved salt) water depends on several factors such as water intake, species, age, physiological condition, season of the year and salt content of the diet.

Several factors should be considered when assessing the quality of an available water source. Generally, water containing more than 1 percent NaCl (common salt) is not considered good quality because this is about the maximum salt content that cattle and sheep can tolerate without decreasing their productivity. If there is a question about the quality of a water source then the source should be tested.

Mineral content is important, especially in arid areas. Depending on the type of minerals that are present, up to 15 000 mg/litre (1.5 percent) of dissolved solids may be tolerated by livestock, but normally the palatability of the water is reduced as the mineral content increases and the animal's performance will decline; a good-quality water source should therefore contain less than 2 500 mg/litre (0.25 percent) of dissolved solids. Some salts, such as nitrates, fluorine and other heavy metals, may become toxic before the levels that affect palatability are reached. Levels of 100 to 200 parts per million (ppm) of nitrates are potentially toxic and 1 g of sulphate per litre may result in diarrhoea. Other materials that are sometimes found in water supplies and may affect palatability or be toxic include pathogenic microorganisms, algae and protozoa, hydrocarbons, pesticides and many industrial chemicals.

WAYS TO IMPROVE WATER QUALITY

Water can be derived from various sources - wells, ponds, rivers/streams, springs, etc. The most commonly used source of water for livestock is surface water (streams, ponds, etc.). Rainwater that has been collected and stored can also be a good source of water in some areas. If water sources of different qualities are available, then the highest-producing cows should be given the best-quality water.

The adequacy of watering space must also be considered. If cows have to wait too long to drink, their water consumption and dry matter consumption will be decreased. The drinking-water source should be located near where the animals are being fed; if animals have to go long distances to water they will consume less. In order to achieve maximum performance, water sources need to be available in close proximity to grazing areas or the areas where cows are being housed. Cattle can be prevented from walking and defecating in the water by piping it into watering tanks. Maximum performance will only be achieved when cattle have *ad libitum* access to a good-quality water source.

VARIABILITY IN FEED COMPOSITION AND ITS IMPACT ON ANIMAL PRODUCTION

In order to meet the nutritional requirements of livestock a precise knowledge of feedstuff composition is necessary. Such information is particularly vital when trying to achieve the high levels of production required in today's competitive markets (where there is growing interest in quality, efficiency and the environment) through the preparation of balanced diets for the animals. Knowledge is also essential in order to mix the right proportions of various ingredients for the manufacture of valuable compound feeds. Ultimately, knowing the chemical characteristics and the nutritional value of raw materials is fundamental in the planning of forage production on the farm so that crop yields can be balanced with the animals' requirements. The general aspects of this have been reviewed by Topps (1989).

From a political point of view, data on feedstuff composition and nutritional value provide essential information to policy-makers that allows them to develop competitive and sustainable agriculture.

Feedstuffs are usually described by their chemical composition as well as by their nutritional value. Information on the composition of a feedstuff is acquired through chemical analysis, and most commonly includes such parameters as dry matter, protein, fibre fractions, organic matter and fat contents. The nutritional value of a feedstuff is assessed from experiments with animals (*in vivo* digestibility/*in situ* degradability, etc.) and provides information on how feedstuffs are digested and metabolized by the animal, mainly through interpreting differences between the input and the output of a series of components. Among these, the digestible/degradable organic matter and the digestible or metabolizable energy values are the ones most frequently represented in databases and used to predict energy supply from feeds and diets.

To provide both chemical and nutritional information, feedstuffs have been analysed in laboratories and animal-based studies and the resulting data collected in tables of feed composition for more than 200 years. The first recorded publication was that of Thaer (1809). More recently, collections of data have been organized into computer programs, creating databases of feedstuffs composition. The first database available on a computer was produced in 1963 at Utah State University in the United States (Harris, Asplund and Crampton, 1968). Today, modern databases are powerful tools with which information can be rapidly retrieved, sorted, updated and printed.

SOURCES OF DATA

Information on feedstuffs composition and nutritional value plays a fundamental role at the farm, feed manufacturer and government levels, so the data inserted into databases need to be reliable and of high quality. The quality of the data depends, in the first place, on the origin of the information, which may have been extracted from the literature, collected from laboratories, obtained from other databases or generated specifically from animal studies and analyses of feeds.

DATA ASSEMBLED FROM THE LITERATURE

Feedstuffs information in the literature usually concentrates more on the data value obtained and does not give a full description of the feedstuffs concerned . When feedstuffs are insufficiently or inappropriately described there is a risk of confusing their real origin. A typical example of this occurs when publications generally refer to the product "distillers' dark grains", which is a by-product of the whisky distilling industry that, depending on the type of distilling process, may be derived from barley (in the malt distilling process) or wheat and/or maize (in the grain distilling process). In this case a true and existing genetic variability is ignored. It is evident that the compositions of the two products will differ, so the provision of additional information on the origin of the feedstuff is essential; it is not enough merely to refer to it as "distillers' dark grains". In the absence of additional information, when trying to obtain information on the protein content specifically of barley distillers' dark grains, a value obtained from the average protein content of samples of both barley dark grains and wheat/maize dark grains would be retrieved from the database, and this value would be meaningless. Data obtained from the literature can therefore often be inappropriate, particularly when they use averaged data which may incorrectly merge different feedstuffs. Data from the literature are recommended only when no other sources are available.

DATA COLLECTED FROM LABORATORIES

When compiling databases of feedstuffs information, the data used have usually been produced in a number of different laboratories. When assembling collections of data, it is necessary to have specific information regarding the analytical procedures used to obtain the data, in order to guarantee that those used to create a database have been obtained through standardized methods, are expressed in standardized units and can, therefore, be compared.

The standardization issue is particularly important for data on the nutritional value of feedstuffs, obtained through *in vivo* digestibility or *in situ* degradability studies. In this case, together with the strictly analytical issue, the laboratories and research institutes involved should have standardized procedures for conducting animal studies. These relate to the numbers of animals and the species used (sheep, cattle, pigs, etc.) and to the feeding and collection protocols employed. However, when conducting *in vivo/in situ* studies, results will always be substantially influenced by variability among individual animals, no matter what level of standardization is achieved.

The standardized analytical procedures used to collect data from laboratories need to be monitored continuously, and the data they produce checked for accuracy and relevance. For this purpose, ring tests among participating laboratories should be carried out in order to evaluate the precision of standard or newly developed techniques (Barber, 1983; Fisher, 1983).

MERGING OF NEW AND OLD DATA

It is common practice to merge new databases with old ones. In these cases it is important that the analytical procedures used to obtain all of the data are understood in order to generate information that is expressed on a common basis and is, therefore, comparable. The evolution of analytical methodology is a substantial issue. Old data may have been obtained with obsolete methods or with surviving analytical procedures that, in the past, produced data that were less accurate than those produced today. Thus, the merging of old data with new may be inappropriate and may reduce the overall quality of the information.

DATA PRODUCED SPECIFICALLY FOR USE IN DATABASES

The data generated specifically for use in databases are likely to be those of the highest quality as all the necessary information will be included and the methods standardized and checked. The chemical composition of feeds can be analysed using the most up-to-date and standard methods and animal studies can be designed appropriately, by deciding which animal species to use and in which physiological state the animals studied should be. Both feeding and collection protocols can also be set with the aim of meeting the specific requirements of the database.

Ideally, an entire database would be produced by analysing specifically the composition of feedstuffs and studying their nutritional value through animal studies. In this way the variability arising from extrinsic factors such as analysis methods and animal protocols would be reduced to the minimum. On the other hand, when using data from a single source it is critical that the techniques and procedures used have been certified for precision and are representative. However, if it is to contain representative information, the database has to be established with an appropriate number of samples.

The costs involved in analysing feedstuffs and, particularly, performing animal measurements are so prohibitive that it is rare for feedstuff information to be produced specifically for the purpose of assembling a database. Moreover, much time is required to obtain the data, particularly those derived from animal studies. Therefore, the data are usually extracted from the different sources listed previously. Ultimately, it is the responsibility of the database manager to judge which information to include in order to generate a meaningful database.

SOURCES OF DATA VARIABILITY

Information on feedstuffs may be associated with different sources and types of variability. Variability can be "intrinsic" and caused by real differences among feedstuffs, such as the genetic origin of the feed or the processes that have been applied to it. Variability can also be "extrinsic", that is caused by differences in sampling and analysis procedures.

INTRINSIC VARIABILITY OF DATA

Each feed has particular chemical and nutritional characteristics which distinguish it from other feeds. However, the same feed can also be derived from different cultivars or influenced by its geographical origin. Moreover, an identical raw material may have been processed in a variety of ways to produce very different products. The wide range of diverse wheat-related materials provides a clear illustration of the need to distinguish among different feedstuffs derived from the same raw material. Terms for wheat-based materials include wheat, durum wheat, winter wheat, spring wheat, processed wheat meal and wheat distillers' dark grains. All of these products and by-products are wheat-based, but they vary substantially in terms of both chemical composition and nutritional attributes and it is therefore expected that they will have different effects when fed to animals.

When assembling a database it is necessary to make sure that the real variability arising from the intrinsic characteristics of the feedstuffs is correctly recognized in order not to affect the quality of the data. Information from feedstuffs databases is most commonly retrieved in the form of averages (or "consolidated data"), so the feeds have to be merged judiciously in order to obtain meaningful information. To achieve reliability, a precise description and the correct naming of feedstuffs are essential, and for this purpose all available information on the type, origin, processing, etc. of the feedstuffs is needed.

One important attribute that is often omitted is information on the forage's stage of maturity. As shown in the example illustrated in the Figure, the content of both neutral detergent fibre (NDF) and starch relate strongly to the stage of maturity of the forage maize, and this is clearly reflected in the dry matter (DM) content of the plant, which increases with maturation. In this case, therefore, it would be incorrect to describe material harvested at different stages simply as forage maize; the different maturity stages should be indicated and, on the basis of these, the different types of product classified.

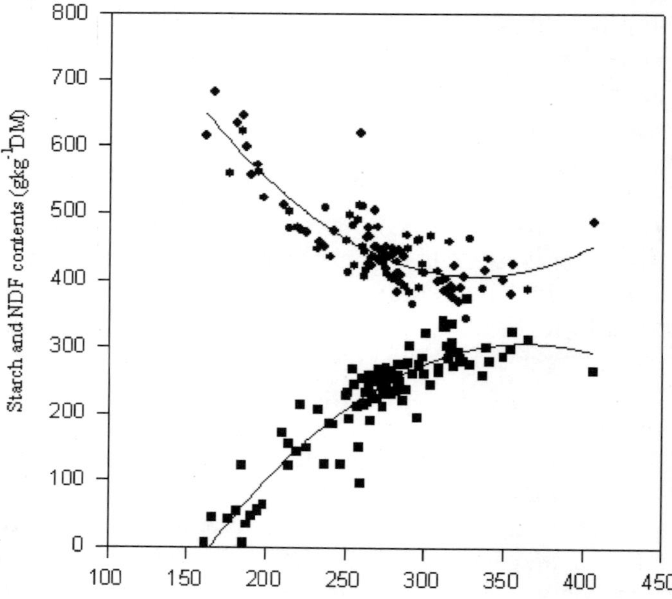

Fig. Relationship between maturity stage and neutral detergent fibre (NDF) and starch contents of maize (from Givens *et al.*, 1995)

With respect to the processes applied to the feeds, when introducing data on, for example, rice bran meal, it is necessary to know how the meal was obtained and which processes were involved in its production. In the example shown in Table 1, at least two different types of products (expelled and extracted rice bran meal) need to be differentiated because they are characterized by different chemical compositions and, consequently, by different nutritional values.

Table : Extracted and expressed rice bran meal: analytical and nutritional differences		
	Extracted meal	**Expressed meal**
Analytical database parameters		
Oven DM *(fresh basis)*	896	902
Crude protein *(g/kg DM)*	54	128
NDF[1] *(g/kg DM)*	450	370
Ether extract *(g/kg DM)*	7.3	90
Ruminant database parameters		
Metabolizable energy *(MJ/kg DM)*	7.1	10.9
DM digestibility coefficient	0.48	0.63
Organic matter digestibility coefficient	0.55	0.70

As shown in Table 1, the process that produces the extracted rice bran meal leads to a material with a much lower fat content compared with the expelled one (7.3 g/kg compared with 90.0 g/kg DM), and this produces a direct effect on the metabolizable energy value. It is apparent that if, instead of specifying the type of process used, the values of the two types of rice bran meal had been averaged, the resulting values would have been meaningless.

Another, more simple, example is related to the on-farm processes applied to forages. Hay is obtained by drying the forage, but the drying process may be achieved by "sun curing" or "barn curing" the material. The different processes can lead to different compositions; for example, related crude protein content varies from 122 g/kg DM for barn-cured hay to 99 g/kg DM for the sun-cured variety . In this case also, information on the type of process applied to the forage is essential in order to maintain the two feeds as distinct entities and, thus, avoid erroneous mean values.

EXTRINSIC VARIABILITY OF DATA

Differences in analytical procedures may exist among different laboratories and also within the same laboratory. If not identified, differences can compromise the information retrieved from the database as it will compare values provided on different bases. In this respect, an important limitation of databases is related to the type and quality of the data they make available to their users.

In general, the diversity of analysis methods adopted by different laboratories is responsible for most of the extrinsic variability found in databases . It is safe to compare or mean parameters only if they have been grouped according to the method of analysis used to obtain them. An example in which incorrect mean values may result is in the estimation of lignin using potassium permanganate, according to the method of Goering and Van Soest (1970), and using acetyl bromide, according to the method of Morrison (1972). These two procedures for measuring lignin not only give different results but are also expressed in different units and it is therefore incorrect, if not impossible, to merge and compare the two values. Recently, Beever and Mould (2000) highlighted large differences in the crude protein and starch contents of maize silages submitted to nine different laboratories. The values observed for one maize silage ranged from 57 to 119 g/kg DM, for crude protein, and from 165 to 272 g/kg DM, for starch. Investigations uncovered the fact that different methods were being used and that some were predicted by near infrared reflectance spectrophotometry (NIRS).

Variability also often arises in data on the nutritional value of feedstuffs that have been obtained through *in vivo/in situ* experiments using animals. The animal species may be a source of this inherent data variability. In particular, it is common practice to classify the nutritional value of feedstuffs on the basis of data obtained through measurement among both sheep and cattle under the general definition of "ruminants". Differences in the passage rate of digesta and, therefore, of feed utilization between these two species are often substantial. Other generalizations commonly made arise from the lack of differentiation among the different physiological states of animals of the same species (dry and lactating cows, for example, or growing and finishing pigs). Such physiological differences may have a great impact on the data obtained, and when not recorded will compromise the quality of those data. Moreover, the use of non-standardized feeding and faecal collection protocols can affect the results obtained substantially.

The *in situ* method used extensively to measure the rumen degradability of feeds is subject to many sources of variability. Huntington and Givens (1995) reviewed many of these, and the *in situ* method has been the subject of a number of ring tests. For example, Madsen and Hvelplund (1994) reported on the protein degradability of five concentrate feeds evaluated *in situ* at 23 different European institutes. Although the mean values obtained were similar to published values, the reproducibility among centres was poor. In particular, the ring test underlined the need to standardize the material used to make the bags and the washing procedures followed.

A last source of variability, in terms of mean data, is related to the number of samples taken of a feedstuff which can vary widely, resulting in consolidated data that are more or less representative.

In conclusion, in order to produce a high-quality database on feedstuff composition and nutritional value, the intrinsic variability generally needs to be recorded and differences among materials need to be clearly identified. This is vital if effectively different feeds are not to be merged and averaged but maintained distinct. On the other hand, extrinsic variability should be kept to a minimum because, when a few standard procedures are each applied to a large number of samples, the resulting data will be more representative and useful than when a large number of different methods have each been applied to only a few samples.

EFFECTS OF DATA VARIABILITY

The use of information obtained from feedstuff databases characterized by low-quality data (with high extrinsic variability and low intrinsic variability) may have various effects depending on the end user of the database (e.g. animal nutritionist, compound feed manufacturer, farm manager, policy-maker). In this respect, in general, the quality of the data is more often influenced by the extrinsic than the intrinsic variability.

FOR THE ANIMAL NUTRITIONIST

Analysis of feedstuffs composition is costly and time-consuming. Nutritional values acquired through studies with animals are particularly labour-intensive. The nutritionist can therefore not normally afford to analyse specifically each of the feedstuffs involved and often needs to base assessments of nutritive value on more readily available and less expensive information.

The animal nutritionist is in charge of designing the animals' diet. The first consequence of unreliable information on feedstuffs, resulting from high extrinsic variability, may be the formulation of a nutritionally unbalanced diet. This may have different effects, depending on nutritional, environmental and economical factors; these effects are highly interrelated since the optimization of feed utilization leads to the optimization of animal output and financial returns.

Nutritional effects. Today, nutritional information on feedstuffs is used to predict animal performance (often with the use of complex models) through estimation of the energy supply to the animal. The incorporation of low-quality data in these models will produce unreliable estimates of animal performance. Furthermore, it is important to maintain the data resulting from *in vivo*measurement of nutritive value separate from those values predicted from chemical composition.

Environmental effects. The most common environmental effect derived from unbalanced diets is caused by nitrogen loss. Particularly for ruminants, the capture of nitrogen depends on the rate of production of microbial protein and is related to the availability of carbohydrates and energy in the rumen. It is therefore important to know the exact amount of degradable nitrogen (together with the carbohydrate and energy availability) when characterizing a feedstuff, in order to capture nitrogen for anabolic purposes and avoid the release of ammonia into the environment.

Table 2 gives an example of how the efficiency of nitrogen conversion in the rumen is affected by the level of nitrogen in the diet. In the Table 2 example, the differences in nitrogen intake are due only to differences in the crude protein content of the grass part of the diet. The balance among nitrogen absorption in the intestine, its conversion into milk protein and its loss in faeces and urine is highly dependent on the capacity of the rumen to capture this nutrient. In the example, increasing the nitrogen intake by approximately 25 percent resulted in nitrogen losses in the urine increasing by 80 percent.

It is therefore evident that even small differences in the concentration of nitrogen in different feedstuffs may give rise to substantial losses of nitrogen to the environment.

Table : Nitrogen (N) balance of cows fed at different N levels

N intake *(g/day)*	N excretion *(g/day)* Milk	Faeces	Urine
626	107	158	361
494	118	178	198

Source: **Van Vuuren and Meijs, 1987.**

Economic effects. If, for example, maize gluten is fed at the rate of 5 kg per cow per day to a herd of 100 cows at a metabolizable energy (ME) level of 1.8 MJ/kg DM (as proposed by AFRC, 1993), it would supply the herd with 5 310 MJ ME/day. At a level of 12.8 MJ/kg DM , the daily ME supply to the herd would be 5 760 MJ. Over a 200-day period, the difference in ME supply would be 90 000 MJ, which represents a saving of some 8 tonnes of compound feed, or some US$2 500.

Unbalanced diets may also produce an economic loss in terms of animal health, feed conversion efficiency and, ultimately, the output of animal products. The wrong proportion of a nutrient in the diet is reflected in milk production (in terms of both quantity and quality) and has a direct effect on the economics of production. Such effects can be seen extremely rapidly in fast-growing poultry, where even small changes in the nutrient balance can lead to drastic economic consequences.

FOR THE COMPOUND FEED MANUFACTURER

Compound feeds are composed of a blend of various raw materials and/or by-products. In designing these products, the feed manufacturer needs to find the balanced combination among different materials that will satisfy the requirements of specific animals in a specific physiological state. In order to achieve this, the manufacturer initially needs to base purchasing decisions on the available information about the chemical composition and nutritional value of feedstuffs.

It is therefore very important at this stage that the information available is representative and reliable, not least so that the economic value of the material can be assessed and compared with its market price.

Subsequently, the composition of the different ingredients will be measured and the nutritional value of the product estimated, but failure to get the initial values correct will ultimately be reflected in a higher cost of production and will reduce sales of compound feeds to farmers.

FOR THE FARM MANAGER

The farm manager needs to plan crop production in order to meet the animals' requirements. Managers therefore need to obtain information on the supposed chemical and nutritional characteristics of various ingredients in advance and, based on this information, plan the correct combination and quantity of different forages. If the information is inaccurate, the crops produced will provide unbalanced proportions of nutrients (i.e. too much protein, too few available carbohydrates, etc.). The immediate consequences will be an inappropriate diet for the animals, with direct effects on production, and the necessity to compensate the lack of some nutrients by purchasing from the market.

FOR THE POLICY-MAKER

The policy-maker needs reliable information in order to be able to direct the policy of the country or region towards competitive and sustainable agriculture. It is evident that, if estimates are based on imprecise information, policy-makers will not be able to make informed or useful decisions.

A further effect of the use of low-quality data by policy-makers is related to the intrinsic variability of feeds, and therefore to real differences in characterizing the materials (genetic differences or differences arising from the processing of raw materials). These differences may be derived from the various ways of describing and naming feedstuffs adopted in different countries. The result is confusion in the trading of feeds, and difficulties in developing and applying export policies.

The lack of harmonization of feed description and naming has been the source of many problems among countries and, in particular, among the Member States of the European Union (EU). Historically, both linguistic and scientific barriers have produced significant differences in feed identification, feed naming and feed description, and false variability often exists because the same name is attributed to different feeds or different names are attributed to identical feeds.

The availability of reliable feed data and information that are uniform among different countries will not only contribute to fair trade in feedstuffs but will also facilitate cooperation in animal nutrition research directed towards feed efficiency, product quality and the environment. Not least, it is indispensable for the correct application of the General Agreement on Tariffs and Trade (GATT) and realization of the EU's agricultural policy. Within the EU, a number of steps have been taken to produce a common approach to feed description and naming .

CONCLUSIONS

Feedstuffs vary because of their genetic make-up and as a consequence of the processes applied to them (intrinsic variability of feedstuffs). It is important that information about these factors is available and that genetically different feeds and those processed under varying conditions are identified and recorded separately. Failure to do so will produce improperly averaged, generalized data that provide meaningless information.

Another source of data variability results from differences in the methodologies used to obtain the information (extrinsic variability of feedstuffs). Chemical analysis procedures and animal study protocols may vary according to the laboratory or institute involved. This type of variability needs to be minimal if reliable information is to be obtained.

To achieve the necessary reliability, information regarding the chemical and nutritional characteristics of a feedstuff needs to be carefully examined before it is incorporated into a database and, once incorporated, it needs to be carefully managed. Failing to do so will produce false variability among feeds, ultimately resulting in errors in predicting animal performance and environmental effects and impairing the economics of animal products.

CONTAMINANTS AND TOXINS IN ANIMAL FEEDS

Animal feeds are routinely subject to contamination from diverse sources, including environmental pollution and activities of insects and microbes. Animal feeds may also contain endogenous toxins arising principally from specific primary and secondary substances produced by fodder plants. Thus, feed toxins include compounds of both plant and microbial origin. Although these toxins are often considered separately, because of their different origins, they share several common underlying features.

Thus, particular compounds within both plant and microbial toxins may exert antinutritional effects or reduce reproductive performance in farm animals. Furthermore, the combined effects may be the result of additive or synergistic interactions between the two groups of compounds. The extent and impact of these interactions in practical livestock feeding remain to be quantified. Feed contaminants and toxins occur on a global scale but there are distinct geographical differences in the relative impact of individual compounds. The term "feed" is generally used in its widest context to include compound blends of straight ingredients as well as forages. With such a broad perspective, it is necessary and more instructive to introduce some focus. Consequently, this article is limited to a review of those contaminants and toxins that represent significant risks to farm livestock. Feed contamination arising from insect fragments and excreta will not be addressed, but the role of such vectors in the transmission of fungal spores and hyphae should not be ignored. Legal control of certain feed contaminants and toxins is in place and operating within a continually evolving framework; the salient issues will be briefly reviewed here.

ENVIRONMENTAL CONTAMINANTS

A wide range of organic and inorganic compounds may occur in feedstuffs, including pesticides, industrial pollutants, radionuclides and heavy metals. Pesticides that may contaminate feeds originate from most of the major groups, including organochlorine, organophosphate and pyrethroid compounds (van Barneveld, 1999). A recent survey indicated that 21 percent of feeds in the United Kingdom contain pesticide residues.

Pirimiphos-methyl, an insecticide used in grain stores, was detected with the highest frequency. Although pesticides are potentially toxic to farm livestock, the primary focus of concern centres on residues in animal products destined for human consumption. Dioxins and polychlorinated biphenyls (PCBs) are examples of industrial pollutants that may contaminate feeds, particularly herbage. Cows grazing pastures that are close to industrial areas produce milk with higher dioxin content than cows from rural farms. In 1999, dioxin-contaminated animal fat was inadvertently added to animal feeds destined for Belgian, French and Netherlands farms. Unacceptable levels of dioxins were found in meat products and eggs from these farms.

Human health considerations are also paramount in the monitoring of radionuclide pollution. Following the Chernobyl accident in 1986, caesium-134 and caesium-137 were released, causing widespread contamination of pastures and conserved forages. As a consequence, milk and sheep carcasses became contaminated and restrictions were imposed on the movement and slaughter of sheep .

Contamination of feeds and herbage with cadmium may occur as a result of applying certain types of fertilizers to crops and pastures. On the other hand, lead contamination arises from industrial and urban pollution, while mercury in feeds arises from the use of fishmeal.

BACTERIAL CONTAMINANTS

There is currently considerable interest in the occurrence of *Escherichia coli* in animal feeds following the association of the O157 type of these bacteria with human illness. In a recent United States study , 30 percent of cattle feed samples obtained from commercial sources and farms contained *E. coli*, although none of the tests for *E. coli* O157 were positive. Replication of faecal *E. coli*, including the O157 type, was demonstrated in a variety of feeds under conditions likely to occur on cattle farms in the summer months. Since faecal contamination of feeds is widespread on farms, it is an important route for exposure of cattle to *E. coli* and other organisms. The potential for exposure to bacteria also exists when poultry litters are fed to cattle (in California, for example, two such poultry waste products are commercially available for use as cattle feed). However, providing the products are adequately heat-processed prior to distribution, the risks of contamination with *E. coli*, *Salmonella* spp. and *Campylobacter* spp. are likely to be minimized or even eliminated (Jeffrey *et al.*, 1998). Nevertheless, it is worth noting that *S. enterica* commonly occurs in cattle feeds in the United States, Europe and South Africa, with contamination rates ranging from 5 to 19 percent (Krytenburg *et al.*, 1998).

Listeria monocytogenes tends to occur in poor-quality silages and big-bale silage. When grass is ensiled under anaerobic conditions, the low pH regime ensures that *Listeria* is excluded from the resulting silage. However, in big-bale silage a degree of aerobic fermentation may occur, raising pH levels and allowing the growth of *Listeria*. These bacteria also survive at low temperatures and in silages with high levels of dry matter. Contamination of silage with *Listeria* is important as it causes abortion, meningitis, encephalitis and septicaemia in animals and humans. The incidence of various forms of listeriosis has been increasing in recent years.

FUNGAL CONTAMINANTS

There are consistent reports of worldwide contamination of feeds with fungi and their spores. In the tropics, *Aspergillus* is the predominant genus in dairy and other feeds (Dhand, Joshi and Jand, 1998). Other species include *Penicillium*, *Fusarium* and *Alternaria*, which are also important contaminants of cereal grains (D'Mello, Macdonald and Cochrane, 1993). Fungal contamination is undesirable because of the potential for mycotoxin production. However, spores from mouldy hay, silage, brewers' grain and sugar-beet pulp may be inhaled or consumed by animals with deleterious effects termed "mycosis". Common examples of such conditions include ringworm and mycotic abortion. The latter may occur in cattle as a result of systemic transmission and subsequent proliferation in placental and foetal tissues.

MYCOTOXINS

Mycotoxins are those secondary metabolites of fungi that have the capacity to impair animal health and productivity (D'Mello and Macdonald, 1998). The diverse effects precipitated by these compounds are conventionally considered under the generic term "mycotoxicosis", and include distinct syndromes as well as non-specific conditions.

A list of the principal mycotoxins occurring in feeds and forages is given in

Table 1, which also indicates the fungal species associated with the production of these contaminants. Mycotoxin contamination of forages and cereals frequently occurs in the field following infection of plants with particular pathogenic fungi or with symbiotic endophytes. Contamination may also occur during processing and storage of harvested products and feed whenever environmental conditions are appropriate for spoilage fungi. Moisture content and ambient temperature are key determinants of fungal colonization and mycotoxin production.

It is conventional to subdivide toxigenic fungi into "field" (or plant-pathogenic) and "storage" (or saprophytic/spoilage) organisms. *Claviceps*, *Neotyphodium,Fusarium* and *Alternaria* are classical representatives of field fungi while *Aspergillus* and *Penicillium* exemplify storage organisms. Mycotoxigenic species may be further distinguished on the basis of geographical prevalence, reflecting specific environmental requirements for growth and secondary metabolism.

Thus, *Aspergillus flavus*, *A. parasiticus* and *A. ochraceus* readily proliferate under warm, humid conditions, while *Penicillium expansum* and *P. verrucosum* are essentially temperate fungi. Consequently, the *Aspergillus* mycotoxins predominate in plant products emanating from the tropics and other warm regions, while the *Penicillium* mycotoxins occur widely in temperate foods, particularly cereal grains. *Fusarium* fungi are more ubiquitous, but even this genus contains toxigenic species that are almost exclusively associated with cereals from warm countries.

Table : Origin of principal mycotoxins occurring in common feeds and forages

Mycotoxins	**Fungal species**
Aflatoxins	*Aspergillus flavus; A. parasiticus*
Cyclopiazonic acid	*A. flavus*
Ochratoxin A	*A. ochraceus; Penicillium viridicatum; P. cyclopium*
Citrinin	*P. citrinum; P. expansum*
Patulin	*P. expansum*
Citreoviridin	*P. citreo-viride*
Deoxynivalenol	*Fusarium culmorum; F. graminearum*
T-2 toxin	*F. sporotrichioides; F. poae*
Diacetoxyscirpenol	*F. sporotrichioides; F. graminearum; F. poae*
Zearalenone	*F. culmorum; F. graminearum; F. sporotrichioides*
Fumonisins; moniliformin; fusaric acid	*F. moniliforme*
Tenuazonic acid; alternariol; alternariol methyl ether; altenuene	*Alternaria alternata*
Ergopeptine alkaloids	*Neotyphodium coenophialum*
Lolitrem alkaloids	*N. lolii*
Ergot alkaloids	*Claviceps purpurea*
Phomopsins	*Phomopsis leptostromiformis*
Sporidesmin A	*Pithomyces chartarum*

An emerging feature is the co-production of two or more mycotoxins by the same species of fungus . This observation has enabled a fresh interpretation of the causes of well-known cases recorded in the history of mycotoxicoses.

AFLATOXINS

This group includes aflatoxin B_1, B_2, G_1 and G_2 (AFB_1, AFB_2, AFG_1 and AFG_2, respectively). In addition, aflatoxin M_1 (AFM_1) has been identified in the milk of dairy cows consuming AFB_1-contaminated feeds. The aflatoxigenic *Aspergilli* are generally regarded as storage fungi, proliferating under conditions of relatively high moisture/humidity and temperature. Aflatoxin contamination is, therefore, almost exclusively confined to tropical feeds such as oilseed by-products derived from groundnuts, cottonseed and palm kernel. Aflatoxin contamination of maize is also an important problem in warm humid regions where *A. flavus* may infect the crop prior to harvest and remain viable during storage.

Surveillance of animal feeds for aflatoxins is an ongoing issue, owing to their diverse forms of toxicity and also because of legislation in developed countries (D'Mello and Macdonald, 1998). In the United Kingdom, analysis conducted during the 1987-1990 period indicated that all imported feedstuffs complied with legislation in force for AFB_1 levels. Elsewhere, however, aflatoxin levels in certain feeds still pose serious risks to animal health. Thus, in India total aflatoxin levels of 3 700 _g/kg were detected in a sample of groundnut cake. Of potentially greater significance is the contamination of maize samples in China and northern Viet Nam with combinations of AFB_1 and *Fusarium* mycotoxins. In China, 85 percent of maize samples were contaminated with both AFB_1 and fumonisin B_1 at levels ranging from 8 to 68 _g/kg and 160 to 25 970 _g/kg, respectively. Feed-grade maize in northern Viet Nam had AFB_1 levels ranging from 9 to 96 _g/kg, and fumonisin B_1 levels in the range of 271 to 3 447 _g/kg (Placinta, D'Mello and Macdonald, 1999). Between 1988 and 1989, analyses of farmgate milk in the United Kingdom showed low levels of AFM_1 contamination, but more than 50 percent of milk samples in the United Republic of Tanzania were found to contain the mycotoxin (D'Mello and Macdonald, 1998). The importance of aflatoxins in animal health emerged in 1960, following an incident in the United Kingdom in which 100 000 turkey poults died from acute necrosis of the liver and hyperplasia of the bile duct ("turkey X disease"), attributed to the consumption of groundnuts infected with *Aspergillus flavus*. This event marked a defining point in the history of mycotoxicoses, leading to the discovery of the aflatoxins. Subsequent studies showed that aflatoxins are acutely toxic to ducklings, but ruminants are more resistant. However, the major impetus arose from epidemiological evidence linking chronic aflatoxin exposure with the incidence of cancer in humans.

OCHRATOXINS

The *Aspergillus* genus includes a species (*A. ochraceus*) that produces ochratoxins, a property it shares with at least two *Penicillium* species. Ochratoxin A (OA) and ochratoxin B are two forms that occur naturally as contaminants, with OA being more ubiquitous, occurring predominantly in cereal grains and in the tissues of animals reared on contaminated feed. Another mycotoxin, citrinin, often co-occurs with ochratoxin. In recent Bulgarian wheat samples, OA and citrinin levels ranged from < 0.5 to 39 _g/kg and from < 5 to 420 _g/kg, respectively. In oats, higher levels of OA were detected (maximizing at 140 _g/kg) while citrinin was below detection limits (D'Mello, 2001).

The ochratoxins and citrinin are nephrotoxic to a wide range of animal species. OA is frequently implicated in porcine nephropathy and in Balkan endemic nephropathy of humans. The role of citrinin in these syndromes has yet to be elucidated.

FUSARIUM MYCOTOXINS

Extensive data now exist to indicate the global scale of contamination of cereal grains and animal feed with *Fusarium* mycotoxins (D'Mello and Macdonald, 1998). Of particular importance are the trichothecenes, zearalenone (ZEN) and the fumonisins. The trichothecenes are subdivided into four basic groups, with types A and B being the most important. Type A trichothecenes include T-2 toxin, HT-2 toxin, neosolaniol and diacetoxyscirpenol (DAS). Type B trichothecenes include deoxynivalenol (DON, also known as vomitoxin), nivalenol and fusarenon-X. The production of the two types of trichothecenes is characteristic for a particular *Fusarium* species. However, a common feature of the secondary metabolism of these fungi is their ability to synthesize ZEN which, consequently, occurs as a co-contaminant with certain trichothecenes. The fumonisins are synthesized by another distinct group of *Fusarium* species . Three members of this group (fumonisins B_1, B_2 and B_3) often occur together in maize.

Virtually all the toxigenic species of *Fusarium* listed in Table 1 are also major pathogens of cereal plants, causing diseases such as head blight in wheat and barley and ear rot in maize. Harvested grain from diseased crops is therefore likely to be contaminated with the appropriate mycotoxins, and this is supported by ample evidence. Surveillance of grain and animal feed for the occurrence of *Fusarium* mycotoxins has been the subject of many investigations over recent years (Tables 2 and 3). The global distribution of these mycotoxins is a salient feature, but striking regional differences should also be noted. Another aspect worthy of comment is consistent evidence of the co-occurrence of various *Fusarium* mycotoxins in the same sample. These issues have been considered at greater length by Placinta, D'Mello and Macdonald (1999) who, for example, referred to a German study in which 94 percent of wheat samples analysed were contaminated by between two and six *Fusarium* mycotoxins and 20 percent of the samples were co-contaminated with DON and ZEN . The most frequent combination included DON, 3-ADON and ZEN. T-2 and HT-2 toxins were detected at levels ranging from 0.003 to 0.250 mg/kg and 0.003 to 0.020 mg/kg, respectively, but these mycotoxins only occurred in combination with DON, NIV and ZEN.

Table. Global distribution of deoxynivalenol (DON), nivalenol (NIV) and zearalenone (ZEN) in cereal grains and animal feed (mg/kg)

Table : Global distribution of deoxynivalenol (DON), nivalenol (NIV) and zearalenone (ZEN) in cereal grains and animal feed (mg/kg)

Country	Cereal/feed type	DON	NIV	ZEN
Germany	Wheat	0.004-20.5	0.003-0.032	0.001-8.04
Poland	Wheat	2.0-40.0	0.01	0.01-2.0
	Maize kernels	4.0-320.0		
	Maize cobs: axial stems	9.0-927.0		
Finland	Feeds and grains	0.007-0.3		0.022-0.095
	Oats	1.3-2.6		
Norway	Wheat	0.45-4.3	max 0.054	
	Barley	2.2-13.33	max 0.77	
	Oats	7.2-62.05	max 0.67	
Netherlands	Wheat	0.020-0.231	0.007-0.203	0.002-0.174
	Barley	0.004-0.152	0.030-0.145	0.004-0.009
	Oats	0.056-0.147	0.017-0.039	0.016-0.029
	Rye	0.008-0.384	0.010-0.034	0.011
South Africa	Cereals/animal feed		0.05-8.0	
Philippines	Maize		0.018-0.102	0.059-0.505
Thailand	Maize			0.923
Korea, Republic	Barley	0.005-0.361	0.005-0.361	
	Maize	mean 0.145	mean 0.168	
Viet Nam	Maize powder	1.53-6.51	0.78-1.95	
China	Maize	0.49-3.10	0.6	-
Japan	Wheat	0.03-1.28	0.04-1.22	0.002-0.025
	Barley			0.010-0.658
	Wheat	0.029-11.7	0.01-4.4	0.053-0.51
	Barley	61.0-71.0	14.0-26.0	11.0-15.0
New Zealand	Maize	max 3.4-8.5	max 4.4-7.0	max 2.7-10.5
USA	Wheat	up to 9.3		
	Wheat (winter), 1991	< 0.1-4.9		
	Wheat (spring), 1991	< 0.1-0.9		
	Wheat, 1993	< 0.5-18.0		
	Barley, 1993	< 0.5-26.0		
Canada	Wheat (hard)	0.01-10.5		
	Wheat (soft, winter)	0.01-5.67		
	Wheat (soft, spring)	0.01-1.51		
	Maize	0.02-4.09		
	Animal feeds	0.013-0.2	0.065-0.311	
Argentina	Wheat	0.10-9.25		

In the Lublin region of southeastern Poland, type A trichothecene contamination of barley grain was linked with the natural incidence of fusarium head blight, in which the predominating organism was *F. sporotrichioides* (Placinta, D'Mello and Macdonald, 1999). Of 24 barley grain samples, 50 percent were positive for T-2 toxin, with a range of 0.02 to 2.4 mg/kg. In five of these samples, co-contamination with HT-2 toxin occurred, with a range of 0.01 to 0.37 mg/kg. Maize ears may also become naturally infected with *Fusarium* pathogens. The findings of one study in Poland indicated that infection with *F. graminearum* can result in contamination of cobs with DON and 15-ADON simultaneously (Placinta, D'Mello and Macdonald, 1999). Concentrations of DON and 15-ADON in *Fusarium*-damaged kernels ranged from 4 to 320 mg/kg and 3 to 86 mg/kg, respectively, but the axial stems of the cobs were more heavily contaminated, at 9 to 927 mg/kg and 6 to 606 mg/kg, respectively. Oat grains produced in Norway by commercial growers were found to be more heavily contaminated with DON than barley or wheat kernels . In addition to NIV , other contaminants included 3-ADON and fusarenon-X. For example, 56 percent of certain oat samples contained detectable quantities of 3-ADON at 0.03 mg/kg or more. Other notable examples of DON contamination include wheat and barley samples from Japan and the United States . It should be stated, however, that even in samples with lower levels of contamination, high incidence rates have been recorded. Thus, 90 and 79 percent of cereal samples in the Netherlands were positive for DON and NIV respectively (Placinta, D'Mello and Macdonald, 1999).

Widespread contamination of maize and animal feed with fumonisins has recently been reported . In most instances the predominant fumonisin was FB_1. The highest values for FB_1 were recorded from maize samples in China, where AFB_1 co-occurred in 85 percent of samples, and in Thailand. Multiple contamination of maize with fumonisins, DON, NIV and AFB_1 was also observed in northern Viet Nam. For FB_2, the highest values in maize were found in samples from Argentina. In the Philippines, Thailand and Indonesia, FB_1 and FB_2 occurred in more than 50 percent of maize samples, and these mycotoxins co-occurred with aflatoxins in 48 percent of samples (Placinta, D'Mello and Macdonald, 1999).

The *Fusarium* mycotoxins induce a wide range of effects in farm livestock (D'Mello, 2000). DON is a potent feed intake inhibitor in pigs; ZEN is associated with reproductive abnormalities in pigs and ruminants. Fumonisins have been linked with specific syndromes, namely porcine pulmonary oedema and equine leukoencephalomalacia. Fumonisin contamination of maize in South Africa has been correlated with the occurrence of oesophageal cancer in humans.

ENDOPHYTE ALKALOIDS

The endophytic fungus *Neotyphodium coenophialum* occurs in close association with perennial tall fescue, while another related fungus, *N. lolii*, may be present in perennial ryegrass (D'Mello, 2000). Ergopeptine alkaloids, mainly ergovaline, occur in *N. coenophialum*-infected tall fescue, while the indole isoprenoid lolitrem alkaloids, particularly lolitrem B, are found in *N. lolii*-infected perennial ryegrass. The ergopeptine alkaloids reduce growth, reproductive performance and milk production in cattle, while the lolitrem compounds induce neurological effects in ruminants.

PHOMOPSINS

In Australia, lupin stubble is valued as fodder for sheep, but infection with the fungus *Phomopsis leptostromiformis* is a major limiting factor because of toxicity arising from the production of phomopsins by the fungus. Mature or senescing parts of the plant, including stems, pods and seeds, are particularly prone to infection. Phomopsin A is considered to be the primary toxin, causing effects such as ill-thrift, liver damage, photosensitization and reduced reproductive performance in sheep (D'Mello and Macdonald, 1998).

SPORIDESMIN

Pithomyces chartarum is a ubiquitous saprophyte of pastures and has the capacity to synthesize sporidesmin A, a compound causing facial eczema and liver damage in sheep.

PLANT TOXINS

Many plant components have the potential to precipitate adverse effects on the productivity of farm livestock (D'Mello, 2000). These compounds are present in the foliage and/or seeds of virtually every plant that is used in practical feeding.

Table : Plant toxins: sources and concentrations

Toxin	Principal sources	Typical concentrations
Lectins	Jackbean	73 units/mg protein
	Winged bean	40-320 units/mg
	Lima beans	59 units/mg protein
Trypsin inhibitors	Soybean	88 units/mg
Antigenic proteins	Soybean	-
Cyanogens	Cassava root	186 mg HCN/kg
Condensed tannins	Acacia spp.	65 g/kg
	Lotus spp.	30-40 g/kg
Quinolizidine alkaloids	Lupin	10-20 g/kg
Glusosinolates	Rapeseed	100 mmol/kg
Gossypol	Cottonseed	0.6-12 g/kg (free)
Saponins (steroidal)	Brachiaria decumbens; Panicum spp.	-
S-methyl cysteine sulphoxide	Kale	40-60 g/kg
Mimosine	Leucaena leucocephala	145 g/kg (seed)
		25 g/kg (leaf)
Phyto-oestrogens	Clover; lucerne; soybean	-

Typical concentrations for selected toxins are presented in Table 4. Plant toxins may be divided into a heat-labile group, comprising lectins, proteinase inhibitors and cyanogens, which are sensitive to standard processing temperatures, and a heat-stable group including, among many others, antigenic proteins, condensed tannins, quinolizidine alkaloids, glucosinolates, gossypol, saponins, the non-protein amino acids S-methyl cysteine sulphoxide and mimosine, and phyto-oestrogens. The role of these substances as antinutritional factors has been considered at length by D'Mello (2000), but the salient points are worth reiterating.

LECTINS

Lectins are proteins capable of damaging the intestinal mucosa. In contrast to most other dietary proteins, lectins resist digestive breakdown and substantial quantities of ingested lectins may be recovered intact from the faeces of animals fed diets containing one of a number of legume seeds (D'Mello, 2000). The prime example of a lectin with potent antinutritional and toxic properties is concanavalin A, a component of the jack bean. Lectins are also present in other legume grains including the winged bean and soybean. Concanavalin A enhances the shedding of brush-border membranes and decreases villus length, thereby reducing surface area for absorption in the small intestine. With other lectins, the lamina propria of the intestine may become infiltrated with eosinophils and lymphocytes. The overall effect is reduced nutrient absorption, but immune function may also be impaired.

PROTEINASE INHIBITORS

The proteinase inhibitors are typical examples of heat-labile factors with antinutritional activity. They constitute a unique class of proteins with the ability to react in a highly specific manner with a number of proteolytic enzymes in the digestive secretions of animals. The trypsin inhibitors of soybean are now well characterized (D'Mello, 1995) and are an important determinant of nutritive value. Proteinase inhibitors are also present in other leguminous seeds such as field beans, winged beans, pigeon pea and cowpea. Effects in animals include reduced protein digestion and endogenous loss of amino acids, with the overall result that performance is impaired.

ANTIGENIC PROTEINS

Certain storage proteins of legume seeds are capable of crossing the epithelial barrier of the intestinal mucosa to elicit adverse effects on immune function in farm animals. In the case of the soybean, the antigenic proteins have been identified as glycinin and _-conglycinin. The antigenic proteins are characterized by their resistance to denaturation by conventional thermal processing procedures and to enzyme attack in the digestive tract of mammals. The most striking effects of antigenic proteins are embodied within the "immune hypersensitivity" syndrome. This condition occurs after feeding heated soybean to sensitized calves and piglets (D'Mello, 1991). The component antigens provoke extensive local and systemic immunological reactions together with severe intestinal damage. The resulting effects include abnormalities in movement of digesta, impaired nutrient absorption and a predisposition to diarrhoea.

CYANOGENS

Cyanogens occur widely in plants and in diverse forms. In sorghum and cassava , the predominant cyanogens are, respectively, dhurrin and linamarin. The latter compound is also present in linseed. Cyanogens are glycosides that readily yield HCN and it is this latter molecule that causes dysfunction of the central nervous system, respiratory failure and cardiac arrest (D'Mello, 2000). Metabolizable energy values for poultry tend to be lower in untreated cassava root meal, presumably because of its cyanogenic potential.

CONDENSED TANNINS

Tannins belong to a group of phenolic compounds with a molecular weight in excess of 500 daltons. Condensed tannins (CTs) are a subset of this group and are widely distributed in leguminous forages and seeds and in sorghum. Cattle and sheep are sensitive to CTs, while goats are more resistant. Adverse effects may be seen in sheep when CTs, including those in lotus or in browse legumes such as *Acacia* species, comprise a significant part of their diets. Primary effects include impaired rumen function and depressed intake, wool growth and live-weight gain. However, at moderate levels (30 to 40g/kg legume dry matter), CTs may result in nutritional advantages in respect of increased bypass protein availability and bloat suppression in cattle. At higher levels (100 to 120 g CTs/kg legume dry matter), reduced gastrointestinal parasitism in lambs has been reported (D'Mello, 2000).

QUINOLIZIDINE ALKALOIDS

The quinolizidine alkaloids occur in lupins and include lupinine, sparteine and lupanine. Bitter cultivars contain relatively high levels of total alkaloids and are not suitable as animal feedstuffs because of their negative effects on intake. In addition, cattle consuming certain lupin species during pregnancy may produce calves with multiple congenital deformities.

GLUCOSINOLATES

Glucosinolates are glycosides of particular significance in brassica forage crops such as kale (Table 4; D'Mello, 2000). Removal of glucose from glucosinolates by plant or microbial enzymes (myrosinase), results in the release of a diverse array of compounds which undergo further breakdown to yield a number of toxic metabolites. The most common breakdown products are isothiocyanates and nitriles but, depending on such conditions as pH, temperature and metallic ion concentrations, a number of other metabolites may also be produced. These products may then cause organ damage, goitrogenic effects or reduced feed intake, particularly in non-ruminant animals.

GOSSYPOL

Gossypol pigment occurs in cottonseed in free and bound forms. In whole seeds, gossypol exists essentially in the free form, but variable amounts may bind with protein during processing to yield inactive forms. Free gossypol is the toxic entity and causes organ damage, cardiac failure and death. Cottonseed meal fed to bulls can induce increased sperm abnormalities and decreased sperm production.

SAPONINS

Saponins are divided into two groups: steroidal saponins, which occur as glycosides in certain pasture plants such as *Brachiaria decumbens* and *Panicum* species ; and triterpenoid saponins, which occur in soybean and alfalfa. Many hepatogenous photosensitization conditions in sheep have been attributed to the intake of forage plants containing steroidal saponins. In contrast, triterpenoid saponins from alfalfa reduce feed degradation in the rumen.

AMINO ACIDS

A wide range of non-protein amino acids occur in the foliage and seeds of plants. Forage and root brassica crops contain S-methyl cysteine sulphoxide (SMCO), while the aromatic amino acid mimosine occurs in the foliage and seeds of the tropical legume *Leucaena leucocephala* (D'Mello, 2000). Uncontrolled feeding of brassica forage to ruminants causes organ damage with haemolytic anaemia, which is attributed to the intake of SMCO. Abrupt feeding of *Leucaena* to sheep causes shedding of fleece, reduced intake, organ damage and death. In cattle, loss of hair, excessive salivation, lethargy, weight loss and enlarged thyroids are common features of *Leucaena* toxicity.

PHYTO-OESTROGENS

Phyto-oestrogens are a diverse group of isoflavonoid compounds found primarily in forage and grain legumes . In clover, formononetin is the major form of phyto-oestrogen. Phyto-oestrogens are actively metabolized in the rumen to form products that vary in their biological activity. Formononetin is converted into a more oestrogenic compound. Phyto-oestrogens have been associated with "clover disease" in sheep, which is characterized by low ovulation and conception rates (D'Mello, 2000).

WEED SEEDS

Contamination of animal feeds with weed seeds is a major problem worldwide. The impact of weed seeds arises from the toxins they contain and from their diluent effects on nutrient density of feeds. The toxins include many of those cited, particularly alkaloids, saponins, amino acids and proteinase inhibitors. Examples of weed seeds that are controlled by legislation in various countries include those of *Datura* spp., common vetch, castor-oil plant and *Crotalaria* spp.

ANIMAL TOXINS

Of the diverse types of naturally occurring animal toxins, the prion proteins of mammalian meat- and bone-meal have recently emerged as important feed contaminants necessitating statutory control. Prion proteins are harmless animal tissue components with the capacity to transform themselves into agents causing fatal neurological lesions in a wide range of species. The significance of prions has been highlighted following the emergence of bovine spongiform encephalopathy (BSE) as a major disease of cattle in the United Kingdom. The onset of this disease was attributed to the feeding of cattle with meat- and bone-meal prepared from the carcasses of scrapie-infected sheep. The latter disease is also caused by prion proteins, as is the human equivalent - new variant Creutzfeldt-Jakob disease (vCJD). The incidence of vCJD in humans has been linked to the consumption of BSE-infected beef. It is this association that has led to extensive and stringent legislation in the European Union (EU) concerning the use of specified animal products in livestock feeding.

UNDECLARED ADDITIVES

Animal products are frequently contaminated with drug residues administered through the feed. Such feed additives may be used for disease control and the enhancement of livestock performance. Residues may also arise through contamination of animal feeds with undeclared drugs. The occurrence of these drugs is mostly due to cross-contamination in feed mills . For example, medicated feed residues may be retained within equipment and then contaminate subsequent batches of feed. Under these conditions, levels of contamination may be low but sufficient to cause detectable residues in animal products.

Lynas *et al.* (1998) examined the extent of feed contamination with undeclared antimicrobial additives in Northern Ireland. Of 247 medicated feeds, 35 percent were found to contain undeclared antimicrobials; and of 161 unmedicated feeds, 44 percent were shown to contain antimicrobials. The contaminants most frequently identified included chlortetracycline, sulphonamides, penicillin and ionophores. Sulphadimidine in contaminated feeds was sufficient to cause violative tissue residues if consumed by animals in the finishing stages. It is possible that feed contamination with undeclared antimicrobials is a global problem warranting further investigation. Drug residues in animal products are undesirable because of human health implications concerning allergies and the development of antibiotic resistance in disease organisms.

REGULATION

It is instructive and relevant to provide a brief review of the regulatory prospects for the control of undesirable substances. Currently, regulations are most comprehensive in Europe and North America, while in developing countries statutory directives may not even exist. Thus, 50 countries, mostly in Africa, have no regulations for mycotoxin control (D'Mello and Macdonald, 1998). This situation may be changed by the new rules imposed on feeds imported into the EU which came into force in August 1999. Non-EU feed manufacturers are now required to have representatives based in the EU who can confirm declarations concerning certain quality and safety standards for imported animal feeds.

For heavy metals and aflatoxins, distinctions in prescribed limits are generally made for straight, complete and complementary feedstuffs. Additional distinctions may apply according to the destination of feeds for a particular class of animal. For controlled pesticides, separate regulations exist for feedstuffs and for fats, with virtually no distinction for the class of animal. Of the wide variety of plant toxins, only gossypol, cyanogens and certain glucosinolates are subject to regulatory control in the EU. Special regulations apply to contamination of feeds with specific bacteria. For example, under United Kingdom regulations, positive identification of *Salmonella* in feeds must be reported to a "veterinary officer of the Minister" .

Specific regulations apply to the control of BSE in cattle. For example, in the United Kingdom, it has been illegal to feed ruminants with any form of mammalian protein since November 1994. The feeding of mammalian meat-and bone-meal (mMBM) to farmed livestock has been prohibited since April 1996. However, pigs and poultry may still be fed diets containing mammalian protein in forms other than mMBM, e.g. processed catering waste. Surveillance results of animal feeds indicate widespread compliance with these regulations, with 99.7 percent of feeds found to be negative for mammalian protein.

EFFECTS OF PROCESSING

Heat processing is a common procedure in feed manufacture, conferring improved properties as regards the safety and nutritive value of animal feeds. For example, heat treatment of dried poultry litter appears to be an effective method for controlling, or even eliminating, contamination with *Salmonella*, *E. coli* and *Campylobacter* (Jeffrey *et al.*, 1998). Thermal processing is also effective for denaturing proteinase inhibitors, lectins and cyanogens. However, for antigenic proteins, more complex procedures involving the use of hot aqueous ethanol extraction are required (D'Mello, 1991).

For aflatoxin-contaminated oilseeds destined for animal feed, ammoniation appears to be the processing method of choice. The feedstuff is treated with either ammonium hydroxide or gaseous ammonia at high temperatures and pressure in commercial feed mills, or at ambient temperature and low pressure in small-scale operations in developing countries. If the ammoniation reactions are allowed to proceed to completion, the detoxification process is irreversible and aflatoxin contamination is virtually eliminated. Providing that the residual ammonia is dissipated, diets containing the decontaminated meals are readily consumed by animals without ill-effects. Depending on the efficacy of decontamination, residues of AFM_1 in the milk of dairy cows are substantially reduced or absent altogether. The adverse effects of tannin-rich forages may be overcome by treatment or spraying of foliage with polyethylene glycol, but the practical application of this procedure still has to be economically evaluated.

CONCLUSIONS

Animal feed, including herbage, may be contaminated with organic and inorganic compounds as well as with particulates. Organic chemicals comprise the largest group and include plant toxins, mycotoxins, antibiotics, prion proteins and pesticides. Inorganic compounds include heavy metals and radionuclides. Particulates such as weed seeds and certain bacterial pathogens are common contaminants of feed. The effects of feed contaminants and toxins range from reduced intake to reproductive dysfunction and increased incidence of bacterial diseases. Residues transferred to edible animal products represents another reason for concern. Comprehensive legislation is in place for the control of several of these chemical compounds and pathogens in feed. However, in many developing countries, particularly in Africa, statutory control of contaminants is at best rudimentary. The scope for decontamination of feeds is limited and generally uneconomic, and prevention is the most effective practical strategy.

7

Edible Oil Industry

EDIBLE OIL REFINERY : COOKING OIL REFINERY : VEGETABLE OIL REFINERY

Edible Oil Refinery and Edible Oil Refining have been the areas of excellence for Tinytech Udyog. We are the basic designers, manufacturers and exporters of complete Edible Oil Refinery Plants to refine the crude oil and make it pure edible. Tinytech Udyog manufactures unique edible oil refinery with complete unique construction. Our refinery plants are specifically designed to give the minimum operation costs and maximum output results.

The edible oil refinery can refine almost all types of oils. The refined oil quality depends on the type of crude oil and its chemical structure. So far, we have exported our refinery plants to 25 countries of the world.

The above photo shows the complete edible oil refinery of 5-ton capacity *erected at our Tinytech showroom.*

Edible Oil Refinery 5 Tons per day.

1. Neutralizer

2. Neturalizer
3. Bleacher
4. Deodourizer
5. Cooler
6. Thermic Fluid Boiler
7. Filter Press
8. Filter Press
9. Raw Oil Tank
10. Bleach Oil Tank
11. Soap Pan
12. Soap Pan

Steam generator and vaccum pump are on the back side and so can not be seen. Berometric Condensor and catchalls with 40ft. tower not shown.

PROCESS DESCRIPTION OF EDIBLE OIL REFINERY

For refining the edible oil, there are three basic processes in the refinery. First process is neutralizing the oil in the neutralizer to remove the Free Fatty Acids (FFA) by adding caustic soda. Oil is heated up to about 60°C by thermic fluid coils and oil is stirred by stirrer. Then soap stock formed due to chemical reaction is allowed to settle at the bottom of the neutralizer from where it is taken out into soap pan. Neutralized oil is drawn into the second vessel called bleacher where color of oil is removed by bleaching process with aid of chemicals such as carbon black and bleaching earth. Oil is generally heated up to 110°C by thermic fluid coils. Stirring is also continued. Bleaching process is done under vacuum. Bleached oil then goes to the filter press where bleaching earth and chemicals are separated and clean bleached oil is then drawn to deodorizer where oil is heated above 110°C through thermic fluid coils and then live steam is given to the oil from the bottom steam nozzles and temperature of oil is raised up to 200 to 220°C through thermic fluid coils. Entire process is done under high vacuum. Thus smell is removed from the oil in the deodorizer. Then it goes to cooler where water circulating coils take away heat and oil is cooled. Again it goes to second filter press where completely refined and transparent color less oil is obtained. Thermic Fluid Boiler, Vacuum Pump, Barometric Condenser, Catchalls, Steam Generator etc. play their role in the refining process. So these equipments are part of the refinery and connected with the vessels through pipelines.

SPECIFICATIONS OF EDIBLE OIL REFINERY

Capacity 5 tons per day i.e. 4 batches of 1250 kg each:

- All the main vessels i.e. two neutralizers, one bleacher and one deodorizer are properly arranged on the first floor of the steel structure. So all these vessels are hanging on the steel structure.

Just below the two neutralizers, two soap pans are resting on the ground floor in which soap stock is collected. There is a steam pipe arrangement in the soap pans also.

- Steel structure has size of 14ft. x 14ft. (i.e. 4.25mtr. x 4.25mtr). First floor is 9ft. above the ground level. There are 8 columns of double channel which supports the entire steel structure. It has proper staircase and railing on all the sides of steel structure at the first floor and also on staircase. Two filter presses are also accommodated on the first floor of the steel structure.
- Two oil tanks i.e. raw oil tank and bleached oil tank are accommodated under the structure on the ground floor. Then cooler, thermic fluid boiler, two steam generators, vacuum pump, water pumps, oil pumps and refined oil tank are arranged on the ground floor around the steel structure i.e. outside the square of 14ft. x 14ft. of the steel structure. So total space occupied is about 30ft. × 30ft. (9mtr. x 9mtr.)
- 40ft. tower is erected just near the deodorizer and its complete structure is supported from the ground floor and also it is attached with the refinery structure. Barometric condenser is arranged at 40ft. height to create proper vacuum.
- All types of pipelines are interconnected as per the requirement of the refinery i.e. oil pipelines (yellow color), vacuum pipelines (blue color), steam pipelines (black color), water pipelines (white color), thermic fluid pipelines (red color). At all appropriate places, proper valves are provided in the pipelines.
- Neutralizer is provided with thermic fluid coil for heating the oil.
- Bleacher is provided with double pipe coil. One is for thermic fluid and another is for cooling water.
- Deodorizer is provided with double pipe coil i.e. in both the coils, thermic fluid is circulated. Steam is ejected from the stainless nozzles provided on the steam pipe cross supported at the bottom.
- Cooler is provided with double pipe coil. Both for cooling water.
- In every vessel temperature gauge is provided. Vacuum gauge is provided on deodorizer, bleacher and cooler.
- Neutralizer is open on the top having conical bottom.
- Bleacher has dished ends on both the sides. Similarly deodorizer has dished ends on both the sides. Cooler has also dished ends on both the sides.

EDIBLE OIL REFINERY WITH FRACTIONATION PROCESS

- There will be chilling plant for fractionation process which will include shell and tube chiller, compressor, motor, pump, condenser, control panel box etc.

- Crystallizing unit which is similar to neutralizer complete with chilling coil.
- Filter press for separation of palm olein and palm stearin.

SOURCES OF EDIBLE OILS

The processing parameters for each type of oil seed or source may vary slightly, but the general process for all oils is very similar. The variation is a result of the type of seed or source, but the ultimate goal is to yield a clean and stable product which is 96 percent or higher pure triglyceride. Animal fats are rendered from tissue using dry heat or steam and are processed in facilities which are under USDA jurisdiction. Vegetable oils are obtained through expression (pressing) or solvent extraction from the source. The fats and oils obtained directly from rendering, expression or extraction are called crude oils. These crude oils contain varying levels of non-triglyceride materials, the majority of which would be considered impurities in most finished oils. This is not to say this is always bad.

The most expensive olive oils are those from the first press. There also are processors who market specialty oils which are only mechanically pressed. However, the great majority of the oils which are sold to food processors and at the retail level are fully refined, that is, they have been processed to remove most impurities or non-triglyceride materials.

REFINING OF CRUDE OIL

Degumming

The first step in the refining process of many oils is degumming. Oils are degummed by mixing them with water to hydrate phosphatides, which are then removed by centrifuging. Degumming may be enhanced by adding phosphoric or citric acid or silica gel. Degumming removes valuable emulsifiers such as lecithin. Cottonseed oils are not degummed, but the process is necessary for such oils as soybean and canola.

Alkali Refining

The degummed oil is then treated with an alkali to remove free fatty acids, glycerol, carbohydrates, resins, metals, phosphatides and protein meal. The oil and alkali are mixed allowing free fatty acids and alkali to form a soap. The resulting soapstock is removed through centrifuging. Residual soaps are removed with hot water washings. Cottonseed oil is also refined using a process called miscella refining. This process allows oil to be refined in the miscella stage at the solvent extraction plant prior to removal of the solvent. The oil produced using this method has higher yields and has what some consider a lighter, more desirable color.

Bleaching

During the bleaching process, trace metals, color bodies such as chlorophyll, soaps and oxidation products are removed using bleaching clays, which adsorb the impurities. Bleached oils are nearly colorless and have a peroxide value of near zero. Depending on the desired finished product, oils are then subjected to one or more processes.

Winterization (Fractionation)

Oils destined for use as salad oils, or oils that are to be stored in cool places undergo a process called winterization so that they will not become cloudy when chilled. The refined, deodorized oils are chilled with gentle agitation, which causes higher melting fractions to precipitate. The fraction which settles out is called stearin. Soybean oil does not require winterization, but canola, corn, cottonseed, sunflower, safflower and peanut oils must be to be clear at cool temperatures.

Hydrogenation

Treatment of fats and oils with hydrogen gas in the presence of a catalyst results in the addition of hydrogen to the carbon-carbon double bond. Hydrogenation produces oil with the mouth feel, stability, melting point and lubricating qualities necessary to meet the needs of many manufacturers. It is important to note that hydrogenation is a selective process that can be controlled to produce various levels of hardening, from very slight to almost solid.

Deodorization

Deodorization is a steam distillation process carried out under a vacuum, which removes volatile compounds from the oil. This may be a batch or continuous process. The end product is a bland oil with a low level of free fatty acids and a zero peroxide value.

This step also removes any residual pesticides or metabolites that might be present, which are more volatile than the triglycerides in the oil. Some manufacturers favor cottonseed oil as it can be deodorized at lower temperatures, which results in more tocopherols (natural antioxidants) being retained. Deodorization produces some of the purest food products available to consumers. Few other products are so thoroughly clean as refined, bleached and deodorized oil.

Interesterification

This process allows fatty acids to be rearranged or redistributed on the glycerol back-bone. This is most often accomplished by catalytic methods at low temperatures. The oil is heated, agitated and mixed with the catalyst at 90°C. There also are enzymatic systems which may be used for interesterification. It does not change the degree of saturation or isomeric state of the fatty acids, but can improve the functional properties of the oil.

Oil Specifications and Selection

The computer industry created the saying "Garbage In, Garbage Out." The same can be applied to food processing. The use of poor quality materials can compromise product quality. One pitfall is the purchase of materials based solely on cost. If the "great deal" does not have the right functional characteristics, the oil's performance in process may be compromised and the finished product may not even be salable. Purchases should never be based on cost alone, although the seasonality of the various oil source harvests, and the supply's effect on price, does affect purchasing decisions. Changing oil prices are one reason why federal law allows labels of fried snacks and prepared foods to read "Made with one or more of the following oils… ."

While food processors work with their suppliers or contract packers in a multitude of fashions, many have initiated programs to validate the companies that supply them.

Five Steps Toward Validation

1. Management from both supplier and buyer establish performance characteristics or specifications. The buyer must be specific in communicating to the supplier his expectations about what the product or service should be. When reviewing suppliers, be sure to check:
   - Production capabilities
   - Record keeping
   - Sanitation/good manufacturing practice compliance
   - Food safety and quality assurance programs
   - Laboratory/quality staff
   - Overall company commitment to quality
2. Review analytical methods to determine the necessary data to be submitted and the format it should take. Many processors provide their suppliers with data acquisition or collection sheets. This makes the processor's life easier, especially when dealing with many suppliers.
3. Measure key attributes and conduct collaborative studies to assure validation and correlation between the methods used by the supplier and buyer laboratories.
4. Run tests of the material(s) in the presence of the buyer and the supplier at the manufacturing plant. This provides both parties with a greater understanding of how the operation will work.

5. The buyer and supplier should agree on a mutually acceptable quality control system such as Statistical Process Control, Total Quality Management, or Hazard Analysis Critical Control Point.

PACKAGING OF FATS AND OILS

Manufacturers of fried foods (snacks, coated products, etc.), salad dressings, many formulated foods and a range of other products use vast quantities of fats and oils in the production of these products. In general, transport packaging is designed to inhibit oxidation; methods include minimizing exposure to ultraviolet light and nitrogen gas blanketing. Bulk deliveries of oil are made via:

Rail cars and/or tanker trucks: To assure the quality of oils delivered in bulk, the containers must be thoroughly cleaned and drained prior to loading. Residual water, cleaning compounds or other contaminants which are allowed to remain in the tanks may compromise the entire tanker or car. All seals and valves should be properly secured and sealed to protect the product and provide an indicator of tampering. When loading or unloading bulk tanks, hoses and pumps must be cleaned. When receiving oils, many operators and refiners of crude pass the oils through a screen or filter to ensure that any contaminants are removed.

Collapsible or foldable containers: Manufactured from metal or plastic and designed to be used with a plastic or laminate inliner. The advantage of these containers is they fold up, increasing the efficiency of the backhaul operations. Also, if a panel is damaged, it, and not the whole container, may be replaced. These bins are now being used in Europe for oils for small bakery operations and for foodservice and catering operations.

Rigid plastic reusable container: Must be cleaned after each use. They usually contain a built-in spigot to allow the containers to drain or to which a pump may be attached. Oil must be fluid in this package.

Plastic containers: Encased or contained in a steel mesh to protect and support the plastic, these containers are meant to be reused and must be washed before refill.

Reinforced fiber containers: In which the oil is filled into a single-use plastic or laminate inliner. The fiber may be reused, but once it gets wet or oily, it must be discarded.

Bag-in-box: Another relatively new package used for frying and salad oils. Used in Europe, the package has yet to catch on in the United States. As the bag empties and collapses, headspace is minimized, which can increase the shelf life of the oil. The container was adopted to reduce waste in the foodservice industry. Other packaging: Smaller quantities, including one- gallon jugs to 35-lb. jugs in a box, are available for foodservice applications and small processing operations.

QUALITY EVALUATION

There are a number of tests used to monitor oil quality. These include chemical, physical and sensory tests. There also are several rapid tests which can be used as quality tools. The quality of the fats and oils used in manufacturing directly affects the finished product. Standards are published by the American Oil Chemists Society (AOCS).

Chemical Tests

Active Oxygen Method (AOM, AOCS Cd 12-57). Measures oxidative stability. Air is bubbled through an oil or fat which is held at 97.8°F. Oil samples are withdrawn at regular intervals and the peroxide value (PV) is determined. The AOM is expressed in hours and is the length of time needed for the PV to reach a certain level. AOM is used as a specification for fats and oils. AOM hours tend to increase with the degree of saturation or hardness. This method, though popular, is being replaced with the Oil Stability Index.

Alkaline Soaps Alkaline soaps, formed by the reaction of metals and free fatty acids in the presence of water, are a chemical marker of oil degradation. They are most commonly formed as a result of reaction with residual caustic cleaners and, during deep-fat frying, from coatings, breadings and from animal blood and bone cells. This test helps in part to predict food quality and frying oil performance.

Anisidine Value (AOCS Cd 18-90) Aldehydes are products of the decomposition of peroxidized fatty acids. The Anisidine Value measures aldehyde levels, using them as a marker to determine how much peroxidized material has already broken down. In conjunction with current peroxide levels, the past and future degradation profile of an oil can be mapped out-especially for oils processed twice to reduce free fatty acids and reheated frying oils.

Fatty Acid Methyl Esters (FAME, AOCS Ce 1-62). Used to determine the fatty acid composition of fats and oils. Triglycerides are converted to methyl esters and then analyzed using gas-liquid chromatography. With new food regulations and the new oils being produced through breeding and genetic engineering, it is essential these values be known.

Free Fatty Acids (FFA, AOCS Ca 5a-40). Using a titration procedure, FFA is a measure of the amount of fatty acid chains hydrolyzed off the triglyceride backbone. It can be a useful marker for the degraded oil on the surface of a fried food, but is considered by many to be a poor indicator of frying oil quality. Results are reported as %FFA, calculated as oleic acid.

Iodine Value (AOCS Cd 1-25). This test measures the degree of unsaturation in fats and is used as a finished product specification for fresh oils. Elemental iodine is added to the double bonds of unsaturated fatty acids and measured. Results are expressed as grams of iodine absorbed per 100 grams of fat.

Oil Stability Index (OSI, AOCS Cd 12b-92). This automatic test measures the rate at which an oil oxidizes when air is bubbled through it. A breakdown product, formic acid, is conveyed into distilled water contained in a cell. The instrument continuously monitors conductivity in the water. The time at which the conductivity rises sharply is the endpoint.

Peroxide Value (PV, AOCS Cd 8b-90). This is the classic test for measuring oxidation in fresh oils, but has limited value for frying oils as the test is highly sensitive to temperature. Peroxides are unstable radicals formed from triglycerides. Processors extract oil from a food to measure the PV; a PV over 2 is an indicator that the product has a high rancidity potential and could fail on the shelf.

Polar Materials (TPM, AOCS Cd 20-91). Many manufacturers consider polar material measurement to be the single most important test for degrading oil. Polar materials are all non-triglyceride materials soluble in, emulsified in, or suspended in the frying oil. Once an oil is exposed to frying temperatures and food, a portion of the triglycerides are converted into myriad degradation products. Since they also include conversion products, %TPM measures cumulative degradation of the oil.

Polymers (AOCS Cd 22-91). Usually the largest single class of degradation products in frying oil, polymers include dimers, trimers, tetramers, etc., and can be formed through oxidative and thermal reactions. The dark "shellacs", which form on fryer walls, heater tubes and belts, are polymeric materials. The official method to test polymer levels uses high-pressure liquid chromatography. They are an excellent chemical marker of oil degradation

Thiobarbituric Acid (TBA, AOCS Cd 19-90). This test is an excellent indicator of fatty acid oxidation products and detects the onset of rancidity reactions. The addition of TBA results in colored pigments when it reacts with aldehydes and other oxidative breakdown products. Absorption is read at 450 nm for the yellow pigments; 530 nm for red.

Physical Tests

Melting Point. Refers to the point at which a pure compound changes from a solid to a liquid (including the ranges of temperature in which fats will melt in the mouth to produce the desired mouthfeel). Commercial oil products do not melt at one sharp point, but rather over a range of temperatures. Among the methods for determining melting points are Complete Melting Point (AOCS Cc 1-25); Wiley Melting Point (AOCS Cc 2-38); Dropping Point (AOCS Cc 18-80); and Slip Point (AOCS Cc 3-25, 3b-92).

Oil Color (Lovibond, AOCS Cc 13c-92). Color is used as a quality index for frying and as a specification in finished oils. The range of oil colors varies, but if an oil from a refiner is darker than expected, it could indicate abuse or improper refining. Measure Lovibond red, yellow and blue when evaluating a frying system and developing quality standards.

Smoke, Flash, Fire Points (AOCS Cc 9a-48). By heating an oil in a cup under strong light, the temperature at which the oil begins to smoke is observed. With continued heating and the use of a small flame, the flash and fire points are determined. These points are key for oils used in deep-fat frying and griddle cooking.

Solid Fat Index/Content (SFI, AOCS Cd 10-57, SFC, AOCS 16b-93). These measurements describe the percentage of a product that is solid at different, defined temperatures. The creation of this curve gives an understanding of properties and performance of oils over a range of temperatures, information that is essential to create basestocks for blending to produce margarines or shortenings. SFI is determined using dilatometry, a technique that measures the changes in volume that occur when a solid goes to liquid. Magnetic resonance imaging is used to determine SFC. It measures the amounts of liquid and solid fat in a sample, based on relaxation of protons after the sample has been pulsed. The SFC test is faster than the SFI test, but is more expensive.

Sensory Tests

Sensory Analysis (AOCS Cg 2-83). This method is a flavor evaluation of vegetable oils. The oils are placed in covered glass beakers, which are then placed in an aluminum block. The block is heated in the dark. Covering the beakers allows volatiles to build up and the samples are evaluated for flavor and odor.

AUTHENTICITY OF VEGETABLE OILS

In past incidents of oil adulteration, palm stearin and olein (fractions of palm oil) have been blended together or with palm oil to give a product of unknown and variable quality; groundnut oils have contained undeclared small quantities (5 percent) of cheaper oils such as soybean oil; rapeseed oil has been added, undeclared, to the more expensive soybean oil and maize (corn) oil; and cottonseed oil has been diluted with palm olein. Historically, detecting such fraud has been difficult because of the small database establishing appropriate purity criteria for authentic edible oils and fats.

OLIVE OILS

Olive oils are distinct from other vegetable oils because they may be consumed without extensive refining. Indeed, refining the product is considered detrimental since the attractive organoleptic properties of oil are diminished in the process. Virgin olive oils attract a higher price than refined olive oils because of their pleasant, rather delicate flavour and aroma and limited production volume. As a result, olive oils are subject to two types of deliberate adulteration. The first is the blending of virgin olive oils with olive oils of lower grade (e.g. refined olive oil or olive-pomace oil). The second is the less subtle mixing of olive oil with liquid vegetable oils. There has been considerable concern regarding the deliberate mislabelling of olive oils since a researcher revealed that most of the olive oils studied were not of the grade claimed (Firestone *et al.,* 1985). As a consequence of such findings the International Olive Oil Council (IOOC) (1993a) and the Codex Alimentarius Commission (1993) have produced standards for virgin and refined olive and olive-pomace oils and certain blends of these products.

USEFUL PURITY CRITERIA

Palm oil is a semi-solid oil at ambient temperatures in northern Europe. This is explained by its fatty acid composition (FAC): the oil contains large quantities (40 to 47 percent) of palmitic acid (C 16:0) and similar amounts of oleic acid (C18:1). The limited presence of polyunsaturated fatty acids permits close packing of the component triglycérides which results in a relatively high slip melting point.

Palm oil can be adulterated with other palm products, and in these cases the determination of fatty acid, sterol and tocopherol compositions is of limited use. However, plotting iodine value against slip melting point produces three distinct groupings for palm oil and its fractions palm stearin and olein, thereby providing a method of identifying impure oils.

Palm stearin has high concentrations of tripalmitin; palm oil contains moderate levels but palm olein has almost none. Accordingly, by determining the triglycéride carbon number, the presence of palm oil or palm stearin in palm olein can be detected.

Double-zero ("00") rapeseed oils, which have become more common since the 1980s, are low in erucic acid, come from seeds low in glucosinolates and have a higher linolenic acid (C18:3) content (10 to 14 percent) than the previously predominant single-zero ("0") rapeseed oils (approximately 8 to 10 percent linolenic acid). The "00" oils are therefore significantly more prone to oxidation and consequently might be considered of lower quality.

Rapeseed (low erucic acid) and soybean oils have similar FAC; however, the differences are sufficient to permit identification of blending. For example, low-erucic acid rapeseed oil contains 52 to 67 percent oleic acid and 16 to 25 percent linoleic acid. Soybean oil contains approximately 18 to 26 percent oleic acid and 50 to 57 percent linoleic acid.

Perhaps the most straightforward method of distinguishing the two oils is by their sterol composition. For example, soybean oil has much higher concentrations of stigmasterol than rapeseed oil. More important, rapeseed oil has high levels of brassicasterol, while soybean oil is almost devoid of this compound.

It has been established that the FAC at the 2-position of the triglycérides is significantly different for these oils. In particular, linolenic acid enrichment factor (EF) is approximately 1,75 for rapeseed oil and 0.9 for soybean oil . Cottonseed, groundnut and sunflower-seed oils are characterized by their lack of linolenic acid (C 18:3) and by the fact that the sum of their oleic and linoleic acid concentrations is approximately 70 to 80 percent of the total. The presence of more than 0.5 percent linolenic acid indicates adulteration, possibly by soybean or rapeseed oil, both of which trade at lower prices than these oils.

Most oils do not contain tocotrienols, the most notable exception being palm oil. When there are tocotrienols in a cottonseed oil the presence of palm oil or a palm oil fraction is indicated. Groundnut and rapeseed oils generally do not contain d -tocopherol, while soybean oil is rich in this compound. If, following measurement of FAC, a groundnut oil appears to contain an adulterant, the determination of d -tocopherol will verify whether or not it is soybean oil.

The mean ratio of a - to d -tocopherol in sunflower-seed oil is approximately 200. In cottonseed, groundnut and maize oils the corresponding ratio is less than 1. Therefore, one might suspect a sunflower-seed oil of containing one of these oils if this ratio is significantly reduced below 200. The use of FAC alone would not permit this detection.

Palm kernel and coconut oils are rich in lauric acid and the short-chain fatty acids C6:0, C8:0 and C 10:0. There are only small differences in the FAC of the two products, so identifying the oil from its FAC is most difficult. However, analysis of the triglycéride carbon number provides a method of categorical differentiation. The carbon number is renormalized to take account of only those triglycérides with carbon numbers between 32 and 42. When the sum of the concentrations of the triglycérides with carbon numbers of 34 and 40 is plotted against the sum of those with carbon numbers of 36 and 38, it is quite apparent whether the oil is coconut or palm kernel oil (King and Zilka, 1986; King, Zilka and Turrell, 1985).

Purity criteria for olive oils

Because of the differences between olive and other vegetable oils, parameters that serve as quality indices only in the case of a particular vegetable oil can be used to help distinguish the different quality grades of olive oil.

Free fatty acid content (FFA). The FFA of an olive oil can be used as a measure of its quality. In refined vegetable oils, the lower the FFA the more acceptable the oil to the human palate. Virgin olive oils cannot be categorized in this way because their characteristic flavour involves a sharp component that results from the FFA present. Therefore, a higher FFA is acceptable in virgin olive oil than would be permitted in refined vegetable oils. IOOC and CAC standards set a limit of 1 percent for FFA in extra-virgin olive oils.

Peroxide value (PV). The PV is an indication of the amount of hydroperoxides present in an oil. These compounds arise from lipid oxidation;

therefore, the PV, expressed as milliequivalent oxygen per kilogram oil (meq/kg), is a measure of oil quality. The PV is greatly reduced by the refining process used for most vegetable oils. Virgin olive oils are not exposed to such processes and the PVs permitted in these products are considerably higher. The IOOC and CAC standards permit extra-virgin olive oils to have PVs of up to 20 meq/kg, while pure olive oils, which by definition are blends of virgin and refined olive oils, must have PVs below 10 meq/kg.

Specific extinction (*SE*). This is a simple and rapid indicator for establishing whether oils labelled as virgin contain refined oils. The SE of an oil will increase on refining because the usual 1:4 méthylène interrupted distribution of double bonds found in linoleic and linolenic acids is altered in part to form a conjugated 1:3 distribution. If the oil has an SE greater than 0.25 at 270 nm, it is considered either to be not virgin or to contain oxidized fatty acids. If an oil is considered suspect, it is treated with alumina, which removes oxidation products, and the SE is determined again. If, after treatment with alumina, the SE is greater than 0.10, the oil is considered to be adulterated with refined oils.

Fatty acid composition. The use of FAC to establish the purity of an olive oil has been criticized because of the very large variations permitted in standards for certain fatty acid ranges . Analysis of the FAC at the 2-position of the triglycéride, a technique used to indicate esterification, is particularly relevant for olive oils. For example, in poor-quality olive oils, fatty acids may be removed from the glycerol by hydrolysis. These can be recovered during oil refining and recombined with glycerol to produce an oil of the same overall FAC but having a different distribution of fatty acids within the triglycérides. In such a case, the esterified oils have a considerably higher concentration of palmitic (C 16:0) and stearic (C 18:0) acids at the 2-position .

This phenomenon has been exploited in setting standards to prevent the addition of esterified oils to virgin oils. For example, the CAC and IOOC standards state that the sum of palmitic and stearic acids at the 2-position should not exceed 1,5 percent in virgin oil or 1.8 percent in refined oils.

Table. Partial fatty acid composition of olive oil - Teneur partielle en acides gras de l'huile d'olive - Composición parcial de los αcidos grasos del aceite de oliva

Fatty acid	Permitted range (*% of total fatty acids*)
C16:0	7.5-20
C18:1	55-83
C18:2	3.5-21

Table. Typical profiles of fatty acids at the triglyceride 2-position for olive and olive-derived oils - Profils typiques des acides gras à la position triglycéride 2 pour les huiles d'olive et les produits dérivés - Perfiles típicos de los αcidos grasos en la posición 2 del triglicérido, en los aceites de oliva y derivados

Fatty acid	Virgin	Esterified	Pomace
C16:0	0.7-1.6	9.0	2.0
C16:1	0.5	1.1	-
C18:0	Trace-0.3	2.6	0.6
C18:1	85.5-89.1	75.6	-
C18:2	1.3-11.7	11.6	-

Sterol composition. This particularly useful parameter identifies adulteration with liquid vegetable oils, which tend to contain considerably higher levels of desmethylsterols than olive oils. Early determinations of sterol composition by gas liquid chromatography (GLC) involved the use of packed columns. The stationary phases that were available at that stage had limited resolving power and only six sterols could be identified from olive oils: cholesterol, brassicasterol, campesterol, stigmasterol, b -sitosterol and D -7-stigmastenol. As improved stationary phases were introduced it became possible to separate D -5-avenasterol from b -sitosterol and D -7-avenasterol from D -7-stigmastenol. Subsequent important chromatographic developments now allow the separation of 16 desmethylsterols from olive oils.

Despite these advances, many standards still require the concentration of b -sitosterol to be greater than 93 percent of the total sterols. Internationally, it has been agreed that this limit should apply to "apparent b -sitosterol", referring to the sum of the concentrations of b -sitosterol, D -5 avenasterol, D -5,23-stigmastadienol, D-5,24-stigmastadienol, chlerosterol and sitostanol.

Although an important aspect of sterol composition is the apparent b -sitosterol composition, the CAC and IOOC have implemented some or all of the following criteria (calculated as percentage of total sterols): cholesterol, 0,5 percent maximum; brassicasterol, 0.2 percent maximum; campesterol, 4 percent maximum; D -7-stigmastenol, 0,5 percent maximum. In addition, the concentration of stigmasterol should be less than that of campesterol.

CODEX STANDARDS TO COMBAT FRAUD

Over the years, the Codex standards for fats and oils have been gradually modified to enhance their usefulness in tackling authenticity problems. The pace of the changes is inevitably affected by the availability of data of sufficient quality for inclusion in the database. One significant source of data used to establish purity criteria for edible oils and fats of major importance has been research in the United Kingdom funded by the Ministry of Agriculture, Fisheries and Food (MAFF) and the Federation of Oils, Seeds and Fats Associations (FOSFA) at the Leatherhead Food Research Association.

To produce meaningful data, it is essential that sufficient samples be collected from representative geographical origins and that the oils be pure. In the MAFF/FOSFA work, over 600 authentic commercial samples of vegetable oilseeds of known origin and history, generally of ten different geographical origins, were studied for each of 11 vegetable oils. The oil from these seeds was extracted in the laboratory, except in the case of palm oil, which was obtained from palm plantations because the parent fruit is perishable and cannot be transported. The extracted oils were analysed to determine their overall FAC. FAC at the 2-position of the triglyceride, sterol and tocopherol composition, triglyceride carbon number and iodine value, slip melting point and solid fat content as appropriate. Prior to 1981, FAC data were not included in Codex standards because data of sufficient quality were not available. In 1981, standards were adopted that included FAC ranges as mandatory compositional criteria. The MAFF/FOSFA work provided the basis for later revisions to these ranges.

In general, as more data became available, it was possible to propose fatty acid ranges much narrower and consequently more specific than those adopted in 1981. FAC of oils that were adopted by the Codex Alimentarius Commission (CAC) in 1981 and ranges for the same oils proposed at Step 4 at the Codex Committee on Fats and Oils (CCFO) meeting held in September 1993.

Further MAFF/FOSFA information has enabled the British secretariat of CCFO to propose the inclusion of data relating to sterol and tocopherol/ tocotrienol (tocol) composition in the new draft standards. The combination of data on fatty acids with those on sterol and tocol composition provides a powerful method of identifying oils and oil blends.

Table. Codex standards for fatty acid composition of oils - Normes Codex pour la teneur en acides gras des huiles végétales - Normas del Codex para la composición en αcidos grasos de los aceites

Fatty acid	Soybean oil		Groundnut oil		Cottonseed oil		Sunflower-seed oil	
	1981	1993	1981	1993	1981	1993	1981	1993
C14:0	< 0.5	< 0.2	< 0.6	< 0.1	0.4-2	0.6-1	< 0.5	< 0.2
C16:0	7-14	8-13.3	6-16	8.3-14	17-31	21.4-26.4	3-10	5.6-7.6
C16:1	< 0.5	< 0.2	< 1	< 0.2	0.5-2	0-1.2	< 1	< 0.3
C18:0	1.4-5.5	2.4-5.4	1.3-6.5	1.9-4.4	1-4	2.1-3.3	1-10	2.7-6.5
C18:1	19-30	17.7-26.1	35-72	36.4-67.1	13-44	14.7-21.7	14-65	14-39.4
C18:2	44-62	49.8-57.1	13-45	14-43	33-59	46.7-58.2	20-75	48.3-74
C18:3	4-11	5.5-9.5	< 1	< 0.1	0.1-2.1	0-0.4	0-0.7	0-0.2
C20:0	<1	0.1-0.6	1-3	1.1-1.7	0-0.7	0.2-0.5	0-1.5	0.2-0.4
C20:1	<1	<0.3	0.5-2.1	0.7-1.7	0-0.5	0-0.1	0-0.5	0-0.2
C22:0	< 0.5	0.3-0.7	1-5	2.1-4.4	0-0.5	0-0.6	0-1	0.5-1.3
C22:1	-	< 0.3	< 2	< 0.3	0-0.5	0-0.3	0-0.5	0-0.2
C22:2	-	-	-	-	-	-	-	0-0.3
024:0	-	< 0.4	0.5-3	1.1-2.2	0-0.5	0-0.1	0-0.5	0.2-0.3
C24:1	-	-	-	< 0.3	-	-	< 0.5	-

Olive oils

In processing, many crude vegetable oils undergo a bleaching step which involves heating the oil to approximately 103°C under vacuum with the addition of a bleaching earth (often acid activated). The objective is to remove pigments and produce an oil of light-yellow appearance. The bleaching process can be used on olive oil, usually in refining of oils of lower value. However, this process produces other changes within the oil. For example, it causes the dehydroxylation of sterols to produce steroidal hydrocarbons such as stigmasta-3, 5-diene. If an oil has undergone high-temperature deodorization as well, the formation of dehydroxylated sterols will be even greater. However, it is unlikely that these compounds will be produced to any great extent in virgin olive oils; thus their presence is indicative of mixing with either refined olive oil or other vegetable oils. The latest IOOC trade standard for olive and olive-pomace oils sets limits for these compounds , and CCFO will consider this relatively new development in due course.

FUTURE DEVELOPMENTS

The standards for oils and fats were developed and recognized throughout the world relatively recently. The current standards will be improved, with better databases of oil composition, as technology develops. For example, $^{13}C/^{12}C$ stable-isotope mass spectrometry seems set to become an important tool in determining adulteration of maize oil products.

Historically, determining the authenticity of maize oil with traditional methods was problematic because its FAC overlaps with that of several other vegetable oils. In addition, the concentration of sterols in maize oils is very great in comparison with that of other vegetable oils, so that the sterol composition of any blend will comprise predominantly those from maize oil. It is possible to form blends of oils whose characteristics according to traditional analysis are very similar to those of pure maize oil.

The determination of the $^{13}C/^{12}C$ stable-isotope ratio (SIR) enables the identification of blends of maize oil with other vegetable oils . The sample oil is burned to form carbon dioxide which is purified by GLC and then analysed by mass spectrometry. The results are presented not as an absolute abundance of each carbon isotope but rather as a ratio of the heavy ^{13}C isotope to ^{12}C, measured as parts per thousand (ppt) with respect to an international standard, carcon dioxide produced from calcite of Pee Dee formation belemnite (PDB) with phosphoric acid.

Table. Levels of stigmasta-3, 5-diene permitted in olive oils by the International Olive Oil Council - Niveaux de stigmasta-3, 5-diene autorisés par le Conseil oléicole international pour les huiles d'olive - Niveles de estigmasta-3, 5-dieno de los aceite de oliva permitidos por el Consejo Oleícola Internacional

Olive oil grade	Maximum permissible level of stigmasta-3, 5-diene*(mg/kg)*
Edible virgin olive oils	0.1
Lampante virgin olive oil	0.5
Refined olive oil	50
Olive oil[a]	50
Crude olive-pomace oil	0.5
Refined olive-pomace oil	120
Olive-pomace oil[b]	120

Table. Carbon stable-isotope ratio for maize oil and other oils - Ratio isotopique du carbone stable pour l'huile de maïs et les autres huiles - Relación del isótopo de carbono estable para el aceite de maíz y otros aceites

Oil	Mean ▲^{13}C *(ppt)*	Range ▲^{13}C *(ppt)*	No. of samples
Maize	-14.95	-13.71 to -16.36	42
Other vegetable	-28.99	-25.38 to -32.39	68
Cereal	-31.26	-30.38 to -32.39	4
Fish	-26.66	-25.37 to -27.95	4
Animal	-30.28	-27.56 to -32.08	5

It is estimated that the determination of the $^{13}C/^{12}C$ SIR and the calculated iodine value (determined from the FAC) will permit the identification of maize oil adulterated with 5 to 10 percent other vegetable oil. This is a powerful way to identify and thus prevent maize oil adulteration, and criteria relating to this technique may be expected to appear in the appropriate Codex standards in the future. Recently, two instrumental methods, one based on chemical theory and the other on computer technology - i. e pyrolysis mass spectrometry and artificial neural networks - have been coupled to give a rapid assessment of adulteration of olive oils with seed oils. Although at present the system appears complex and expensive, it may one day form part of an internationally recognized standard to help prevent olive oil adulteration.

THE PRODUCTION AND PROCESSING OF MARINE OILS

The title of this document reflects the development that the Omega-3 market now includes fish oils, fish liver oils, some mammal (seal), crustacean (krill) and molluscan (squid) oils as well as single cell oils from marine and freshwater algae, genetically modified yeast and genetically modified oilseeds. The document will mainly discuss fish body oils but will include information on the production of krill, cod liver oil, and other methods of producing marine oils.

FISHERIES INFORMATION

In order to understand the production of marine oils it is important to understand where these products come from. The potential collapse of global fisheries and some have even predicted that by 2048 the wild fisheries will be depleted. These predictions have unsettled the markets that depend on marine oils and in some cases have led to panic buying and speculation in these markets which eventually leads to major swings in the prices of these products.

When you look at the historic global landings of fish and crustaceans over the period 1950 - 2008 (the latest year for this data), you find that the global fisheries production seems to be growing at a rate of about 11.5% per year. However closer examination of the data shows that most of the growth from 1992 to the present is due to aquaculture and over that same period growth in the global capture fisheries has been relatively static. Extension of the data indicates that if everything remains the same, the capture and aquaculture lines will cross in 2030 or so. The ocean and inland capture fisheries to aquaculture production over the period 1990 - 2008.

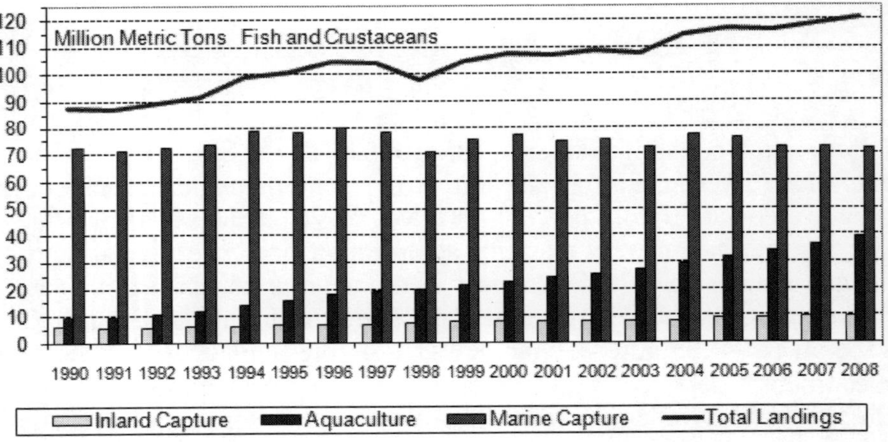

Fig. Global capture vs. farmed fish and crustacean production.

Aquaculture is an important consideration when discussing marine oils since on the one hand it is the major consumer of fishmeal and oil and on the other could be a potential source of fishmeal and oil, from the by-products, when the fish are processed.

THE ETHYL ESTER VS. TRIGLYCERIDE FORM OF FISH OILS

There is no question that one of the major advances in nutritional medicine has been the introduction of highly purified fish oil products. Very sophisticated distillation and filtration processes can now eliminate virtually all of the toxic compounds such as mercury, lead, and pesticides from crude fish oil.

There are several different methods to "molecularly distill" crude fish oil into these purified forms. To say a fish oil is molecularly distilled has become synonymous with the highest quality in the mind of many consumers, but the term really does little to assign quality any more than the term automobile tells a consumer the difference between a high priced luxury sedan versus a cheap import. Another misconception promoted by marketing propaganda is that the triglyceride form of fish oils is superior to the ethyl ester (EE) form.

Triglyceride vs. Ethyl EsterTriglyceride vs. Ethyl Ester

A triglyceride consists of a glycerol "backbone" with three 3 fatty acids attached. Fish oils naturally contain triglycerides containing DHA, EPA, and a saturated fat. During the production of all concentrated fish oils through "molecular distillation," the fatty acids are liberated into free ethyl ester forms. Some fish oil products are made by synthesizing the free fatty acids back to a triglyceride form while others, including the pharmaceutical forms, maintain the purified oil in the ethyl ester (EE) form. Some companies selling fish oils claim that the triglyceride form is more natural, has better stability, and is better absorbed than the EE form. None of these claims is true. The recombined triglycerides are not necessarily in their natural form, they are not more stable, and they certainly are not better utilized by the body. My personal opinion is that the EE form actually possesses some advantages:

In order for the body to utilize the DHA or EPA in a triglyceride form they must be liberated from the glycerol backbone. The EE form provides an easier to assimilate form for many and is significantly less likely to cause burping up of a fishy smell. Think of the EE form as a "pre-digested" form of fish oil.

While early absorption studies showed an advantage to the triglyceride form, it turns out the studies were not taking into account the fact that the EE form is processed in a more efficient manner. Very detailed absorption studies have shown that the EE form is actually more bioavailable in that it is more easily processed by the cells that line the intestines and is also more easily incorporated into cell membranes.

Though the triglyceride form is very effective, the EE form may produce even better clinical results. For example, studies looking at the effects of fish oils on reducing factors that promote dangerous blood clots as well in the important effect of lowering triglycerides show some greater benefits with the EE form. In one study, while the EE and triglyceride forms at equal concentrations showed a similar effect on raising blood levels, the EE form showed significant advantages in lowering triglycerides and reducing platelet aggregation than the triglyceride form.

The EE form is backed by considerably more in depth scientific research and it is the form preferred when higher dosages of EPA and DHA are required. Our own detailed quality control analysis at Natural Factors has shown exceptional stability in soft gelatin capsules and studies have shown feeding humans either pure DHA or EPA EE at a dosage of 4 grams does not increase lipid peroxides or cause oxidative damage.

The bottom line

While there are certain advantages to the EE form, the truth is that both the EE form and the triglyceride form produce great benefit to human health because they both provide EPA and DHA. That is the critical effect that both forms provide. The reasons why these fatty substances are so important revolve around their role in cellular membranes. A diet that is deficient in omega-3 fatty acids, particularly EPA and DHA, results in altered cell membranes. Without a healthy membrane, cells lose their ability to hold water, vital nutrients, and electrolytes. They also lose their ability to communicate with other cells and be controlled by regulating hormones. They simply do not function properly. Cell membrane dysfunction is a critical factor in the development of virtually every chronic disease, especially cancer, diabetes, arthritis, and heart disease. Not surprisingly, fish oil supplementation whether as the EE or triglyceride form have shown tremendous beneficial or protective effects against all of these disases. Again, the majority of this clinical research has been conducted with the EE form.

Practical recommendations

How much fish oil should you take? According to the latest scientific evidence, a daily dosage of 1,000 mg of EPA and DHA (combined) is sufficient to produce significant protection against heart disease and strokes. When there is a therapeutic indication for EPA and DHA such as in elevated triglycerides, rheumatoid arthritis, depression, and asthma the daily dosage is usually 3,000 mg of EPA and DHA. Keep in mind that these dosage recommendations are based upon the level of EPA and DHA versus the amount of fish oil in the capsules or liquid, so you must read the label carefully to make sure you are getting the correct amount. The specific fish oil product that I recommend is RxOmega-3 Factors from Natural Factors.

8

Cereal Crops

INTRODUCTION

The crucial difference between cultivated cereal crops and their wild relatives is in ear fragility at maturity. Easy shattering of spikes into spikelets upon maturity is essential for seed dispersal and survival in the wild, whereas forms with non-brittle ears survive only under cultivation. It is generally assumed that most Triticeae crops have been domesticated from their wild relatives by selection of non-shattering individuals which sporadically appear in wild populations as rare mutants However, there are no documented cases of the appearance of non-brittle mutants in wild populations, except observations of introduction from cultivars into weedy forms. The appearance of non-brittle mutants seems to be a rare event which may be induced under specific conditions. Interspecific hybridization may activate transposition of mobile genetic elements which may be one potential source of increased mutation rates. A hypothesis was proposed that rye and wheat forms with varying ear fragility may have arisen as a result of interspecific hybridization processes between different wild species (Jaaska 1975). Taking into account that non-brittle mutants will persist in the wild only for a limited number of generations after their appearance, it follows that rye and barley should have been domesticated *in statu nascendi* from the ancient hybrid populations of their wild relatives.

RYE

Despite considerable disagreement among taxonomists about the delimitation of rye species and their intraspecific taxa the rye genus *Secale* L. may be treated as consisting of three valid biological species

- The Outcrossing annual *Secale cereale* L. s.l, including the European cultivated rye (subsp. *cereale*), the Transcaucasian cultivated and weedy rye with a tough rachis (subsp. *segetale* Zhuk.), and various weedy and wild forms of the annual self-incompatible rye with a brittle rachis such as subsp. *ancestrale* Zhuk. s.l, including weedy subsp, *ancestrale* Zhuk. s.str, weedy subsp. *afghanicum* (Vav.) Hammer, weedy subsp. *dighoricum* Vav., and wild subsp. *vavilovii* (Grossh.) Kobyl. s.str., non s.l. of Kobyljanskij

- The Outcrossing perennial *Secale strictum* Presl., syn. *S. montanum* Guss., with several subspecies: subsp. *strictum* (= *S. dalmaticum* Vis.), subsp. *anatolicum* (Boiss.) Hammer, subsp. *kuprijanovii* (Grossh.) Hammer, subsp. *ciliatoglume* (Boiss.) Hammer, and subsp. *africanum* (Stapf) Hammer.
- *Secale Sylvestre* Host. - a cleistogamous annual of sandy dunes and coasts.

A cleistogamous annual, originally collected by Kuckuck in Iran and attributed to *S. vavilovii* may deserve a specific rank as *S. iranicum* Kobyl., syn. *S. vavilovii* Grossh. sensu Khush, non sensu Grossheim or sensu lato of Gandilyan owing to its reproductive isolation as a result of its cleistogamous breeding system. Likewise, South African endemic perennial rye may be recognized as *S. africanum* Stapf because of its autogamous breeding system.

Grossheim described *S. vavilovii* as a short-statured (stems 20-35 cm) wild annual with short (4-8 cm) fragile spikes which he collected in Nakhitshevan from a dry habitat on volcanic ash soil. Populations of short wild annual rye were later found to occur in different dry regions of Armenia by Gandilyan who attributed the short stature to a phenotypic adaptation to a dry and nutrient-poor habitat.

On those grounds he proposed to treat all wild and weedy annual ryes with a brittle rachis as *S. vavilovii* s.l. separately from the cultivated *S. cereale* s.str. To give these forms a specific rank is questionable because they are not reproductively isolated from non-brittle weedy *S. cereale* subsp. *segetale*. Their inclusion under *S. cereale* subsp. *vavilovii* s.l. as proposed by Kobyljanskij contradicts the botanical nomenclature rules because of the priority of subsp. *ancestrale* Zhuk.

At the subspecies level Vavilov expressed a view that cultivated rye evolved from a wild perennial rye through the appearance of annual weedy forms which in turn were domesticated by unconscious selection of non-brittle forms under cultivation in barley and wheat fields. Later he reported finding a weedy rye in Afghanistan with fragile ears which he attributed to *S. cereale* var. *afghanicum* and proposed that it might be an initial form from which semi-brittle and non-brittle forms of weedy rye were spontaneously selected under cultivation in wheat and barley fields in northern areas and higher altitudes He also further argued that *S. cereale* may have evolved from a perennial *S. montanum* with wild *S. vavilovii* Grossh. acting as a link between them. rye was domesticated in the Near East region as a secondary weedy crop (subsp. *segetale*) and only thereafter spread to European countries and was used as a distinct crop. Alternatively, the present-day weedy ryes with brittle and semi-brittle rachis are products of introgressive hybridization of the cultivated non-brittle subsp. *segetale* with wild rye subsp. *vavilovii* s.str. Segregants from this hybridization acquired a weedy trait from subsp. *segetale* and became field weeds. Artificial hybrids between wild, weedy and cultivated forms of *S. cereale* are completely interfertile and show regular meiosis (that they comprise a single biological species. It is generally accepted that all annual rye species have evolved from the perennial *S. strictum*. *Secale cereale* and *S. strictum* differ by two large translocations between three of the seven chromosomes, but intraspecific taxa have the same chromosome arrangement in both species Polymorphism for reciprocal translocations has been described in populations of *S. cereale* The evolution of *S. cereale* from *S. strictum* should thus involve fixation of two reciprocal translocations which would be possible only by the involvement of an autogamous intermediate. Stutz (suggested that cleistogamous annuals *S. sylvestre* and *S. vavilovii* sensu Khush (= *S. iranicum*) might represent intermediate stages in the evolution of *S. cereale* from *S. strictum.*

Secale sylvestre has the same chromosomal arrangement as *S. strictum,* but a low crossability with it, or differs in only a small chromosomal translocation, whereas *S. iranicum* was found to have the same chromosomal arrangement as *S. cereale* (Nürnberg-Krüger Stutz suggested that cleistogamous annual *S. sylvestre* has been derived from *S. strictum* and has then given rise to a similarly cleistogamous annual *S. iranicum* by fixation of two chromosomal translocations, while *S. cereale* was assumed to emerge from *S. iranicum* by acquisition of the outcrossing breeding system by introgression from *S. strictum.*

Variability among the rye species established that *S. cereale* and *S. strictum* display partially homologous polymorphism of many isozymes with most allozymes shared between them. that *S. iranicum* is fixed for one of the allozymes found in *S. cereale* and *S. strictum,* whereas *S. sylvestre* has unique allozymes of acid phosphatase ACP-B, anodal peroxidase PRX-C, and aromatic alcohol dehydrogenases AAD-A and AAD-E In the it has been concluded that *S. sylvestre* is a lateral branch of evolutionary divergence form S. *strictum* and not an intermediate leading to *S. iranicum* and *S. cereale.*

Morever, *S. strictum* and *S. sylvestre* are well isolated in nature by growing in different ecological habitats and do not hybridize freely. Instead, I suggest that some unknown inbreeding form of subsp. *vavilovii* related to *S. iranicum* might be an intermediate from which both brittle- and tough-rachis forms of *S. cereale* evolved by introgression of self-incompatibility from *S. strictum* It was also assumed that non-brittle rye *S. cereale* subsp. *segetale* might be domesticated *in statu nascendi,* directly from some such hybrid populations currently extinct, while fragile subsp. *vavilovii* s.str. has persisted in the wild. Later, *S. sylvestre* was found to differ from the other rye species also in allozymes of cathodal peroxidases CPX-4 and CPX-5 and chloroplast DNA whereas *S. cereale* and *S. strictum* revealed homologous polymorphism and could not be definitely distinguished by allozymes and chloroplast DNA Zhukovsky (1pointed out that there have been no reports of spontaneous appearance of non-brittle forms for more than 100 years of cultivation of wild and weedy ryes in different botanical gardens and collections. The reason may be in the recessive nature of the non-brittle mutation combined with the outcrossing breeding system of rye The rare non-brittle mutants will remain phenotypically unexpressed in outcrossing rye populations in heterozygous genotypes until two parents with recessive non-brittle alleles cross and segregate into homozygotes in a progeny.

The probability for this depends on the frequency of non-brittle mutations which may be extremely low. Therefore, the involvement of an inbreeding intermediate would be an important premise for the appearance of recessive non-brittle mutants phenotypically expressed in homozygotes. Zhukovsky also has proposed a hypothesis that weedy subsp. *segetale* might have arisen from interspecific hybridization between wild perennial and annual ryes with the appearance of non-brittle forms in the hybrid progeny. He assumed that interspecific hybridization might be the crucial mutagenic factor which has caused the appearance of semi- and non-brittle forms of rye. Stutz "on the slopes of Mt. Ararat, *S. vavilovii* makes contact and hybridizes rather freely with *S. montanum.*" The seed obtained from crosses between *S. cereale* and *S. strictum* were found to germinate only when *S. cereale* was the mother parent indicating that the introgression is possible from the perennial rye. Sympatric populations of wild perennial and annual ryes in the Near East region should be examined for the fragility, chromosome rearrangements and molecular characters in order to have more information about the origin of wild, weedy and cultivated forms of *S. cereale.* Electrophoretic variants of aliphatic and aromatic alcohol dehydrogenase (ADH and AAD), aspartate aminotransferase (AAT), acid phosphatase (ACP), esterase (EST) and anodal peroxidase (APX) isoenzymes in rye species: major electrophoretic variants (allozymes) are numbered in the order of their decreasing mobilities and listed in the order of decreasing occurrence; rare allozymes are labelled by letter 'r'; unique allozymes are in italics.

Species	ADH -A	AAD -A	AAD -E	AAT -B	AAT -C	ACP-B	EST A	EST B	APX C
S. strictum	2;1r	1	2;1;3r	1	2;1	4;4f;5;3	2f;2;3	3;1;2	1
S. cereale									
subsp. *cereale*	2	1	2;1	1	2;3	4;1;3;2	2	1	1
subsp. *segetale*	2	1	2,1	1	2;3	4;1;3;2	2	1	1
subsp. *ancestral*	2	1	2;1	1;2r	2;3	4;3;1;2	2;2f;3r	1;3;2	1
S. iranicum	2	1	1	1	2	4	2	1	1
S. sylvestre	2	*2*	*1f*	1	2	*4f*	2;0	1	2

BARLEY

The cultivated barley *Hordeum vulgare* L., incl. *H. distichon* L. and *H. hexastichon* L., and its closest wild relative *H. spontaneum* C. Koch are autogamous annuals which with the allogamous perennial *H. bulbosum* L. share basic genome a number of allozymes Their hybrids are completely interfertile and have normal chromosome pairing in meiosis. Cultivated barley and its closest wild relative, *H. spontaneum,* are now commonly recognized as subspecies of *H. vulgare* s.l.

However, taking into account their autogamous breeding system, which itself provides a reproductive barrier between them, and the fact that the biological species concept is not strictly applicable to uniparentals, they could formally be accepted at a species level as separate phylogenetic lineages. There is a general agreement among investigators that cultivated barley has originated from its closest wild relative *H. spontaneum* through the latter's domestication Different views, however, have been expressed with respect to the place, time and mechanisms of the origin of different forms of cultivated barley, particularly six-row forms

Monophyletic origin of the cultivated barley as a two-row form by domestication of *H. spontaneum* and the secondary origin of the six-row barley from a cultivated two-row form is now generally accepted thanks to experimental evidence on the secondary origin of the Tibetan semi-brittle six-row barley by hybridization between the cultivated six-row barley and wild *H. spontaneum.* The semi-brittle forms in the present-day mixed populations of weedy and cultivated barley are evidently derived by introgression from the cultivated barley. Genetic studies of hybrid progeny between *H. vulgare* and *H. spontaneum* have shown that ear fragility is controlled by two closely linked genes (*Bt* and *Bt2*) with a recessive mutation at either loci giving rise to non-brittle ears In the case of a simple *in statu nascendi* domestication of barley by selecting out non-brittle mutants, the cultivated barley has evidently been domesticated repeatedly from different genotypes of wild barley, *i.e.* it has a polytopic origin.

This, however, does not explain a strikingly wider morphological variability among cultivated barley than in other cereals. Indeed, morphological variation within *H. spontaneum* is limited to only three botanical varieties which differ in the apex shape and awn length of lateral spikelets. At the same time, the cultivated barley is remarkably more variable with over 100 botanical varieties described among primitive barley landraces Although a remarkable morphometric variation was observed among a set of 77 accessions of wild barley under cultivation around Moscow (Russia) under unusual climatic conditions, it still remained relatively limited and no non-brittle cultivar-like forms were observed Characters of the wild parent dominate in hybrids with cultivated barley and segregation appears in later generations.

No morphologically new types were found among the progeny of hybrid generations between various morphological types of *H. spontaneum.* Therefore, the question as to why cultivated barley is so morphologically variable still remains unanswered. Comparative studies of isoenzyme variation among a set of morphologically different accessions of *Hordeum vulgare* s.str. and *H. spontaneum* showed that both-had the same allozymes of essentially monomorphic isoenzymes and displayed variation of 10 polymorphic esterase isozymes. This shows that the isozyme loci which were monomorphic in wild barley have remained also in the cultivated barley, *i.e.* cultivation has not induced new variation at the isozyme loci in contrast to those controlling variable morphological characters. The same also has been demonstrated with respect to wild and cultivated wheats and The cultivated barley and its wild progenitor could not definitely be distinguished by any of the isoenzymes studied except by a frequency of allozymes of some isoesterases.

Hordeum bulbosum displays extensive intrapopulation polymorphism of several isozymes which were largely monomorphic in *H. vulgare* and *H. spontaneum.* The allozyme genepool of the two annuals was found to be a subset of most frequent allozymes of *H. bulbosum* This result is consistent with a view that *H. spontaneum* might have evolved from *H. bulbosum* by fixation of genes controlling self-compatibility and annual habit, polytopic origin of *H. spontaneum,* as well as against later, repeated introgression from the bulbous barley. Moreover, crossing experiments between *H. vulgare* s.l. and *H. bulbosum* have shown that hybrids could be obtained only by the embryo rescue technique, had disturbed meiosis, were sterile and frequently haploid owing to spontaneous elimination of *bulbosum* chromosomes

Electrophoretic variants of aliphatic and aromatic alcohol dehydrogenase (ADH and AAD), aspartate aminotransferase (AAT) and esterase (EST) isoenzymes in cultivated barley (*vulgare*) and its wild relative species (*spontaneum, bulbosum*): major electrophoretic variants (allozymes) are numbered in the order of their decreasing mobilities and listed in the order of decreasing occurrence; rare variants are labelled by letter 'r'.

Isozyme	***Vulgare***	***Spontaneum***	***Bulbosum***	***Vulgare***	***Spontaneum***
ADH-A		1	1	1;2r	
ADH-B	1	1	1		
ADH-D	3	3	3;2;1		
AAD-A	1	3	3;4;2;1		
AAD-B	2;0	2;0	2;2s;1;0		
AAD-E	2	2	2;1;3		
AAT-A	1	1;2	1		
AAT-B	1	1	1;2;3;0		
AAT-C	2	2	2;3;1		
EST-A				1	1
EST-B				1	1
EST-D				3;2;4;0	2;3;4;1;0
EST-E				2	2;1r;3r
EST-F				1;2;0	2;1;3;4
EST-H				2;0	2;1;0;3

EST-I	2;0;1;3	2;0;3;1
EST-J	1;0	1;0
EST-K	3;0;2	0;1

Hordeum spontaneum and *H. bulbosum* are reproductively isolated by strong sterility barriers. Observations that crossability and chromosome elimination varies depending on the genotype of parental species suggested that introgression from the bulbous barley in some genotype combinations may be possible.

ADAPTATIONS OF CEREALS

Cereals are grains produced by plants belonging to the grass family. They account for over fifty per cent of human energy and protein needs, and cereal plants occupy two-thirds of all cultivated land. Cereals were the earliest cultivated plants and for over ten thousand years have been the staple food for many human societies. Their importance is related to a number of features. They are relatively easy to grow, store and transport and they have a high nutritive value. The food values of some important cereals compared with those for some other plant foods.

The amount of energy that can be obtained from and the total amount of protein and lipid present in 100 g. Most of the energy comes from starch and other carbohydrates and so the figures in the second column are a good measure of the amount of these substances present. Note how the energy figures and those for proteins and carbohydrates which relate to cereals are much higher than the figures for the other plants. Part of the reason for this is that cereal grains contain a very low proportion of water.

FARMING METHODS

INTENSIVE FARMING

After World War II intensive farming techniques flourished. Using high-yielding hybrid cultivars and large inputs of inorganic fertilisers; newly-developed chemical pesticides, and machine power, crop yields increased to 3 or 4 times those produced using the more extensive (low-input) methods of 100 years ago. Large areas planted with monocultures (single crops) are typical. Irrigation and fertiliser programmes are often extensive to allow the planting of several crops per season. Given adequate irrigation and continued fertiliser inputs, yields per hectare from intensive farming are high. Over time, these yields decline as soils are eroded or cannot recover from repeated cropping. More fertiliser leaches from the soil and enters groundwater as a pollutant. Unemployment rises as workers are replaced by machines and the farmer becomes more and more dependent on fossil fuels and external inputs – he becomes a 'land-slave'. On the other hand, famine has become a thing of the past.

Extensive (or Organic) Farming

Organic farming is a sustainable form of agriculture based on the avoidance of synthetic chemicals and applied *inorganic* fertilisers.

It relies on mixed (crop and livestock) farming and crop management, sometimes combined with the use of environmentally friendly pest controls (*e.g.* biological controls and flaming), natural pesticides (nicotine and derris) and livestock and green manures. Note that 'Organic' is not the same as 'pesticide-free'; to have that you must grow your own - and eat the occasional pest yourself! Organic farming uses crop rotation and *intercropping,* in which two or more crops are grown at the same time on the same plot, often maturing at different times.

MACRONUTRIENT DEFICIENCY SYMPTOMS

When plants are harvested the nutrients are removed with them. In a natural ecosystem the plants would eventually die and decay, with the nutrients being returned to the soil. Farmers need to use fertilisers containing these nutrients to maintain productivity. Farmers can use organic fertilisers or inorganic fertilisers.

The most commonly used fertilisers are the soluble inorganic fertilisers containing nitrate, phosphate and potassium ions (NPK). Inorganic fertilisers are very effective but also have undesirable effects on the environment. Since nitrate and ammonium ions are very soluble, they do not remain in the soil for long and are quickly leached out, ending up in local rivers and lakes and causing eutrophication.

Element	*Function in plant*	*Deficiency symptoms*
Nitrogen	growth, proteins & nucleic acids	stunted growth, yellow leaves
Phosphorus	nucleic acids, ATP, membranes	poor root growth, blue-green colour to leaves
Potassium	Enzyme activator	Poor flowering; susceptible to disease;brown edges to leaves
Iron	Manufacture of chlorophyll	white veins in young leaves
Magnesium	contained in chlorophyll	yellowing with green veins on old leaves
Sulphur	amino acids (and flavours in onions, garlic etc)	yellowing and stunting of plant in spring

They are also expensive. An alternative solution, which does less harm to the environment, is the use of organic fertilisers, such as animal manure (farmyard manure or FYM), composted vegetable matter, crop residues, and sewage sludge. These contain the main elements found in inorganic fertilisers (NPK), but in organic compounds such as urea, cellulose, lipids and organic acids. Of course plants cannot make use of these organic materials in the soil: their roots can only take up inorganic mineral ions such as nitrate, phosphate and potassium. But the organic compounds can be digested by soil organisms such as animals, fungi and bacteria, who then release inorganic ions that the plants can use Some advantages of organic fertilisers are:

Since the compounds in organic fertilisers are less soluble than those in inorganic fertilisers, the inorganic minerals are released more slowly as they are decomposed. This prevents leaching and means they last longer. The organic wastes need to be disposed of anyway, so they are cheap. Furthermore, spreading on to fields means they will not be dumped in landfill sites, where they may have caused uncontrolled leaching. The organic material improves soil structure by binding soil particles together and provides food for soil organisms such as earthworms.

This improves drainage and aeration. Some disadvantages are that they are bulky and less concentrated in minerals than inorganic fertilisers, so more needs to be spread on a field to have a similar effect. They may contain unwanted substances such as weed seeds, fungal spores, heavy metals. They are also very smelly! Increasing the amount of fertiliser increases yield, but only up to a point:

PROBLEMS WITH FERTILISERS

This is the process that takes place when freshwater is 'enriched' by nutrients, especially nitrates and phosphates.The aquatic ecosystems naturally progress from being oligotrophic (clean water with few nutrients and algae) to eutrophic (murky water with many nutrients and plants) and sometimes to hypertrophic (a swamp with a mass of plants and detritus). This is in fact a common example of succession.

In the context of pollution "eutrophication" has come to mean a sudden and dramatic increase in nutrients due to human activity, which disturbs and eventually destroys the food chain. The main causes are fertilisers leaching off farm fields into the surrounding water course, and sewage (liquid waste from houses and factories).

These both contain dissolved minerals, such as nitrates and phosphates, which enrich the water. Subsequently, this may lead to excessive plant growth ('algal blooms') and this, in turn, can lead to the deoxygenation of the water and the death of much of the animal life. In cold Arctic waters this does not happen, though the water may still have high mineral content and so be eutrophic.The main source of nitrogen is farming – either nitrates (from fertiliser over-use) or urea (from over-use of slurry/manure).

Correct timing of fertiliser application can reduce these problems. Cold soils prevent crops absorbing nutrients, so there is no point applying them in winter or cold spring weather. Heavy rain leads to the nutrients being washing into groundwater before the plants have had a chance to absorb them; so do not apply if heavy rainfall is forecast.The main source of phosphates is sewage. Phosphates are added to detergents to improve washing performance – particularly in hard water areas. Sewage is also warm too, so the combined effect on plant growth downstream is quite marked. Aeration of the sewage outfall (by weirs or spraying) will increase oxygen levels and improve water quality for animal life, but do nothing to the mineral load added to the water.

9

Benefit of Forest Products

PRODUCTION FORESTRY IN INDIAPRODUCTION FORESTRY IN INDIA

DEFINITIONS

In the context of the current study, production forestry may be understood to be the raising of block plantations on private lands, leased forest lands or leased community lands with the following purposes:

- Supply of timber as raw material to wood-based industry, and
- Supply of fuelwood/small timber for mitigation of the huge demand-supply gap in energy needs in rural areas.

The size or the ownership pattern of the land in question may vary. It may be useful to consider the following additional definitions (and explanatory notes) by Food and Agriculture Organization (FAO), Rome for a better understanding of production forestry.

FOREST

Land spanning more than 0.5 hectares (ha) with trees higher than 5 metres (m) and a canopy cover of more than 10 percent, or trees able to reach these thresholds in situ. It does not include land that is predominantly under agricultural or urban land use.

Explanatory notes:

- Forest is determined both by the presence of trees and the absence of other predominant land uses. The trees should be able to reach a minimum height of 5 m in situ. Areas under reforestation that have not yet reached but are expected to reach a canopy cover of 10 percent and a tree height of 5 m are included, as are temporarily unstocked areas, resulting from human intervention or natural causes, which are expected to regenerate.
- Includes areas with bamboo and palms provided that the criteria of height and canopy cover are met.

- Includes forest roads, firebreaks and other small open areas; forest in national parks, nature reserves and other protected areas such as those of specific scientific, historical, cultural or spiritual interest.
- Includes windbreaks, shelterbelts and corridors of trees with an area of more than 0.5 ha and width of more than 20 m.
- Includes plantations primarily used for forestry or protection purposes, such as rubber-wood plantations and cork oak stands.
- Excludes tree stands in agricultural production systems, for example in fruit plantations and agroforestry systems. The term also excludes trees in urban parks and gardens.

OTHER WOODED LAND

Land not classified as Forest, spanning more than 0.5 ha; with trees higher than 5 m and a canopy cover of 5-10 percent, or trees able to reach these thresholds in situ; or with a combined cover of shrubs, bushes and trees above 10 percent. It does not include land that is predominantly under agricultural or urban land use.

Production

Forest/Other wooded land designated for production and extraction of forest goods, including both wood and non-wood forest products.

Production Forest

Forest actually designated for production of forest goods i.e. where the extraction of forest products, usually wood and fibre, are the predominant management objective. It includes both wood and non wood forest products.

Productive Plantation

Forest/Other wooded land of introduced species and in some cases native species, established through planting or seeding mainly for production of wood or non wood goods.

Explanatory notes:

- Includes all stands of introduced species established for production of wood or non-wood goods.
- May include areas of native species characterized by few species, straight tree lines and/or even-aged stands.

The second set of definitions are borrowed from common technical parlance, with special reference to what is in vogue in entities in the wood-based industry, such as paper mills.

Farm Forestry

The practice of raising trees as crop, to primarily harvest and sell the timber without reference to the size of the holding(s).

Agroforestry

The practice of growing timber along with pure agricultural food and cash crop species and/or horticultural species Finally, terms such as industrial plantations and tree farming are also to be found in the literature in this domain.

FOREST PRODUCTS: WOOD & CORK

Forest products have been of service to humans from the very beginnings of our history. The most familiar, and the most important, of these products is wood. Wood is used in all types of construction, as a fuel and as a raw material of the paper and rayon industries. Other products include rubber, cork, many of our tanning materials and dyes, resins gums, oils, drugs and even sugar, starch and some chemicals. Additionally, the seeds and fruits of many trees may serve as food for humans or their livestock. In addition to being of value to humans, forests themselves have many utilitarian features. They help to regulate climate and temperature. They aid in the conservation of the water supply and in flood control by preventing water runoff. Their roots hold the soil firmly in place and control erosion. They may also act as shelter area against drying winds. They afford a range for livestock, a shelter for wild life and offer many recreational aspects for humans, the importance of which cannot be underestimated.

FOREST PRODUCTS AS FUEL

Fuel is an indispensable necessity of life both in home and industry. Any material that burns readily in air can be utilized, but this includes a great variety of plant products. The most important of these are wood, peat and coal, which represent different stages in the carbonization of the original plant tissue.

WOOD

Farms and rural communities have accounted for about 90 percent of the total amount of wood used for fuel. Wood makes an excellent fuel because it is about 99 percent combustible when dry and so leaves only a small amount of ash. It is also flaming fuel and well adapted for heating large surfaces. The value of different kinds of wood for heating purposes depends on the amount of moisture present. Therefore, seasoned wood is better than green wood. Hardwoods have the greatest fuel value, particularly such woods as hickory, eucalyptus, oak, beech, birch, maple and ash. Longleaf pine in the southern United States is mainly used while in the western area Douglas fir, western yellow pine, western hemlock and western larch are used.

PEAT

Peat is made up of deposits of vegetable matter that have accumulated in swamps and bogs and slowly decomposed, becoming somewhat carbonized and compacted. The various plant tissues can still be discerned. The process of peat formation is continuous, and peat is a valuable fuel in countries where wood is scarce. It is more bulky to manipulate and leaves from 5-15 times as much ash. At the lower depths of some peat bogs a soft brown coal called lignite may be found. This also has the original plant structures still visible.

COAL

Coal comprises the fossilized remains of plants that lived in former geological periods. The original plant tissue has been more fully decomposed and converted into carbon. Coal is much harder and more compact than peat or lignite, and has a greater heating power. It also yields a larger amount of smoke and ash. Anthracite or hard coals are the oldest and contain about 95 percent carbon. Bituminous or soft coals are more recent in origin and thus are less completely carbonized.

They tend to soften and fuse at temperatures below the combustion point. Cannel coal consists of fossilized spores. It is very compact and oily and burns with a candle like flame. Unlike other coals it does not soil in one's hands. Coal is a comparatively inexpensive source of power and heat and also of many useful chemical products.

Among the latter, which are obtained by destructive distillation, are oils, such as benzol and naphtha; coal gas that is used for fuel and illuminating purposes; ammonia; coal tar, the source of dyes, antiseptics and many other materials; and coke Coke bears the same relationship to coal that charcoal does to wood. It is obtained by the smothered combustion of coal in piles or special ovens, usually as a by-product of the illuminating-gas industry. It is almost pure carbon and burns without smoke or flame. Coke is an excellent fuel that is especially used in metallurgy.

PETROLEUM

There are no traces of the original structure present in petroleum, and it has been generally believed that petroleum had an organic origin and was formed under pressure from the minute floating plant and animal life of former shallow seas. Crude petroleum has many uses, but the substances derived from it by fractional distillation are of much greater importance. Among these products are gasoline, kerosene, plastics, petroleum jelly, medicines and paraffin.

LUMBER

Lumber from wood has been in use for building purposes and other construction since early times. In the United States the first sawmill was established in Maine in 1631. Thereafter a huge industry has developed. The word "lumber" refers to wood that has been prepared to some extent for future use. The larger pieces of lumber that are used in heavy construction are often called "timber." The standard unit of measuring lumber is the board foot, which is the equivalent of a piece of wood 1 in. thick, 12 in. wide and 1 ft. long.

LUMBER INDUSTRY

The location of the lumber industry and species utilized are usually in constant change. In the United States it has always been in a region where large stands of virgin timber were available. Until 1830 the state of Maine was the main lumber-producing area, and for the next 40 years New York and Pennsylvania took the lead. By 1870 the center shifted to the Lake States, with first Michigan and later Wisconsin. After 1910 the Southern states became the leading producers, with southern pine replacing the northern hardwoods and white pine. Then the center moved to the Pacific Northwest and began utilizing the immense stands of Douglas fir and other softwoods. The Southern states continue to produce most lumber, although Washington and Oregon are still prime providers.There have been over 150 native American species utilized in the lumber industry.

However, the softwoods have furnished about 78 percent of all the lumber cut. For many years the eastern white pine, Pinus strobes, was the outstanding timber tree and this was one of the most valuable trees in the world. The demand for white pine was so great that the supply soon became diminished and was eventually replaced by other species. Oak and hemlock have also had a prominent role. By the end of the 20thCentury the most important tree species were southern yellow pine, Douglas fir, western yellow pine, oak hemlock, white pine and red gum. Douglas fir and yellow pine produce twice as much as all the other combined. Many woods that at one time were considered worthless have later become important. Examples include sycamore, beech, red gum and tupelo.

LUMBER UTILIZATION

Usually about eight percent of the lumber cut each year is exported; 32 percent is used for structural timbers and rough lumber for construction; 33 percent goes to the planning mills and 27 percent is used in other woodworking industries.

Export Lumber

Lumber has been an important North American foreign trade since the early days of European colonization The demand for American timber has been especially great in Japan.

Structural Timbers

These are the large sizes of lumber from sawmills that are used for buildings, bridges and other types of heavy construction. They include girders, stringers, beams, joists, rafters, posts, caps, planks, caps, roofing, boards for sheathing, and flooring. In the early days before steel, immense quantities of heavy timbers were used in ship building.

Structural timbers are obtained mainly from the softwoods because large sizes are readily available. The timbers are usually sawed from the heart of the tree, and even though defects may be present, the bulk is so massive that the strength is not impaired. Strength is the main requirement of a good structural timber, especially the resistance to stresses that can be estimated. Numerous timber testing experiments have made possible the estimation of the working stresses with great accuracy.

Durability, soundness and ease of working are other desirable qualities. The main species used in the United States for structural timbers are southern yellow pine, eastern white pine, hemlock, Douglas fir, western yellow pine, spruce, redwood and larch.

SH] Planing-mill Products

These are usually associated with sawmills and they use a large amount of lumber representing over 60 different species. Their products are sometimes classified as "factory lumber," that is lumber which has been recut to smaller dimensions and reworked.

The principal products of the planning mills are doors, sashes, window frames, blinds and interior finishes. The best wood for millwork has a straight grain and a soft uniform texture. It should not shrink or swell and it should be easy to work and capable of taking varnishes and paints. The less expensive products are made from white pine, Douglas fir, yellow pine and other softwoods. Expensive items include birch, oak, red gum, maple, walnut, mahogany and other hardwoods with a fine figure.

Veneers are now being used extensively for door panels. Interior finishes include baseboards, columns, cornices, mantels, grills, stair work, posts, balusters, scrollwork, porch work and trimming. Most of the North American and imported woods that are decorative and have good wearing qualities are used for these purposes.

A more recent development of the planning mills has been hardwood flooring. Only the most durable woods that also have attractive designs are used. These are kiln dried and seasoned. The woods used include beech, maple, oak, tupelo, birch and yellow pine.

Other Woodworking Industries

There are numerous industries that have many variable requirements and products. Most use only a relatively small amount of wood, but a few of the more important industries include railroad car, box and crate, furniture, vehicle, agricultural implement and woodenware industries.

H] BOXES & CRATES

Items such as crates, baskets, boxes and other containers are used for the transport of canned goods, farm products and many other articles. For box-making the wood should be light, east to work, strong, with good nail-holding power and a surface that can be printed upon. Lower grades of softwood lumber and the softer hardwoods are mainly used. The principal species are southern pine, western yellow pine, red gum, hemlock, white pine and spruce.

FURNITURE & FIXTURES

This requires wood of special hardness, strength and durability. It should not shrink or warp, and must be ornamental and capable of a high polish. Birch, Maple, Oak, Red Gum, Walnut are the principal species, although chestnut, beech, Elm, tulip and basswood are also used.

A large number of imported woods that have attractive color or figure are utilized also. There have been over 60 species used. Veneers are of increasing importance for they can be used to cover less expensive and less attractive woods.

H] RAILROAD CARS

There has been a lot of lumber used annually for the construction of railroad cars with over 40 different species of wood being used. Oak, Maple, Hemlock, Cypress and several ornamental species are of some importance although Yellow Pine and Douglass Fir have been used the most. By the 21st Century railroad cars have begun to be constructed with plastic walls and that has greatly diminished the need for wood in this industry.

H] VEHICLES

Wood was used extensively in the manufacture of vehicles in the first half of the 20th Century, but has been largely substituted by plastic in the 21st Century.

Misc. Industries

Other industries using wood during the industrial age have been agricultural implements, caskets, coffins, refrigerators, kitchen cabinets, ship and boat building, matches, woodenware and novelties, musical instruments, tanks and silos, signs and supplies, professional and scientific instruments, electrical machinery and apparatus, machine construction, toys, laundry appliances, handles, supplies for dairymen, poultrymen and beekeepers, tobacco boxes, patterns and flasks, sporting and athletic goods, boot and shoe findings, shade and map rollers, brooms and carpet sweepers, picture frames and moldings, motion-picture and theatrical scenery, brushes, plumber's woodwork, shuttles, spools and bobbins, trunks and valises, sewing machines, pumps, wood pipe and conduits, airplanes, toothpicks, printing materials, playground equipment, dowels, clocks, paving materials, saddles and harness, gates and fencing, butcher blocks and skewers, bungs and faucets, firearms, scales, elevators, whips, canes and umbrellas, tobacco pipes and artificial limbs. By the 21st Century either metal or plastics have substituted most of these.

POSTS

Fence posts are used mainly on farms and along roads and railroad right of ways. The old rail fences have almost disappeared. Posts are usually cut 7 feet in length and from 4-6 inches in thickness. They are used in the round or are split. Strength, light weight and durability in the soil and w4eather are the main requirements. Woods that have been utilized for posts are mainly cedar, redwood, chestnut, oak, tamarack, black locust, ash, osage orange and cypress. Posts are usually treated with preservatives before being placed into the ground.

MINE TIMBERS

There is much wood used in mines for shafts and for supporting structures, including collars, caps and props. Of particular importance for safety are strength and durability, and the wood is used in an environment that is conducive to decay. Woods that are normally used for this purpose are pine, oak, tamarack, chestnut, beech hemlock, maple and Douglas fir. These timbers rarely enter the trade for most of the supply is obtained locally from whatever is available.

POLES & PILING

Many poles are used annually to suspend electricity, telegraph and power-transmission lines. Similar amounts are used for work in harbors including trestle and bridge construction. These poles are used in the round and because they are prone to decay at ground level, only those species with durable sapwood are preferred.

These are also treated with preservatives. Strength, light weight and accessibility are prime qualities, and shape is also important. In addition to these stated requirements, pilings must be able to withstand heavy top loads and can withstand blows as they are pounded into the ground. Species preferred are lodgepole pine, Douglas fir, southern pines and cedar. Sometimes chestnut, cypress, oak, larch, redwood, locust and elm are also used.

CHARCOAL & WOOD DISTILLATION

H] WOOD CHARCOAL

Wood has been heated in order to convert it into carbon or charcoal since ancient times. It was probably the first chemical process used by humans. Charcoal is still a valuable fuel as it has twice the heating power of wood and burns without flame or smoke. It is widely used in many European, Asian and Latin American countries, especially where forests are abundant and is the chief domestic fuel in most tropical countries. Charcoal is also used in medicine, as a reducing element in the iron and steel industry, and in the manufacture of chemicals, explosives, gunpowder and some cosmetics. It is the best material for absorbing impurities and foul odors from both water and the atmosphere. It has been used extensively in gas masks. The best yields of charcoal are obtained from the denser hardwoods, such as maple, beech, birch, oak, hickory and mesquite.

Willow charcoal is especially popular for explosives. The conversion of wood into charcoal was formerly accomplished in open-air pits by a process of partial combustion. This method is wasteful as all the volatile material contained in the wood is lost. Beehive kilns and portable ovens have also been used. By the 21st Century charcoal burning has been largely replaced by wood distillation, and the valuable gases and other by-products are recovered as well as the charcoal.

WOOD DISTILLATION

This process is very old and was known to the ancient Egyptians. It is today important not only in rendering available the volatile wood elements, but as a factor in forest conservation. One of the main sources of wood for destructive distillation is the waste left by lumbering operations, sawmills, and planning mills. There are two distinct types of wood distillation.

Hardwood Distillation

This process uses the denser and heavier hardwoods and has been in use since the beginning of the 19th Century. The wood is heated in large oven retorts. The immediate products are charcoal, pyroligneous acid, which condenses from some of the gases given off, tar and oil, and noncondensable wood gases. The tar and oils are allowed to settle out and the pyroligneous acid is passed through a series of stills where more tar and oils are removed. Eventually slaked lime is added and in a final distillation wood alcohol (methanol) passes off and acetate of lime is left as a residue. A modification of the process results in the recovery of acetic acid directly from the pyroligneous acid. The average yield per cord is 900-1080 lbs of charcoal, 180-200 lbs. Of acetate of lime or 103-125 lbs. Of acetic acid, 9.5-11 gallons of wood alcohol, 22-25 gallons of wood tar and oils, and 7,000-11,500 cubic feet of wood gas. Acetate of lime is used primarily in the manufacture of acetic acid, which has wide applications in the paint, textile, leather, film and plastics industries, and acetone, which is extensively used as a solvent. Wood alcohol finds it greatest use as a solvent, especially in the varnish and paint industry; it is the source of a variety of chemical products as well, such as aniline dyes and formaldehyde. It has a variety of uses as a fuel, illuminant, denaturant and ingredients of medical, chemical and other industrial preparations. The wood tar and oils are used as a fuel or as the source of many industrial oils. Wood gas also serves as a fuel and may be converted into a substitute for gasoline.

Softwood Distillation

This utilizes resinous woods, mainly southern yellow pine. The products are charcoal, wood turpentine, oils, and tar and wood gas. Softwood pyroligneous acid contains only small amounts of wood alcohol and acetic acid. The wood turpentine is used to some extent in the manufacture of varnishes, paints and synthetic camphor. The tar and oils also have industrial uses, one important product being creosote.

USES FOR WOOD

Wood is also used as a raw material for the paper and textile industries and as a source of tanning and dye materials, food, alcohol and other products.

CORK

This is a forest product of great antiquity. It is obtained commercially mainly from the cork oak, Quercus suber, a tree native to the Mediterranean region. This oak varies from 20-60 ft. tall and about 4 ft. in diameter, with a short trunk and densely spreading crown. The evergreen leaves resemble those of holly, but are velvety and spongy. The acorns are used to feed pigs. The cork oak ranges from the Atlantic to Asia Minor and is especially numerous in Spain, Portugal, Algeria, Tunisia, southern France, Italy, Morocco and Corsica. The tree thrives on rocky siliceous soil on the lower slopes of mountains. Cork or corkwood consists of the outer bark of the tree, which can be harvested without injury to the tree. It is renewed annually. Harvesting consists of making vertical and horizontal cuts with hatchets or saws, and then prying off large pieces of the bark.

The rich dark-red color of the exposed areas is one of the typical sights in a cork forest that is being used for commercial purposes. The stripping is usually done in midsummer when weather conditions are favorable. The bark of both the trunk and larger branches is usually used, although in some countries the cutting area is restricted to the first 6 feet of the trunk. Cork is first removed when the trees are about 20 years old. This first yield, which is known as virgin cork, is very rough and coarse and of little value. Subsequent strippings occur every nine years. The second yield is better, but the best quality of cork is not obtained until the third cutting and thereafter. The trees live for 100-

500-years.and give an average yield of 40-500 lbs per tree. The best grade of cork consists of inch-thick layers obtained from young vigorous trees. The stripped pieces of cork are dried for several days and weighed and then shipped to a processing area.

They are then boiled in large copper vats. This removes the sap and tannic acid, increases the volume and elasticity, and flattens the pieces. It also loosens the outermost layer, which is scraped off. The rough edges are trimmed and the flat pieces are sorted and baled. Cork has many properties that make it valuable in industry. Despite its bulk, it is very light and exceedingly buoyant due to the fact that it is composed entirely of dead watertight cells. It can be readily compressed and is very resilient. Even after 10 years of use cork stoppers can recover 7s5 percent of the original volume. It is durable, a low heat conductor, and is resistant to the passage of moisture and liquids. It also absorbs sounds and vibration and has certain frictional properties.

Uses of Cork

A great variety of products are manufactured from cork. Sometimes the natural cork is utilized; in other cases composition cork, made of coarse or finely ground pieces treated with adhesives and molded. Articles that have been made from natural cork include bottle stoppers, hats and helmets for use in tropical areas, tips for cigarettes, carburetor floats, handles for golf clubs, penholders, fishing rods, mooring buoys, floats, life preservers, life jackets, surf balls, baseball centers, decoys, mats, tiles, etc. Corkboard, made by heating natural cork, is used as an insulating material for houses, cold-storage plants, and refrigerators. It serves as a means of improving the acoustics of rooms and rendering them soundproof. It is very resilient and thus is a valuable material for machinery isolation. Composition cork is used for the lining of crown caps, the metal tops for sealing bottles, gaskets, toes, counters, and innersoles for shoes, polishing wheels, friction rolls, and several types of floor covering. Linoleum is made from cork or wood flour, linseed oil, resins, such as rosin or kauri gum, pigments, and burlap.

The oil is boiled and allowed to solidify by dripping on pieces of cloth. The solidified oil is ground up and melted with resins. This mixture is cooled and hardened, and after several days of curing it is mixed with the work, which has been ground to a fine dust, and with the dry color pigments. It is then pressed into burlap cloth with hydraulic presses. The linoleum is then seasoned in ovens and finished by giving it a protective surface of nitrocellulose lacquer. Linotiles are individual tiles made from ground cork and linseed oil, but much thicker and denser than linoleum.

COOPERAGE

The manufacture of wooden containers bound together with hoops of wood is an old industry that dates to Biblical and Roman times. However, production has been in a steady decline through the 20th Century due to the competition from other types of containers. Two main classes of cooperate are slack cooperage, to hold dry substances, and tight cooperage, to hold liquids.

SLACK COOPERAGE

This includes a great variety of barrels, casks, tubs, pails, buckets, churns, kegs and other containers. They have been used to transport meat, fish, tobacco, fruit, flour, vegetables, cement, sugar, glassware, crockery and etc. A single barrel usually consists of 15 staves, one set of heading and six hoops. These various parts may be manufactured in different factories and regions. There are many grades of slack cooperage that ranges from sugar and flour barrels, with tongued and grooved staves, to the loose-fitting and less expensive cement barrels. Wood to make slack cooperage should be inexpensive, easy to work, light, elastic and free from twisting and warping. Limbs, tops, defective logs and other forms of waste lumber may be used. Veneers have been used to some extent. Heads and staves are usually made from pine, red gum, beech, maple, oak, Douglas Fir and ash.

TIGHT COOPERAGE

Kegs and barrels to be used for containers for beer, oil, wine and other liquids require more careful construction. Woods that will impart no taste or odor to the liquids and which are impermeable are essential. White oak has been the main wood used, especially when the liquids are to remain the barrels for a long time. Red oak, red gum, yellow birch, white ash, sugar maple and Douglas fir are frequently used. The finished product is then usually treated on the inside with paraffin to insure that no leakage will occur. The hoops are mainly of strap steel.

HEAVY COOPERAGE

Vats and large tanks constitute heavy cooperage. They are made with staves and heads of white oak, cypress, Douglas fir or redwood and bound together with metal straps.

RAILROAD TIES

The average life of an untreated railroad tie is only 5-6 years, so that the demand continues for replacement ties. These are usually hewn from a seasoned wood but they may be sawed. Strength, durability in the soil and the ability to resist impact, crushing and spike pulling are important traits. Treated ties are just as serviceable as those made from naturally durable woods. Most ties in North America are made from southern pine, red gum, oak and Douglas fir. Other species include cedar, chestnut, cypress, maple, beech, tamarack and hemlock.

VENEERS

These are thin slices or sheets of wood with a uniform thickness. Although they may be cut as thin as 1/110th inch, the commercial product is usually about 1/20th in. thick, with 3/8th in being maximum. Veneers were known to the early civilizations of Rome and Egypt, but in America their use was retarded for many years because wood was so abundant and inexpensive. To make veneers the logs or pieces of wood are peeled, boiled and then cut with a knife. The rotary process prepares most.

This involves turning a log on a lathe against a stationary knife that produces a continuous sheet of veneer. The design in this type of veneer is not particularly striking because the sheet is cut parallel to the annual rings. In the slicing process the logs are quarter sawed and thus show a more attractive grain.

The logs are first quartered and then sliced with a stationary knife to yield separate sheets. This process is less wasteful and is used for the more expensive kinds of wood. In the sawing process the quartered logs are cut with a circular saw.

Although the veneers thus produced are thicker, the most valuable woods are sawed because the fibers do not tare and the material can be more readily worked. Freshly cut veneers are usually wet and must be thoroughly dried before adhesives can be applied. Veneers were used primarily only to cover up inferior woods in the furniture and cabinet industries. They were made primarily from walnut, mahogany and other woods that had a beautiful color and grain.

By the end of the 20th Century many species were being used and the veneers were utilized in the manufacture of baskets, boxes, cooperage, door panels, trunks, mirrors, musical instruments, etc. Veneers make possible high strength and minimum weight.

Any wood is suitable that comes in large sizes, has a symmetrical grain and design and few defects and is inexpensive. A variety of both domestic and foreign woods are used, but more than one-half of the total output in North America is made from either Douglas fir or red gum. There are three kinds of hardwood veneers manufactured. Face veneers are sliced or sawed from selected logs and are used for only the finest work. Primary among native species are black walnut, quartered red and white oak, red gum and sugar maple. Commercial veneers are rotary-cut and are used for plywood, concealed parts of furniture, etc.

Birch, Maple, Beech, basswood, tulip, tupelo, cottonwood, sycamore and oak have all be used.

Container veneers are the least expensive and are made from any inexpensive wood into barrels, crates, boxes, etc. Softwood veneers, either rotary-cut or sliced, are made primarily on the Pacific Cost. Over 80 percent are made from Douglas fir, but Sitka spruce, western yellow pine and Port Orford cedar have been used. Softwood veneers are for structural plywood or interior paneling.

PLYWOOD

This involves gluing together 3-9 thin veneers. The grain of each successive layer is at an angle to the next, so the strength is redistributed and the dimensional instability of one layer is compensated for and reduced by the others.

Thus, the finished produce is very strong and stable and much less likely to warp or twist than ordinary wood. Screws and nails may be driven close to the edge with no danger of splitting the plywood. In the manufacture of a 5-ply plywood panel, the face, back, cross band and core sheets are prepared. Applying an adhesive and pressing the glued stock into a panel and finally drying and finishing the product follow this.

Softer woods are usually used because they can be glued more easily. One simple kind of plywood has a 3/8^{ths} inch core of poplar with 1/10th inch birch veneers on each side. Various plant and animal adhesives are used as well as large quantities of synthetic resins. Modifications of the ordinary process result in molded or curved plywood and in wood alloys. Plywood is recognized as an engineering material with its own peculiar properties. It has extensive uses in the home for doors, flooring, walls, partitions, cabinets, shelves, furniture and interior trim. Large quantities have been used also to make concrete forms, prefabricated houses, airplanes, boats, railroad cars and the bodies of trailers and station wagons.

WOOD ALLOYS

In making wood alloys or densified wood, such as uralloy, compreg and impreg, from plywood the natural wood structure is impregnated with synthetic resins and bonded under high pressure. The resins establish strong physical and chemical bonds with the wood fibers and create a material with new properties, which is also very strong, stable, hard and resistant to decay.

RECONSTRUCTED WOOD

This is characterized by a reorganization of the fibers where they are taken out of their original unidirectional grain and rearranged in multidirectional patterns. This may be accomplished by chemical or physical means. An example of a wood that has been reconstructed by physical means is Masonite. Wood chips are subjected to high pressure in a steam vessel and are then exploded with the abrupt release of the pressure. This tears the fibers apart and also reactivates the lignin, a natural plastic, which fixes and binds the fibers in their new orientation. At first Masonite was used as an insulating fiberboard because it was an excellent insulator against heat, sound and electricity. Then it was learned that the application of heat and pressure converted the boards into a homogeneous grainless synthetic board with extreme hardness and water resistance.

SHINGLES & SHAKES

WOOD SHINGLES

Shingles are thin pieces of wood used to protect the roofs and sides of buildings from weathering. Handmade shingles rank among the first of the wood products manufactured by humans. Single wood must be durable, light in weight, easy to split and able to hold nails without loosening, and it must not warp.

Straight, even-grained woods are preferred. The durability of shingles is increased by treatment with a preservative. Red cedar has been the preferred wood in North America. Northern white and southern white cedars, redwood and cypress are also used. If available, eastern white pine is an excellent material.

By the 21stCentury many substitutes entered the market that were longer lasting and less fire prone. However, the lighter weight of shingles make them less expensive to install on existing roofs and aeration is superior to synthetic products, especially in warmer climates.

WOOD SHAKES

Shakes are split shingles and much thicker. They were important in colonial times, but now are used primarily for special architectural effects and in more remote regions. In North America red cedar, sugar pine and redwood are widely used.

EXCELSIOR

This consists of thin curled strands or shreds of wood and is made by placing wood on frames and pressing it against rapidly moving knives or steel teeth. The material was first known as wood fiber. Excelsior is light and elastic and makes an excellent material for packing and shipping glassware and other breakable articles. It is resilient and free from dust and dirt, and may be used for stuffing upholstery and mattresses. A very fine grade of excelsior, wood wool, is used in filters and in the manufacture of matting and rugs. The use of excelsior has steadily decreased as synthetic plastics became available as packaging materials.

SAWDUST & SHAVINGS

Sawdust is used primarily for fuel, usually in the form of briquettes or fireplace logs. It is also valuable for many industrial purposes. It serves as a bedding for kennels and stables, as a floor covering to absorb moisture, for cleaning, drying and polishing metal, as a packing medium, as a soil conditioner and an insulating material. It has played a part in the making of leather and the conditioning of fur and is an ingredient of composition flooring, artificial wood, abrasives, wallboard, floor-sweeping compounds, etc. Shavings find their greatest use as fuel and as packing material. White pine shavings are especially desirable.

WOOD FLOUR

This consists of finely ground sawdust, shavings and other forms of wood waste that has been used in the manufacture of linoleum, plastics, nitroglycerin, veneer bonds, composition flooring, insulating brick, etc. It is used as filler, an absorbent or a mild abrasive. Light colored woods with low resin content are used. White pine has been the main species.

10

Oils Products

ORIGIN OF ESSENTIAL OILS

Essential oils are found in many different parts of the plant.

The following list names some common essential oils and the part of the plant where they can be found:

- Sandalwood- wood
- Geranium- leaves
- Lavender- flowering tops
- Lemon- fruit rind
- Rose, Jasmine- flowers
- Juniper- berries
- Frankincense- gum
- Carrot- seeds
- Ginger- roots

Usually, there is only one essential oil in each plant. However, there are plants which have more than one essential oil in their different parts - fruit, leaves, flowers. The popular example is the Bitter Orange tree (*Citrus aurantium*), which has Bitter Orange oil from the fruit rind, Petitgrain oil from the leaves, and Neroli oil from the flowers.

Not all plants contain essential oils. Of the many thousands that do, only around 200 essential oils are produced commercially for use.

Essential oils are rarely produced solely for aromatherapy use. In fact, aromatherapy use accounts for less than 5% of the world oil production. The main uses are perfumes, food, fruit juices, alcoholic beverages, confectionary, cosmetics, pharmaceutical preparations, and everyday use items such as shampoos and soap. In some cases the complete essential oil is used (Bergamot in Earl Grey tea) and in other cases, one or more constituents are used (menthol from Peppermint oil).

Essential oils, also known as 'volatile oils.' are odoriferous substances widely distributed throughout the plant kingdom. They occur in some 60 plant families and almost any part of a plant may yield oil.

QUANTITY AND STABILITY OF EXTRACTION

Depending on the quantity and stability of the compound, essential oils are mainly extracted by three methods:

i. Distillation by hot water or steam
ii. Pressed by hand or using machinery
iii. Extraction using such volatile solvents as hot oils, fats (maceration), or cold neutral fats (effleurage)

ODOUR AND HIGH VOLATILITY OF ESSENTIAL OILS

Because of their odour and high volatility, essential oils have a variety of uses, for example, soaps and cosmetics, pharmaceuticals, confectionery, aerated water, scented tobacco and incense, among others.

ESSENTIAL OILS THE SAME AS THE PLANT (HERB)

Essential oil actions are often assumed to be the same as the plant (herb) they come from. This is often not the case as the essential oil only contains some of the many constituents in the plant. Therefore, the essential oil will only have some of the healing properties of the whole plant. However, because an essential oil is a concentrated extract from the plant, it is a more powerful substance and, unlike herbs, is only used in very small quantities (drops).

PLANT SPECIES

There are many different species or varieties of each plant. For example, there are several hundred different varieties of Lavender. Only one or two specific species of each plant are cultivated for their essential oil. Generally, these species are not the ones you will find growing in your back yard or available from the local garden centre. The species of the plant is identified by the Latin botanical name written after the English common name (Lavender *Lavandula angustifolia*). Some plants share a common English name, but the botanical name will identify the plant species.

Species identification is very important for aromatherapy as different botanical species of plants have different healing properties. Not only can a different species have different healing properties, it can have no healing properties at all and can even cause a problem if used. An example is Marjoram - one species provides an effective treatment for insomnia, another is likely to cause significant skin irritation and be mentally stimulating....hardly conducive to a good nights sleep.

PRODUCT DESCRIPTION AND APPLICATION

The essential oil of orange has a dominant volatile component, limonene, about 90%. In addition, citral, citronellal and methyl anthranilate are parts of the essential oil. The essential oil of orange is used in beverages, ice creams, perfumes and cosmetics. Orange oil is a resource based product that will substitute import with export potential.

MARKET STUDY AND PLANT CAPACITY

Orange oil is used as a flavoring agent in deserts, soft drinks, ice creams and odorants in perfumery and cosmetics. The local demand for orange oil is met through imports. In order to determine the current effective demand for essential oil of orange, the imported quantity of essential oils of orange and other essential oils of a kind used in non alcoholic drink industries and in preparation of flavoring food.

Table : Import of Essential Oil of Orange and Other Essential Oils Used in Non Alcoholic Drinks and Flavoring Food

Year	Quantity (kg)
2000	279,069
2001	353,601
2002	478,172
2003	521,573
2004	616,090
2005	830,799
2006	964,083

As could be seen from Table import of essential oils of orange and other essential oils used in non-alcoholic beverages and in preparation of flavoring food has been increasing from year to year. The amount of import which was 279,069 kg during year 2000 has increased to 521,573 kg and 964,083 kg by the year 2003 and 2006, respectively. Annual average growth rate during the past seven years was more than 20%.

Since the consumption of the product in the past seven years has been annually increasing by about 20% current effective demand is estimated at 1,157 tons by taking year 2006 as a base.

Demand Projection

The demand for essential oils of orange will increase with the expansion and establishment of the food and soft drinks industries. Due to the favorable climate created for domestic and foreign investors a number of food and soft drinks factories are in pipe line for establishment. Although the demand for the product has been increasing by more than 20% in the past seven years a conservative growth rate of 8% is taken to project the future demand.

Table : Projected Demand For Essential Oil Of Orange (Ton)

Year	Quantity (kg)
2008	1,250
2009	1,350
2010	1,457
2011	1,574

2012	1,700
2013	1,836
2014	1,983
2015	2,142
2016	2,313
2017	2,498

Pricing and Distribution

Based on Customs Authority data (year2006) a factory gate price of Birr 120 per k.g is recommended. The product can be sold directly to the end users mainly for food and soft drinks factories.

ECONOMICS OF ESSENTIAL OILS

The economics working behind essential oils has three components. First, the cultivation of herbs and plants used to extract essential oils; second, the actual process of extraction of the oils; and, third, the marketing and actual sale of these oils. Different plants have different oil content and they differ in their sales also. For example, according to the National Institute for Chemical Pharmaceutical Research and Development, Romania, world production of coriander oil in 2003 was estimated at £6 million and the essential oil content of dried coriander is 0.15% to 1.7%. In contrast, market for lavender oil was estimated at £5 million and the essential oil content of the two types of lavender varies between 0.55% and 1.5%.

There is major emphasis laid on the cultivation aspect as the subsequent yield of essential oils depend entirely on the quality of cultivation. According to a report of the NRDC published in the early years of this decade, the cost of cultivation of herbs in developing countries per hectare comes to around US$ 500 to 1,000. In comparison, revenue per hectare is estimated at around $3,000 to 6,000. This demonstrates how beneficial the essential oils business can prove. Ranga, however, says it is virtually impossible to reach a figure for the whole sector. Different crops have entirely different cycles and products are also sold at varying prices. These oils have rates varying from Rs 200 to Rs 2.25 lakh for a kilogram, he says.

There is no set pattern of procuring crops either. Manufacturers can have contract farming in place to fulfill requirement, but for some herbs they rely on wholesale market supply, according to Ranga. He adds, "For some others, backward integration of farms also exists. Most of the distillation units are located at places where these plants are grown." It is easy, therefore, to perceive there is no single leader across the sector. Some may be producing more of rose oil or sandalwood oil, while others may focus on lemongrass oil or mint oil and yet some others on vetiver oil or eucalyptus oil.

"Even mint is of four different kinds and eucalyptus of two kinds," Ranga says. According to Ranga, "It is difficult to reach an overall figure for production and sale." This explains why statistics are hardly available for the industry as such. As far as economics of extraction of essential oils from plants is concerned, it depends a lot on the set-up, capacity and design of distillation units. With some precautions, the same distillation unit can be used for extracting essential oils from different plants.

According to a study conducted by the global market research firm Frost and Sullivan in 2006, the rise in consumer demand for natural food products, coupled with the associated need for flavoring compounds from natural sources, have provided a major boost to the essential oils and oleoresins market. Frost and Sullivan estimated that the market size of Europe and the US for essential oils would grow to 666 million by 2009, with the actual volume consumed by the two in 2009 being 105,800 tons.

According to the United Nation's COMTRADE database, global imports of essential oils stood at $2 billion in 2005. As listed by them, the top ten import markets in 2005 were the USA ($391 million), France ($199 million), the UK ($175 million), Japan ($152 million), Germany ($117 million), Switzerland ($103 million), Ireland ($75 million), China ($65 million), Singapore ($61 million) and Spain ($61 million). The fastest-growing markets, based on import spending between 2000 and 2005 include Vietnam (14% per annum), Poland (35%), Nigeria (16%), Turkey (25%), South Africa (14%), Indonesia (14%), Saudi Arabia (14%), India (19%), Spain (13%), Singapore (35%), Switzerland (14%), and Japan (13%).

While India is a major exporter of many essential oils; it also imports from several countries. Figures from the Nahva Seva Port, Mumbai between December 2008 and March 2009 show India to have imported a number of essential oils from countries like the US, Brazil, the UK, China and Indonesia. It imported aromatic chemicals worth over Rs 6 crore from the US during this period through this port alone. At the same time, India also exported essential oils to several countries, including to the US, the UK, China, Argentina and other European countries.

A study conducted over a decade ago in 1996-97 had estimated the demand for essential oils for the year at 14,900 tons. The growth rates it estimated then were for domestic and export markets at 9 and 25% respectively. The demand and supply gap was then projected at 8,000 tons. Since then the number of players have swelled not just in India, but overseas also. Ranga says it is difficult to guess at the actual produce and supply. What is perceived, however, is that there is a good demand for essential oils.

"There is intense competition in the market now," says Ranga. "Pricing is very competitive and the scope for new players in the market is not quite bright." However, he points out that the new entrants have plenty of opportunities in the organic oil segment. Demand for organic products is rising these days, he says. Though no special certification is required for setting up distillation units for producing essential oils, an organic certification will definitely be advantageous. If someone still wants to pursue the traditional segment of the business, one must adopt new biotechnology innovations to make a mark. Ranga believes entrepreneurs more willing to adopt and accommodate new technologies will emerge leaders in the long run.

EXPORT OF ESSENTIAL OILS

There are two important sassafras oils of commerce: Brazilian sassafras oil, obtained from the trunkwood of *Ocotea pretiosa*, and Chinese sassafras oil from *Cinnamomum camphora*. Both contain 80 per cent or more of safrole. True sassafras oil, from the roots of North American *Sassafras albidum*, is no longer produced commercially, although it was once the main flavour constituent of "root beer". Its use for such purposes, and in other foods and drinks, has been banned for some years because of fears of health risks associated with consumption of safrole. Only Brazilian and Chinese oils are discussed here, together with oils from *Piper* species, which show considerable promise as alternative, sustainable sources of safrole. Sassafras oil was formerly used in numerous household fragrance applications such as floor waxes, polishes, soaps, detergents and cleaning agents. Its ability to blend with other oils and its powerful masking properties made it valuable for such purposes.

However, the principal use today is as a raw material for the isolation of safrole. This is then converted by the chemical industry into two important derivatives: heliotropin, which is widely used as a fragrance and flavouring agent, and piperonal butoxide (PBO), a vital ingredient of pyrethroid insecticides. Natural pyrethrum in particular would not be an economical insecticide without the addition of PBO as a synergist and the future of the natural pyrethrum industry is linked to the continued availability of PBO.

DESCRIPTION OF TURPENTINE

Turpentine is the volatile oil distilled from pine resin, which itself is obtained by tapping trees of the genus *Pinus*. The solid material left behind after distillation is known as rosin. Both products are used in a wide variety of applications but only turpentine is discussed in detail here (rosin is briefly referred to in Products Other Than oil, below).

Turpentine, rosin and derivatives of these which have been obtained via tapping of living pine trees (whether natural stands or plantations) are known collectively as gum naval stores (and the turpentine and rosin as gum turpentine and gum rosin, respectively). This distinguishes them from turpentine and rosin which have been recovered as by-products from chemical pulping of pines and which are referred to as sulphate naval stores; and wood naval stores, which are similar materials obtained from aged pine stumps. Neither sulphate nor wood naval stores are discussed further.

Traditionally, turpentine has been employed as a solvent or cleaning agent for paints and varnishes and this is still often the case today, particularly in those countries where the pine trees are tapped. There are also some specialized uses, in the pharmaceutical industry, for example.

Most turpentine nowadays, however, is used as a source of chemical isolates which are then converted into a wide range of products. Many of these, including the biggest single turpentine derivative, synthetic pine oil, are employed for fragrance and flavour use, although there are also many important non-aromatic applications such as polyterpene resins. Pine oil is used in disinfectants, cleaning agents and other products having a "pine" odour. Derivatives such as isobornyl acetate, camphor, citral, linalool, citrinellal, menthol and many others are used either in their own right or for the elaboration of other fragrance and flavour compounds. Many of the odours and flavours in use today, which are associated with naturally occurring oils, may well be derived, instead, from turpentine.

A few of the minor constituents of turpentine, such as anethole, are employed for fragrance or flavour use without the need for chemical modification.

SUPPLY AND DEMAND TRENDS OF MARKETS

No more than some general comments and an indication of markets are given here. Trade statistics are complex and difficult to analyse in terms of gum turpentine alone: firstly, because it is not always disaggregated from sulphate turpentine and secondly, because there is considerable trade in turpentine derivatives, with a consequent loss of identity in terms of the type of turpentine used as feedstock.

Greenhalgh estimated world production of all types of turpentine to be approximately 250,000 tonnes in 1979. Of this, about 110,000 tonnes was gum turpentine, most of the remainder being sulphate turpentine. COPPEN estimated annual production of gum turpentine from the seven major producers at 140,000 tonnes based on 1987-89 data (Table). Most recently, DAWSON (1994) has estimated total world production of turpentine at 335,000 tonnes, of which around 100,000 tonnes is believed to be gum turpentine.

The USA and the People's Republic of China are the world's largest producers and consumers of turpentine. Most American requirements are met by domestic sulphate turpentine production but gum turpentine is also imported for fractionation and conversion into derivatives. Chinese requirements are met by her own production of gum turpentine. Japan, Western Europe (particularly France, which imports Portuguese turpentine for fractionation), India and some Latin American countries (Mexico and Brazil, for example) are all major consumers of turpentine, but many other countries import or use domestically produced turpentine to a greater or lesser degree. Small producers such as

Kenya and Thailand consume all their turpentine (a hundred tonnes or so each) locally. Others, such as Indonesia, which produces around 6,000 tonnes pa, export a major part of their production. Recent export of gum turpentine from Indonesia, and their destinations. There are a large number of importing countries but India is by far the biggest importer - over 4,000 tonnes in 1992 and making up for her own declining production.

Any new producer, therefore, or, indeed, an existing one who is able to expand production, is likely to find a ready market. Importers and end-users of turpentine (and rosin) are always anxious to widen their supply base. In addition, there is usually an ample domestic market.

SOURCES OF NATURAL ESSENTIAL OILS

Plant organs containing natural essential oils. Essential oils are generally derived from one or more plant parts, such as flowers (e.g. rose, jasmine, carnation, clove, mimosa, rosemary, lavander), leaves (e.g. mint, *Ocimum* spp., lemongrass, jamrosa), leaves and stems (e.g. geranium, patchouli, petitgrain, verbena, cinnamon), bark (e.g. cinnamon, cassia, canella), wood (e.g. cedar, sandal, pine), roots (e.g. angelica, sassafras, vetiver, saussurea, valerian), seeds (e.g fennel, coriander, caraway, dill, nutmeg), fruits (bergamot, orange, lemon, juniper), rhizomes (e.g. ginger, calamus, curcuma, orris) and gums or oleoresin exudations (e.g. balsam of Peru, balsam of Tolu, storax, myrrh, benzoin).

Specialized plant structures that produce and store essential oils. Depending upon the plant family, essential oils may occur in specialized secretary structures such as glandular hairs (Labiatae, Verbenaceace, Geraniaceae), modified parenchymal cells (Piperaceae), resin canals (conifers), oil tubes called vittae (Umbelliferae), lysig-enous cavities (Rutaceae), schizogenous passages (Myrtaceae, Graminae, Compositae) or gum canals (Cistacae, Burseraceae). It is well known that when a geranium leaf is lightly touched, an odor is emitted because the long stalked oil glands are fragile. Similarly, the application of slight pressure on a peppermint leaf will rupture the oil gland and release oil. In contrast, pine needles and eucalyptus leaves do not release their oils until the epidermis of the leaf is broken. Hence, the types of structures in which oil is contained differ depending on the plant type and are plantfamily specific. Unfortunately, not enough is known even today about these oil secretary structures to carefully categorize them. From the practical standpoint, they can be categorized into superficial and subcutaneous oils. Based on the currently available information, it may be inferred that oils of the Labiatae, Verbenaceae and Geraniaceae families are the only superficial oils known; consequently, the others are considered subcutaneous oils.

During handling, some flowers continue to produce aroma while other quickly loose their odor. Flowers collected at different times may also give different perfumery values. Regarding the rose, halfopen flowers with plump anthers give higher oil yield than fully opened flowers with shrivelled anthers. Humidity, wind, rain and surface temperature also affect the oil yield considerably. Harvesting schedule affects both quantity and quality of the oil.

ESSENTIAL OIL CONSTITUENTS

Major constituents of essential oils, from which it is clear that most essential oils consist of hydrocarbons, esters, terpenes, lactones, phenols, aldehydes, acids, alcohols, ketones, and esters. Among these, the oxygenated compounds (alcohols, esters, aldehydes, ketones, lactones, phenols) are the principal odor source. They are more stable against oxidizing and resinifying influences than other constituents. On the other hand, unsaturated constituents like monoterpenes and sesquiterpenes have the tendency to oxidize or resinify in the presence of air and light. The knowledge of individual constituents and their physical characteristics, such as boiling point, thermal stability and vaporpressure-temperature relationship, is of paramount importance in technology development of oxygenated compounds.

Methods of Producing Essential Oils

Methods for producing essential oils from plant materials. Regarding hydrodistillation, the essential oils industry has developed terminology to distinguish three types: water distillation; water and steam distillation; and direct steam distillation.

Originally introduced by Von Rechenberg, these terms have become established in the essential oil industry. All three methods are subject to the same theoretical considerations which deal with distillation of twophase systems. The differences lie mainly in the methods of handling the material.

Some volatile oils cannot be distilled without decomposition and thus are usually obtained by expression (lemon oil, orange oil) or by other mechanical means. In certain countries, the general method for obtaining citrus oil involves puncturing the oil glands by rolling the fruit over a trough lined with sharp projections that are long enough to penetrate the epidermis and pierce the oil glands located within outer portion of the peel (*ecuelle* method). A pressing action on the fruit removes the oil from the glands, and a fine spray of water washes the oil from the mashed peel while the juice is extracted through a central tube that cores the fruit. The resulting oil-water emulsion is separated by centrifugation. A variation of this process is to remove the peel from the fruit before the oil is extracted.

Often, the volatile oil content of fresh plant parts (fl ower petals) is so small that oil removal is not commercially feasible by the aforementioned methods. In such instances, an odorless, bland, fixed oil or fat is spread in a thin layer on glass plates. The flower petals are placed on the fat for a few hours; then repeatedly, the oil petals are removed, and a new layer of petals is introduced. After the fat has absorbed as much fragrance as possible, the oil may be removed by extraction with alcohol. This process, known as enfl eurage, was formerly used extensively in the production of perfumes and pomades.

COCONUT

The coconut palm, *Cocos nucifera*, is a member of the family Arecaceae (palm family). It is the only accepted species in the genus *Cocos*. The term coconut can refer to the entire coconut palm, the seed, or the fruit, which, botanically, is a drupe, not a nut. The spelling cocoanut is an archaic form of the word. The term is derived from 16th century Portuguese and Spanish *cocos*, meaning "grinning face", from the three small holes on the coconut shell that resemble human facial features.

Found throughout the tropic and subtropic area, the coconut is known for its great versatility as seen in the many domestic, commercial, and industrial uses of its different parts. Coconuts are part of the daily diet of many people. Coconuts are different from any other fruits because they contain a large quantity of "water" and when immature they are known as tender-nuts or jelly-nuts and may be harvested for drinking. When mature they still contain some water and can be used as seednuts or processed to give oil from the kernel, charcoal from the hard shell and coir from the fibrous husk.

Theendosperm is initially in its nuclear phase suspended within the coconut water. As development continues, cellular layers of endosperm deposit along the walls of the coconut, becoming the edible coconut "flesh". When dried, the coconut flesh is called copra. The oil and milk derived from it are commonly used in cooking and frying; coconut oil is also widely used in soaps and cosmetics. The clear liquid coconut water within is a refreshing drink. The husks and leaves can be used as material to make a variety of products for furnishing and decorating. It also has cultural and religious significance in many societies that use it.

Plant

Cocos nucifera is a large palm, growing up to 30 meters (98 ft) tall, with pinnate leaves 4–6 meters (13–20 ft) long, and pinnae 60–90 cm long; old leaves break away cleanly, leaving the trunksmooth. Coconuts are generally classified into two general types: tall and dwarf. On very fertile land, a tall coconut palm tree can yield up to 75 fruits per year, but more often yields less than 30 mainly due to poor cultural practices. In recent years, improvements in cultivation practices and breeding has produced coconut trees that can yield more.

Fruit

Botanically, the coconut fruit is a drupe, not a true nut. Like other fruits, it has three layers: the exocarp, mesocarp, and endocarp. The exocarp and mesocarp make up the "husk" of the coconut. Coconuts sold in the shops of nontropical countries often have had the exocarp (outermost layer) removed. The mesocarp is composed of a fiber, called coir, which has many traditional and commercial uses. The shell has three germination pores (stoma) or "eyes" that are clearly visible on its outside surface once the husk is removed.

A full-sized coconut weighs about 1.44 kilograms (3.2 lb). It takes around 6000 full-grown coconuts to produce a tonne of copra.

Roots

Unlike some other plants, the palm tree has neither a tap root nor root hairs, but has a fibrous root system.

Inflorescence

On the same inflorescence, the palm produces both the female and male flowers; thus, the palm is monoecious. Other sources use the termpolygamomonoecious.

The female flower is much larger than the male flower. Flowering occurs continuously. Coconut palms are believed to be largely cross-pollinated, although some dwarf varieties are self-pollinating.

GROUNDNUT

Geographical Origin

Groundnut (Arachis hypogaea L.) is believed to be the native of Brazil to Peru, Argentina and Ghana, from where it was introduced into Jamaica, Cuba and other West Indies islands. The plant was introduced by Portuguese into Africa from where it was introduced into North America. It was introduced into India during the first half of the sixteenth century from one of the Pacific islands of China, where it was introduced earlier from either central America or South America.

Economic Importance

The oil content of the seed varies from 44 to 50 per cent, depending on the varieties and agronomic conditions. Groundnut oil is an edible oil. It finds extensive use as a cooking medium both as refined oil and Vanaspati Ghee. It is also used in soap making, and manufacturing cosmetics and lubricants, olein steering and their salts. Kernels are also eaten raw, roasted or sweetened. They are rich in protein and vitamins A, B and some members of B_2 group. Their calorific value is 349 per 100 grammes. The H.P.S. type of groundnut kernels are exported to foreign countries. The residual oilcake contains 7 to 8 per cent of N, 1.5 per cent of P_2O_5 and 1.2 per cent of K_2O and is used as a fertilizer. It is an important protein supplement in cattle and poultry rations. It is also consumed as confectionary product. The cake can be used for manufacturing artificial fiber. The haulms (plant stalks) are fed (green, dried or silaged) to livestock. Groundnut shell is used as fuel for manufacturing coarse boards, corksubstitutes etc. Groundnut is also of value as rotation crop. Being a legume with root nodules, it can synthesise atmospheric nitrogen and therefore improve soil fertility.

Botanical Description

Groundnut (Archis hypogaea L.) is a member of sub-family, Papilionaceae of the family Leguminosae. Archis hypogaea L. consists of two subspecies each containing two botanical varieties.

Plants of the botanical variety hypogaea are spreading (runner) to upright (erect bunch) in growth habit, have alternate branching, lack inflorescences on the main stem, possess appreciable fresh seed dormancy, flowers are longer and mature later than those of subspecies fasligiata. Variety hirsuta has been used only to a little extent.

Plants of this subspecies fasligiata are upright, have sequential branching and inflorescences in the main-stem leaf axils, possess little fresh seed dormancy, and are of shorter duration than those of the subspecies hypogaea. Subspecies fasligiata includes both the Spanish and Valencia types

Groundnut, in general, has a short-statured plant, with the main axis being upright (15 to 40 cm long) but the major part of the plant consists of the primary branches. Secondary and tertiary branches are found in the semi-spreading and spreading (Virginia) types, giving them a prostrate stature. The leaves are alternate, stipulate and quadri-foliate. The flowers are orange yellow, typically papilionaceous, with a long calyx tube within which is held the style borne on a superior ovary.

The calyx and corolla lobes are borne in the axils of the leaves on the fruiting branches. They are bisexual, Zygomorphic, complete and sessile. Petals are five, with one large standard, two wings and two fused keel petals. There are two steering and eight fertile anthers, four of which are globose and four oblong (dimorphic).

Groundnut is predominantly a self-pollinated crop and pollination takes place early in the morning. As soon as the fertilization is complete, the flowers fade. After fertilization, an intercalary meristem becomes active at the base of the ovary above the point of attachment of the hypanthium, producing new tissue below itself and resulting in an elongated stalk in the peg. The pegs are positively geotropic, enter the soil and bend in a horizontal plane. Generally two, and occasionally one, three or four, fertilized ovules are borne at the tip of the peg which later swells to become the pod. The testa is generally pink, but varieties with red, white, purple and blotched testa, with various gradations of colours are available.

Distribution, Area and Production

The major groundnut-producing countries of the world are India, China, Nigeria, Senegal, Sudan, Burma and the USA. Out of the total area of 18.9 million hectares and the total production of 17.8 million tonnes in the world, these countries account for 69% of the area and 70% of the production. India occupies the position, both in regard to the area and the production, in the world. About 7.5 million hectares is put under it annually and the production is about 6 million tonnes. 70% of the area and 75% of the production are concentrated in the four states of Gujarat, Andhra Pradesh, Tamil Nadu and Karnataka. Andhra Pradesh, Tamil Nadu, Karnataka and Orissa have irrigated area forms about 6% of the total groundnut area in India.

Climate and Soil

Groundnut is grown throughout the tropics and its cultivation is extended to the subtropical contries lying between 45 degrees N and 35 degrees S and up to an altitude of 1000 metres. The crop can be grown successfully in places receiving a minimum rainfall of 1,250 mm. The rainfall should be well distributed well during the flowering and pegging of the crop. The total amount required for presowing operations (preparatory cultivation) is 100 mm; for sowing, it is 150 mm and for flowering and pod development an evenly distributed rainfall of 400-500 mm is required. The groundnut crop, however, cannot stand frost, long and severe draught or water stagnation.

Groundnut is grown on wide variety of soil types. However, the crop does best on sandy loam and loamy soils and in the black soils with good drainage. Heavy and stiff clays are unsuitable for groundnut cultivation as the pod development is hampered in these soils.

RAPESEED AND MUSTARD

Under the names rapeseed and mustard, several oilseeds belonging to the crucieferae are grown in India:

- Brown mustard, commonly called rai (raya or laha)—Brassica juncea (L.) Czern. & Coss
- Sarson
- Yellow sarson—B. campestris L. var. sarson Prain
- Brown sarson—B. campestris L. var. dichotoma Watt
- Toria (lahi or Maghi Labi)—B. campestris L. var. toria Duth.
- Taramira or tara (eruca sativa Mill.)

In trade, sarson, toria and Taramira are known as rapeseed, and rai as mustard.

Banarsi rai (B. nigra Koch.) which does not fall under any of the four groups is a garden crop used as spice. The cultivation of white mustard (Brassica alba syn. Sinapis alba) is no longer found in India. Rai and Yellow sarson are self-fertile and the rest of the cruciferous oilseeds, viz. brown sarson, toria, taramira, Banarasi rai and white mustard, are self-incompatible.

The acreage under yellow sarson is scantily (mainly in Bihar) and constantly on the decrease. In the recent past, the accreage under brown mustard is steadily on the increase (over 65%) at the expense of other Brassica due to its higher production, greater to pests and diseases and moisture stress.

Origin

Brassica juncea L. (rai) was originally introduced from China into north-eastern India. From where it has extended into Afghanistan via the Punjab. Eastern Afghanistan, together with the adjoining north-western India is one of the independent centres of brown sarson (Brassica campestris var. brown sarson). Yellow sarson (B. campestris var. yellow sarson) is commonly grown in the eastern parts of India where it shows much diversity of forms. Taramira is a relatively recent introduction into India. It is believed to be a native of southern Europe and North Africa.

Economic Importance

Rapeseed and mustard yield the most important edible oil content of the seeds of different ranges from 30 to 48 per cent. In the case of white mustard, the oil content ranges from 25 to 33 per cent. The oil obtained is the main cooking medium in Northern India and can not be replaced by any other edible oil. The seed and oil are used as a condiment in the preparation of pickles and for flavouring curries and vegetables. The oilcake is mostly used as cattle feed. The leaves of young plants are used as a green vegetable. The use of mustard oil for industrial purposes is rather limited on account of its high cost.

Botanical Description

Rapseeed and mustard include annual herbs ranging in height from 0.45 to 1.75 m. Roots, in general, are long and tapering. Toria is more or less a surface-feeder and brown sarson has long roots, with a limited lateral spread, enabling its successful cultivation under drier conditions. Yellow sarson has both extensive and lateral spread. The height of the stem varies from 45 cm (in some varieties of toria) to 1.75 m (in yellow sarson). In toria and brown sarson, the branches arise at an angle of 30° to 40°. In yellow sarson, branches arise laterally at an angle about 10° to 20° and give the plant a narrow and pyramidal shape. The inflorence is coroymbose raceme. In the case of sarson the four petals are spread apart, whereas in brown sarson and toria the petals overlap or may be placed apart, depending upon the variety. The flowers bear a hypogynous syncarpous ovary. In brown sarson and toria, the ovary is bicarpellary, whereas in the case of yellow sarson, it may also be tri or tetra-carpellary.

The fruit is a siliqua. The pods are two-valved, three-valved or four-valved, depending upon the number of carpels in the ovary. The flowers begin to open from 8 a.m. and continue up to 12 noon.

Distribution, area and Production

The crop is grown both in subtropical and tropical countries. In Asia, it is chiefly grown in China, India and Pakistan. It is also grown in Europe, Canada and the USSR, but the forms of rapeseed and mustard grown there are different from those grown in India.

India occupies the first position, both with regard to acreage and production of rapeseed and mustard in the world. In India the Braddica crops occupy the second largest position after groundnut, with 3-5 million hectares, producing about 2 million tonnes of seed annually. The chief states producing them are Uttar Pradesh, Punjab, Haryana, Assam, Bihar, Madhya Pradesh, Rajasthan, West Bengal and Orissa.

Climate and Soil

The rapeseed and mustard crops are of the tropical as well as of the temperate zones and require relatively cool temperatures for satisfactory growth. In India, they are grown in the rabi season from September-October to February-March. The rapeseed and mustard crops grow well in areas having 25 to 40 cm of rainfall. Sarson and toria are preferred in low-rainfall areas, whereas raya and toria are grown in medium and high-rainfall areas respectively.

The rapeseed and mustard thrive best in light to heavy loams. Raya may be grown on all types of soil, but toria does best in loam to heavy loam. Sarson is suited to light-loam soil and taramira is mostly grown on very light soils.

Cultivation

A fine seed-bed is required to ensure good germination. In irrigated areas, the first ploughing is done with a medium sized soil-turning plough, followed by two to four ploughing with a desi plough or a cultivator. Sohaga (Planking) is given after every ploughing.

In rain fed areas, one to two ploughings with a desi plough or a cultivator, each followed by planking, may be given. Toria, in particular, requires a fairly moist seed-bed for good germination, but excessive moisture should be avoided. The rate in the case of mixed cropping depends on the proportion of the rapeseed to the main crop.

When sown pure, 5 kg of seed per ha is used for all rapeseeds and mustard. When sown mixed with other crops, the time of sowing rapeseed and mustard is governed by the sowing of the main crop. The first half of September is best for sowing toria (if wheat is to follow, it should be sown by the end of August), 25th September to 15th October for sarson, 30th September to 15th October for raya, and tarantira is sown throughout October. The seed from healthy and desirable plants, grown in isolation in the case of self-sterile form, should be used. Whenever moisture in the field is inadequate, the seed is mixed with moist soil and kept overnight. For distributing evenly, the seed is usually mixed with sand before sowing.

In mixed cropping rapeseed and mustard are sown in rows 1.8 to 2.4 metres apart across the main crop. The pure crop of rapeseed or mustard is sown at a depth of 4 to 5 cm in lines, 30 cm apart, with a drill, or with a (tube) attached to the plough. Thinning is done three weeks after sowing to maintain a plant-to-plant distance of 10 to 15 cm.

One hoeing in the case of toria in the third week after sowing and 1-2 hoeings in the case of sarson and raya are adequate. Forty kg of W per ha is optimum for all rapeseed and mustard crops in rain fed areas. Under irrigated conditions doses of 40 and 80 kg of W per ha are considered optimum for toria, sarson and rapeseed respectively. For tarantira, 20 kg of W per ha is ancient. All the fertilizers should be drilled before sowing. Among the Brassicae, raya is most responsive to irrigation, followed by yellow sarson. Two irrigations, one at flowering and the other at pod formation, result in the maximum yield in the case of toria, sarson and raya. Its flowering is most economical, if there is water scarcity. Tarantira is not irrigated.

Harvesting is done as soon as the crop begins to turn yellow. Tma, which takes 75 to 90 days to mature, is the earliest crop to be harvested. Harvesting is done with hand-sickler. Threshing is done by beating with a wooden stick the seed bearing part of the plants, taken in convenient bundles or by trampling them under the feet. Winnowing is done with by slowly dropping the threshed produce from a basket held shoulder-high. The seed after being dried in the sun is stored in gunny bags or bins.

Pets and Diseases

The most serious pests of rapeseed and mustard are the mustard aphid (Lipaphis erysinbi (Holt) syn. Rhopalosiphun pseudobrwsicae (Davis), mustard sawfly (Athalia proximo King) and cutworm (Agrotis ypsi" Poott.). To control aphidy the spraying of Methyl Demeton 0.02% or limetboate 0.03% two or three times, depending on the intensity is recommended. The mustard sawfly is controlled by dusting 10% BHC at the rate of 25 kg per ha. Cutworms are controlled by drilling into the soil 5% dust of Aldrin or Heptachlor or Chlordane at the rate of 25 kg per ha.

Alternaria blight (Alternaria brassicae Bork.) is the most widespread and destructive disease of rapeseed and mustard, whereas rust (Cystopus candidus) is serious in certain areas. Spraying with Dithane M-45 or Difolaton at the rate of 11 kg per ha is recommended for controlling these diseases. Orobanche, a phanerogamic parasite, has also been reported to be serious in Punjab and in certain parts of Uttar Flradesh. Hand-pulling of the plants of the parasite and a long rotation are recomnended.

Yield

The average yield of rapeseed and mustard is about 500 kg per ha. Under good crop management, toria, which is a short-duration crop, gives a yield of about 450 to 650 kg per ha, sarson 800 to 1,000 kg and rai 1,000 to 1,200 kg per hectare.

Oil and Protein Quality in the Brassicae

The oil of rapeseede and mustard possesses a Sizable amount of crucie acid (38 to 57%), together with linolenic acid up to 4.7 to 13.0 %. The oleic and linolenic acid, which have nutritive value, together constitute only about 27 per cent. It is desirable to increase the quantity of oleic and linolic acid and erucic acid. A lower proportion of erucic acid will make the oil more palatable, nutritive besides reducing metabolic disorders. The Protein contained in rapeseed and mustard normally ranges between 24 and 30%. On the whole-seed basis and between 35 and 40% on the meal basis. But the presence of toxic glucosinolates in the mustard cake is unsuitable as source of human protein and is at present use as a manual and as a cattle feed.

SANDALWOOD OIL

The term sandalwood has been applied at various times to oils from several different sources. Today, almost all the sandalwood oil traded internationally is so-called East Indian sandalwood oil distilled from the heartwood and roots of *Santalum album*. Australian sandalwood oil from *S. spicatum* and West Indian and African "sandalwood" oils are no longer produced. Unless otherwise stated the following discussion relates to the East Indian type from *S. album* (referred to, here, simply as sandalwood oil).

Sandalwood oil has a characteristic sweet, woody odour which is widely employed in the fragrance industry, but more particularly in the higher-priced perfumes. It has excellent blending properties and the presence of a large proportion of high-boiling constituents in the oil (about 90 per cent santalols) also makes it valuable as a fixative for other fragrances. In India, where it is produced, it is used in this manner for the manufacture of traditional attars such as rose attar; the delicate floral oils are distilled directly into sandalwood oil.

WORLD SUPPLY AND DEMAND TRENDS

MARKETS

India and Indonesia are the two major producers and exporters of sandalwood oil but reliable production data are not available. Domestic consumption, which is certainly high in India and probably greater than the combined total for the rest of the world, is therefore also difficult to estimate. World production/consumption is probably of the order of several hundreds of tonnes annually. The United States and France are the two largest importers of Indian sandalwood oil. Imports into the former Soviet Union have fallen in the last two years and no early recovery of this market is expected. Imports into the Middle East have increased. The USA is also the chief destination for Indonesian exports and thus represents the biggest market for sandalwood oil outside India.

Demand for sandalwood oil fell sharply in the 1970s as a result of very high prices and competition from synthetic substitutes. However, this largely affected the lower-priced formulations and the natural oil has retained its market in the top grade products. Demand now is influenced mostly by supply factors and the way in which this affects prices.

SUPPLY SOURCES

Indian exports over the last six years have averaged about 40 tonnes pa, with no distinct trend over the period. Production is based almost entirely on exploitation of wild trees.

The lack of production or domestic consumption data make it impossible to judge the state of the supply base and whether this (and the level of exports) is likely to change in the future.

Table Exports of Sandalwood Oil from India, and Destinations, 1987/88-1992/93 (Tonnes)

	1987/88	1988/89	1989/90	1990/91	1991/92	1992/93
Total	39	26	34	37	65	42
Of which to:						
France	11	8	14	10	8	9
USA	10	5	5	6	14	8
Soviet Union	7	2	4	7	2	-
Japan	3	2	2	2	4	2
UK	2	1	2	3	3	3
Switzerland	3	2	2	2	1	2
W. Germany	1	2	1	1	3	1
United Arab Emirates	1	~	2	4	5	3
Singapore	~	~	~	~	21	~
Oman	–	–	~	~	~	9

Indonesia is the only other supplier of East Indian-type sandalwood oil.

Recorded annual exports over the six years 1987-92 (Table) averaged 15 tonnes.

Table Exports of Sandalwood oil from Indonesia, and Destinations, 1987-92 (Tonnes)

	1987	1988	1989	1990	1991	1992
Total	22	19	12	13	10	13
Of which to:						
USA	16	12	7	10	1	6
Netherlands	2	3	3	–	6	–
Singapore	~	2	–	–	3	3
Switzerland	1	–	–	–	–	3

Australian production of oil from *Santalum spicatum* ceased in 1971. Exports for the ten years to that date averaged less than 3 tonnes annually.

QUALITY AND PRICES

There is an international (ISO) standard for sandalwood oil (ex *Santalum album*) which stipulates a minimum free alcohols (santalol) content of 90 per cent (m/m). Ranges within which various physico-chemical properties must fall are also given.

In the United States, an EOA standard specifies the same minimum santalol content. As a perfumery oil, the aroma characteristics are all-important and these are judged by the buyer to be acceptable or not for individual consignments.

Sandalwood oil is one of the most highly priced items in the essential oil trade, reflecting the nature of the raw material source and the tightness of supplies. In the late 1980s it was fetching almost US$200/kg. Throughout 1992 the price of oil of Indian origin offered by London dealers was about US$140-150/kg; Indonesian oil was about US$5 lower. In mid-1993 the price of Indian oil rose again to US$180/kg and this was still the price in early 1994.

PLANT SOURCES

BOTANICAL/COMMON NAME

Family Santalaceae:
Santalum album Linn.
(Sandalwood)

Other *Santalum* species occurring in Australia and islands of the Pacific have been, or are, harvested for their fragrant wood, although none (with the possible exceptions of very small quantities of *S. austrocaledonicum* and *S. yasi*) are currently used as sources of internationally traded oil. These include *S. spicatum* and *S. lanceolatum* (Australia), *S. ellipticum* (Hawaii), *S. yasi* (Fiji and Tonga), *S. macgregorii* (Papua New Guinea), *S. austrocaledonicum* (Vanuatu and

New Caledonia) and *S. insulare* (French Polynesia).

DESCRIPTION AND DISTRIBUTION

S. album is a small to medium-sized evergreen tree, sometimes reaching up to 18 m in height and 2.5 m in girth. It is a root parasite and successful regeneration (both natural and artificial) requires, amongst other things, suitable host plants.

S. album occurs naturally in India, Sri Lanka and the Malay Archipelago (Indonesia and surrounding islands). In India it is found in the drier regions in the south of the country, especially the states of Karnataka and Tamil Nadu, up to 1400 m. Formation of heartwood, from which the oil is obtained, is said to be best between 600 m and 900 m. Moderate rainfall (850-1200 mm) spread over several months and much sunshine are conducive to good growth. Sandal has become naturalized in parts of Rajasthan, Maharashtra, Madhya Pradesh and Uttar Pradesh and has been introduced into a number of other Indian states. The wood of trees outside their natural range, however, is very variable with respect to oil content and sometimes has little or no aroma.

In Indonesia, *S. album* occurs on the neighbouring islands of Timor, Sumba, Flores, Alor and Roti, although there is now only a significant population on Timor.

EFFECTS OF OIL PRODUCTION ON THE NATURAL RESOURCE

Cultivation of sandal in India has had limited success. While it might be expected that the destructive nature of sandalwood oil production, which entails the uprooting of mature trees, would put inexorable pressure on the wild resource there is little or no quantitative information available on which to judge the extent to which this might have occurred. Sandal trees freely produce seed and natural regeneration occurs both via seedlings and through root suckers which are produced when the tree has been felled and the stump extracted from the ground. The absence of heartwood in young trees provides little reason for felling trees less than 20-25 years old so they are allowed to grow to at least this age. The extent of heartwood formation is at its maximum at around 30-50 years.

The greatest threat to Indian sandal may be loss through spike disease rather than oil production. Trees of all ages and sizes are liable to be attacked and, if infected, succumb to the disease within about three years.

In Indonesia, continuous harvesting combined with very little regeneration (due to fires, shifting cultivation and uncontrolled cattle grazing) has led to a serious decline in the *S. album* population.

Elsewhere, too, the consequences of destructive harvesting (either for oil production or for sale of the log for incense production are being increasingly recognized and some attempts have been made to quantify loss of the resource. In 1985 it was estimated that live *S. spicatum* stands in Western Australia were sufficient for a further 23 years harvesting before depletion, although favourable technical and economic changes could extend this period. Collection of dead wood (which forms an increasing proportion of the harvested logs) will contribute to a further extension.

HARVESTING/PRIMARY PROCESSING

In India, trees above 60 cm girth are harvested during the post-monsoon period. In areas affected by spike disease only dead and dying trees are harvested. After uprooting, the wood is cut into billets which are then transported to a central depot. The sapwood and heartwood parts of the trunk are clearly demarcated and sapwood is removed accordingly. Roots are primarily heartwood and require no initial division. The value of the wood and the high price that it fetches make smuggling something that the authorities have to contend with. In preparation for distillation the billets of wood are chipped and then reduced to a powder. Most sandalwood oil is now produced by steam distillation of the powder. In former times direct water distillation, in which the raw material is immersed in water and distilled, was used. The high-boiling nature of the oil makes distillation rather slow and it takes many hours to complete.

YIELDS AND QUALITY VARIATION

The yield of heartwood varies from locality to locality and the age of the tree. In India, trees of 100 cm girth have been reported to yield between 85 kg and 240 kg of heartwood according to the area from which they come.

The yield of oil is highest in the roots, about 10 per cent (as received basis), and lowest in chips which are a mixture of heartwood and sapwood (1.5-2 per cent). The oil content of the heartwood varies from tree to tree and is higher for older trees. In India, yields of about 0.9 per cent have been reported from the heartwood of 10-year old trees, while mature trees of 30-50 years age have yielded 4 per cent oil. The oil content also varies according to the colour of the heartwood. Light-coloured wood yields 3-6 per cent oil, while dark brown wood yields about 2.5 per cent oil.

Oil from the younger trees also has a slightly lower proportion of santalols than the mature trees (ca 80 per cent cf 90 per cent), another reason for not harvesting at too young an age.

VALUE- ADDED PROCESSING

No further processing of the oil is carried out until it is prepared for fragrance use by the end-user.

PRODUCTS OTHER THAN OIL

Sandalwood is much prized as a wood for carving and is used for making souvenirs and other items requiring fine workmanship. In India sapwood of sandal is used for wood turning, particularly toy making; the wood comes mainly from trimmings and immature trees killed by spike disease.

Sawdust from heartwood prepared for distillation is valuable enough to be collected and sold for use as an incense for religious purposes as well as for scenting clothes and cupboards.

Outside India, where exports of logs are prohibited, there is a thriving market for sandalwood as an incense in joss-stick manufacture. Australia supplies most of this market at present, mainly from *S. spicatum* which has a low oil content and which is, therefore, less attractive as a direct source of oil. Exports of logs from Western Australia were almost 2,000 tonnes in 1989, valued at A$11.5 million. Log exports from other sources have amounted to a few hundred tonnes or less from individual species.

The cotyledons and kernel of sandal seeds contain a fixed oil which has drying properties. Oil-free sandal seed meal is rich in protein and could be utilized as an animal feed if available in sufficient quantities.

DEVELOPMENTAL POTENTIAL

The nature of sandalwood oil and its origin in the heartwood of mature trees makes it an oil that although high in value is not attractive as a short or medium-term source of income for those who might consider cultivating the tree. In India, under natural conditions in the forest, sandal is slow-growing. Growth rate may be increased by improvement of soil fertility and other measures but vigourous growth leads to much reduced heartwood formation. Assuming that existing propagation and cultivation problems can be overcome, opportunities for utilizing sandal as anything other than a long-term cash crop are likely to depend on the identification of elite trees as a source of material for planting.

This in turn requires the establishment of a wide-ranging screening programme to search for such trees, not only within *S. album* but amongst other species of *Santalum*. Production of oil from superior trees might then offer possibilities for commercial exploitation in the smaller island communities of the Pacific.

RESEARCH NEEDS

Although sandal is highly valued, most research in India has focused on spike disease and little work has been done on the silvicultural and genetic aspects of sandal cultivation. Despite much effort, however, complete characterization of the mycoplasma-like organism believed to be responsible for the disease has still not been achieved. Research is still required to elucidate the precise cause of the disease and the best form of treatment if the risk of infection is not to make sandal cultivation for oil production an unacceptable investment risk.

Research needs include the following:

- Investigation of the intrinsic variability in oil yield and quality within natural populations of *S. album* at the provenance and individual tree level. Indonesia and other sources outside India (where most research to date has been undertaken) should be particularly targeted for sampling. It is known for other genera which occur naturally in Asia (*Pinus*, for example) that marked differences can occur between continental and insular populations of the same species.
- Correlation of heartwood and oil content of trees from natural populations of *S. album* outside India. Very little information is available on the growth characteristics of Indonesian trees and the rate at which they produce heartwood.
- Provenance trials to determine the relative performance of different *S. album* populations.
- Consolidation of tree improvement work already begun in India involving selection of plus trees for high oil content and resistance to spike disease.
- Investigation of oil yields and quality for species of *Santalum* other than *S. album*. The latter species appears to be richer in oil than most others but a systematic study of inter- and intra-species variability is needed to fill the gaps in the present state of knowledge. Where oil yields appear promising, quality assessment should be extended to end-user evaluation; chemical analysis alone is not sufficient to judge the commercial acceptability of oils intended for perfumery use.
- Development of improved propagation techniques and cultivation practices.
- Investigation of the suitability of other tree crops as hosts for cultivated sandal which might themselves serve as sources of income until the sandal is ready for harvesting.

ROSEWOOD OIL

Rosewood oil is obtained by felling wild, Amazonian species of *Aniba* and steam distilling the comminuted trunkwood. The oil ("bois de rose") possesses a characteristic aroma and is a long-established ingredient in the more expensive perfumes. Although formerly it was used more widely as a fragrance, particularly in soaps, where the strong top-note could be used to advantage, its relatively high price now makes it uncompetitive with the cheaper, larger volume oils.

Rosewood oil is rich in linalool, a chemical which can be transformed into a number of derivatives of value to the flavour and fragrance industries, and up until the 1960s rosewood oil was an important source of natural linalool. With the advent of synthetic linalool this use largely disappeared. For those applications where natural linalool is preferred, rosewood oil has been displaced by cheaper alternatives (Chinese Ho oils from *Cinnamomum camphora*). There does remain, however, a very small niche market for the preparation of linalool derivatives possessing an "ex rosewood" character.

Use in aromatherapy formulations, a relatively recent application, has become less attractive as environmental concerns have grown over the destructive nature of rosewood oil production in Brazil.

WORLD SUPPLY AND DEMAND TRENDS

MARKETS

In the 1960s, exports of rosewood oil from Brazil alone were around 500 tonnes pa. Today, the world market for rosewood oil is about 100 tonnes pa, the decline in use arising largely from its displacement by synthetic linalool. Dem Demand is reported to be stable, those who moved away from using rosewood oil in their formulations having done so many years ago. However, any marked and prolonged upward move in the price of the oil above recent levels could adversely affect demand. Some of the top-of-the-market perfumery houses have expressed concern over the destructive manner of producing rosewood oil and a transition to sustainable production would be welcomed by such users.

Recent exports from Brazil, now the only supplier of rosewood oil, are shown in Table.

Table Exports of Rosewood oil from Brazil, and Destinations, 1986-92 (Tonnes)

	1986	1987	1988	1989	1990	1991	1992
Total	48	39	95	78	60	74	68
Of which to:							
USA	28	22	na	na	40	na	na
Switzerland	6	6	na	na	11	na	na
France	10	9	na	na	3	na	na
W. Germany	1	1	na	na	2	na	na
UK	1	1	na	na	1	na	na
Netherlands	–	–	na	na	1	na	na
Spain	–	1	na	na	1	na	na

The United States is the principal importer, followed by Switzerland, France and a number of other EC countries. Regional demand is very small and in 1990 was limited to Argentina (0.4 tonnes). The magnitude of rosewood oil consumption in Brazil is uncertain; 20-30 tonnes of oil are purchased annually by the fragrance sector, much of it by local branches of multinationals, but it is likely that a large proportion of this is exported, either as the crude oil or in formulations (which are not identifiable in trade statistics).

SUPPLY SOURCES

Production of rosewood oil in Peru, Colombia and the Guianas, where *Aniba* also grows, declined to negligible quantities after the advent of synthetic linalool in the 1960s. Brazil is now the only supplier to the world market.

Since the fall in production brought about by the loss of linalool markets and, more recently, by the use of cheaper Chinese Ho oils, production levels have been of the order of 100 tonnes pa. Annual fluctuations are mainly the result of differences in rainfall and river levels which determine accessibility to the wild resource. Harvesting of the trees is concentrated around a number of well-defined tributaries of the Amazon in northern Amazonas and southern Para states. While it should be possible to maintain present production levels in the medium term, the disinclination of youngererations of producers and labourers to undertake the arduous tasks involved in harvesting wild trees, and the increasing costs of collection as wild stands become more remote, suggest that production in the longer term may decline. Attempts at cultivation of *Aniba* to date have not been successful but the lack of any direct alternatives to rosewood oil in established, top-of-the-range perfumery formulations makes it desirable to pursue such objectives.

QUALITY AND PRICES

All major importing countries have published standard specifications for Brazilian rosewood oil and there is also an international (ISO) standard. These specify the botanical source and physico-chemical requirements, including the alcohol content (usually in the range 84-93 per cent determined as linalool). These standards are minimum trade requirements and for perfumery applications individual batches of oil must conform to the aroma expectations of the buyer. *Notwithstanding the above, there are two grades of Brazilian rosewood oil recognised in trade:*

- "Manaus" oil, which is shipped from Manaus, the export centre for the industry, and generally conforms to the standards described above.
- "American" oil, which is stretched by addition of synthetic linalool to give a slightly lower priced oil.

FOB prices for Brazilian rosewood oil have been in the range US$18-32/kg over the period 1987-93. Prices in late 1993 were about US$23/kg; they are expected to rise slightly in 1994 as a result of temporary shortfalls in wood supplies (arising from low river levels).

PLANT SOURCES

BOTANICAL/COMMON NAMES

Family Lauraceae:
Aniba rosaeodora Ducke
Aniba duckei Kostermans
(syn. *A. rosaeodora* var. *amazonica*)
Rosewood (En.), pau rosa (Br.), bois de rose femelle (Fr.).

There is some disagreement as to the exact botanical status of these species. In Brazil, where most of the research on *Aniba* has been carried out, some groups regard *A. rosaeodora* as a synonym of *A. duckei* while others take the reverse view. A third opinion holds that morphological differences that exist within the genus are insufficient to justify separation into two species. Oil producers themselves recognise two plant sources but make no attempt to keep the distilled oils separate.

A number of other *Aniba* species co-occur with *A. rosaeodora* (*A. duckei*) but are not exploited because the oil content is low or the composition/aroma is poor.

DESCRIPTION AND DISTRIBUTION

A. rosaeodora (*A. duckei*) is a large, evergreen tree reaching up to 30 m in height. All parts of the tree are fragrant although only the trunkwood is traditionally harvested and distilled.

Aromatic *Aniba* species are indigenous to the northern and western areas of Greater Amazonia. In Brazil it is found in the States of Amazonas, Pará and Amapá. Elsewhere in the region it occurs in Peru, Colombia, Ecuador, Suriname and French Guiana.

EFFECTS OF OIL PRODUCTION ON THE NATURAL RESOURCE

The perceived threat to the species posed by the destructive nature of harvesting has led to increasingly tight controls on the industry in Brazil. Government regulations exist which are intended to minimise this threat although there are difficulties in enforcing them. The results of recent field surveys in Brazil by Faculdade de Ciências Agrárias do Pará (FCAP) based in Belem indicate, in fact, that the species is not presently faced with extinction. Substantial wild stands exist deep within forest areas which are unlikely to be exploited for logistical or economic reasons.

However, the older, more accessible areas which have been utilised by the rosewood oil industry are effectively devoid of mature trees and there is no significant natural regeneration. This, together with the general problem of deforestation caused by land clearance, has led to a loss of germplasm diversity and a narrowing of the genetic base on which future domestication of the species will depend.

HARVESTING/PRIMARY PROCESSING

Harvesting is carried out by teams of collectors under contract to the distillery owners. Exploration of new areas is led by someone experienced in identifying and distinguishing the different *Aniba* species by appearance and odour. Access trails are created as individual stands of suitable trees are located. Whereas, formerly, trees up to 2 m diameter were readily available, these are now only found in the less accessible areas and trees as small as 15 cm diameter are harvested in order to maintain the supply of wood to the distillery. Occasionally, branches over 4 cm thick may also be collected. More recently, species of *Aniba* other than *A. rosaeodora* (*A. duckei*) have been felled as an expedient to bulk distillation raw material.

After felling, trees are cut into one metre lengths and transported to the river bank (which may be up to 20 km from the collection site). Logs are stock-piled and when river levels are high enough (dependent on the season) they are shipped downstream to the distillery. Most distilleries in Brazil are very basic and designed to be "mobile" so that they can be sited on the river bank and moved around by raft as conditions dictate or allow. In preparation for distillation the logs are cut up into small pieces and then mechanically reduced to chips.

Distillation is carried out in mild or galvanised steel vessels which may vary in size from 200-1,000kg capacity (of chips). Steam generation is by boiler fuelled with spent chips.

YIELDS AND QUALITY VARIATION

Yields of oil vary according to the quality of the wood feedstock (collection area and species mix) and its moisture content, but typically are around 1 per cent (w/w).

Although there are known to be batch-to-batch differences in linalool content, no systematic studies have been undertaken to determine the intrinsic variability of oil composition within natural populations of *Aniba*. The need for this has become more urgent with the recent inclusion of non-traditional species in the feedstock and the attention now being given to cultivation as a means of achieving sustainable oil production.

VALUE-ADDED PROCESSING

No further processing of the oil is carried out either by the primary distiller or any intermediate before it is formulated for fragrance use by the end-user.

PRODUCTS OTHER THAN OIL

Indians use the wood of *Aniba* for making canoes but its value for rosewood oil production mitigates against its use for other purposes.

DEVELOPMENT POTENTIAL

For reasons given above, the consumption of rosewood oil is now determined more by supply and price factors than by other market forces. With the inevitable rise in costs of production consequent upon a labour-intensive operation and the need to go deeper into the forest to locate suitable trees, there is every inducement to consider cultivation as a means not only of ameliorating the loss of biodiversity of *Aniba* in the primary forest but of ensuring the survival of the rosewood oil industry itself in the longer term. Such a solution would also offer the prospect of increased sales of oil and cash-earning opportunities for some of the poorer rural communities, albeit at a very modest level and on a small scale. Reclamation of small areas of degraded land by rosewood cultivation would be an added environmental attraction.

RESEARCH NEEDS

The problems to be overcome before domestication can be considered a realistic, economic option should not be underestimated. Unlike some other Amazonian species which have attracted attention because of their much larger potential market (as sources of fruits or oil seeds, for example), comparatively little research has been carried out on *Aniba*. Prior to 1990, studies were carried out on distribution, botany, propagation and silviculture by various Brazilian institutions (including INPA, CENARGEN and EMBRAPA).

In addition, some commercial distillers had conducted their own trials by planting seedlings within the natural forest. Growth performance with tunnel planting (in cleared strips) within the forest has been poor.

Since 1990, a new, systematic programme of research has been carried out by FCAP, with technical assistance from UK institutions (NRI, OFI and ITE) and funded by the UK's Overseas Development Administration (ODA). This has involved germplasm collections from threatened sites, research on improved propagation methods and establishment of field trials. Results indicate superior growth rates in open-field situations compared to forest tunnel planting. The longer-term aim of this work is to evaluate the techno-economic potential for formal cultivation, including the viability of producing a marketable leaf oil from non-destructive harvesting (coppicing or pollarding).

Specific needs identified by FCAP for future research on rosewood include the following:

- Development of an economic means of mass propagation of planting stock.
- Determination of the practicality and requirements for field establishment
  and the optimum management regimes for short-rotation harvesting of trunkwood and for frequent harvesting of leaf.
- Appraisal of the market for leaf oil (either as a direct substitute for

traditional wood oil or as a new, alternative source of low-priced natural linalool).

- Determination of the economics of production of wood and leaf oils.
- Investigation of the options for formal cultivation (as a monoculture or in mixed cropping systems on under-utilized or abandoned land) and the socio-economic aspects of production.
- Identification and selection for propagation of elite germplasm.

11

Timber and Wood Products

ROLE OF TREES

A tree is a large, perennial, woody plant. Though there is no set definition regarding minimum size, the term generally applies to plants at least 6 m (20 ft) high at maturity and, more importantly, having secondary branches supported on a single main stem or trunk with clear apical dominance Compared with most other plant forms, trees are long-lived. A few species of trees grow to 100 m tall, and some can live for several thousand years.

Trees are important components of the natural landscape and significant elements in landscaping and agriculture, supplying orchard crops (such as apples). Trees also play an important role in many of the world's mythologies

CLASSIFICATION

Fig. An Oak Tree in Denmark

A tree is a plant form and trees occur in many different orders and families of plants. Trees thus show a wide variety of growth form, leaf type and shape, bark characteristics, reproductive structures, etc.

The earliest trees were tree ferns and horsetails, which grew in vast forests in the Carboniferous Period; tree ferns still survive, but the only surviving horsetails are not of tree form. Later, in the Triassic Period, conifers, ginkgos, cycads and other gymnosperms appeared, and subsequently flowering plants in the Cretaceous Period. Most species of trees today are flowering plants and conifers.

The listing below gives examples of many well-known trees and how they are typically classified.A small group of trees growing together is called a grove or copse, and a landscape covered by a dense growth of trees is called a forest.

Several biotopes are defined largely by the trees that inhabit them; examples are rainforest and A landscape of trees scattered or spaced across grassland (usually grazed or burned over periodically) is called a savanna.

MORPHOLOGY

Fig. Leaves are an Important Feature of Trees

The basic parts of a tree are the roots, trunk(s), branches, twigs and leaves. Tree stems consist mainly of support and transport tissues (xylem and phloem). Wood consists of xylem cells, and bark is made of phloem and other tissues external to the vascular cambium.

Fig. Tree Roots Anchor the Structure and Provide Water and Nutrients

Trees may be broadly grouped into exogenous and endogenous trees according to the way in which their stem diameter increases. Exogenous trees, which comprise the great majority of modern trees (all conifers, and all broadleaf trees), grow by the addition of new wood outwards, immediately under the bark. Endogenous trees, mainly in the monocotyledons (*e.g.* palms), grow by addition of new material inwards.

As an exogenous tree grows, it creates growth rings. In temperate climates, these are commonly visible due to changes in the rate of growth with temperature variation over an annual cycle. These rings can be counted to determine the age of the tree, and used to date cores or even wood taken from trees in the past; this practice is known as the science of dendrochronology. In some tropical regions with constant year-round climate, growth is continuous and distinct rings are not formed, so age determination is impossible. Age determination is also impossible in endogenous trees.

The roots of a tree are generally embedded in earth, providing anchorage for the above-ground biomass and absorbing water and nutrients from the soil. It should be noted, however, that while ground nutrients are essential to a tree's growth the majority of its biomass comes from carbondioxide absorbed from the atmosphere the trunk gives height to the leaf-bearing branches, aiding in competition with other plant species for sunlight.

In many trees, the arrangement of the branches optimizes exposure of the leaves to sunlight. Not all trees have all the plant organs or parts mentioned above. For example, most palm trees are not branched, the saguaro cactus of North America has no functional leaves, tree ferns do not produce bark, etc. Based on their general shape and size, all of these are nonetheless generally regarded as trees. Indeed, sometimes size is the more important consideration. A plant form that is similar to a tree, but generally having smaller, multiple trunks and/or branches that arise near the ground, is called a shrub. However, no sharp differentiation between shrubs and trees is possible. Given their small size, bonsai plants would not technically be 'trees', but one should not confuse reference to the form of a species with the size or shape of individual specimens. A spruce seedling does not fit the definition of a tree, but all spruces are trees. Bamboos by contrast, do show most of the characteristics of trees, yet are rarely called trees.

CHAMPION TREES

The world's champion trees can be considered on several factors; height, trunk diameter or girth, total size, and age. It is significant that in each case, the top position is always held by a conifer, though a different species in each case; in most measures, the second to fourth places are also held by conifers.

Tallest Trees

The heights of the tallest trees in the world have been the subject of considerable dispute and much (often wild) exaggeration. Modern verified measurement with laser rangefinders combined with tape drop measurements made by tree climbers, carried out by the U.S. Eastern Native Tree Society has shown that most older measuring methods and measurements are unreliable, often producing exaggerations of 5% to 15% above the real height. Historical claims of trees of 114 m, 117 m, 130 m, and even 150 m, are now largely disregarded as unreliable, fantasy or outright fraud.

The following are now accepted as the top five tallest reliably measured species:

- *Coast Redwood Sequoia sempervirens*: 112.83 m, Humboldt Redwoods State Park, California
- *Coast Douglas-fir Pseudotsuga menziesii*: 100.3 m, Brummit Creek, Coos County, Oregon
- *Sitka Spruce Picea sitchensis*: 96.7 m, Prairie Creek Redwoods State Park, California
- *Giant Sequoia Sequoiadendron giganteum*: 93.6 m, Redwood Mountain Grove, California
- *Australian Mountain-ash Eucalyptus regnans*: 92.0 m, Styx Valley, Tasmania (Forestry Tasmania

Stoutest Trees

The girth (circumference) of a tree is – or at least should be – much easier to measure than the height, as it is a simple matter of stretching a tape round the trunk, and pulling it taut to find the circumference. Despite this, U.K. tree author Alan Mitchell made the following comment about measurements of yew trees in the British Isles: " the tree at Tisbury has a well-defined, clean, if irregular bole at least 1.5 m long. It has been found to have a girth which has dilated and shrunk in the following way: 11.28 m (1834 Loudon), 9.3 m (1892 Lowe), 10.67 m (1903 Elwes and Henry), 9.0 m (1924 E. Swanton), 9.45 m (1959 Mitchell).... Earlier measurements have therefore been omitted".

As a general standard, tree girth is taken at 'breast height'; this is defined differently in different situations, with most foresters measuring girth at 1.3 m above ground, while ornamental tree measurers usually measure at 1.5 m above ground; in most cases this makes little difference to the measured girth. On sloping ground, the "above ground" reference point is usually taken as the highest point on the ground touching the trunk, but some use the average between the highest and lowest points of ground. Some of the inflated old measurements may have been taken at ground level. Some past exaggerated measurements also result from measuring the complete next-to-bark measurement, pushing the tape in and out over every crevice and buttress.

Modern trends are to cite the tree's diameter rather than the circumference; this is obtained by dividing the measured circumference it assumes the trunk is circular in cross-section (an oval or irregular cross-section would result in a mean diameter slightly greater than the assumed circle). This is cited as dbh (diameter at breast height) in tree literature. A further problem with measuring baobabs Adansonia is that these trees store large amounts of water in the very soft wood in their trunks. This leads to marked variation in their girth over the year, swelling to a maximum at the end of the rainy season, minimum at the end of the dry season. Although baobabs have some of the highest girth measurements of any trees, no accurate measurements are currently available, but probably do not exceed 10-11 m diameter.

The stoutest species in diameter, excluding baobabs, are:

- *Montezuma Cypress Taxodium mucronatum*: 11.42 m, Árbol del Tule, Santa Maria del Tule, Oaxaca, Mexico
- *Giant Sequoia Sequoiadendron giganteum*: 8.85 m, General Grant tree, Grant Grove, California
- *Coast Redwood Sequoia sempervirens*: 7.44 m, Prairie Creek Redwoods State Park,

Largest Trees

The largest trees in total volume are those which are both tall and of large diameter, and in particular, which hold a large diameter high up the trunk. Measurement is very complex, particularly if branch volume is to be included as well as the trunk volume, so measurements have only been made for a small number of trees, and generally only for the trunk. No attempt has ever been made to include root volume.

The top four species measured so far are:

- *Giant Sequoia Sequoiadendron giganteum*: 1489 m^3, General Sherman tree
- *Coast Redwood Sequoia sempervirens*: 1045 m^3, Del Norte Titan tree
- *Western Redcedar Thuja plicata*: 500 m^3, Quinault Lake Redcedar
- *Kauri Agathis australis*: 400 m^3, Tane Mahuta tree (total volume, including branches, 516.7 m^3)

However, the Alerce Fitzroya cupressoides, as yet un-measured, may well slot in at third or fourth place, and Montezuma Cypress Taxodium mucronatum is also likely to be high in the list. The largest angiosperm tree is an Australian Mountain-ash, the 'El Grande' tree of about 380 m^3 in Tasmania.

Oldest Trees

The oldest trees are determined by growth rings, which can be seen if the tree is cut down or in cores taken from the edge to the centre of the tree. Accurate determination is only possible for trees which produce growth rings, generally those which occur in seasonal climates; trees in uniform non-seasonal tropical climates grow continuously and do not have distinct growth rings. It is also only possible for trees which are solid to the centre of the tree; many very old trees become hollow as the dead heartwood decays away. For some of these species, age estimates have been made on the basis of extrapolating current growth rates, but the results are usually little better than guesswork or wild speculation.

The verified oldest measured ages are:

- *Great Basin Bristlecone Pine Pinus longaeva*: 4844 years
- *Alerce Fitzroya cupressoides*: 3622 years
- *Giant Sequoia Sequoia sempervirens*: 3266 years
- *Huon-pine Lagarostrobos franklinii*: 2500 years
- *Rocky Mountains Bristlecone Pine Pinus aristata*: 2435 years

Other species suspected of reaching exceptional age include European Yew Taxus baccata (probably over 3000 years) and Western Redcedar Thuja plicata.

The oldest verified age for an angiosperm tree is 2293 years for the Sri Maha Bodhi Sacred Fig (Ficus religiosa) planted in 288 BC at Anuradhapura, Sri Lanka; this is also the oldest human-planted tree with a known planting date.

MAJOR TREE GENERA

Flowering Plants (Magnoliophyta; Angiosperms)

Dicotyledons (Magnoliopsida; Broadleaf or Hardwood Trees)

- Altingiaceae (Sweetgum family)
  - Sweetgum, Liquidambar species
- Anacardiaceae (Cashew family)
  - Cashew, Anacardium occidentale
  - Mango, Mangifera indica
  - Pistachio, Pistacia vera
  - Sumac, Rhus species
  - Lacquer tree, Toxicodendron verniciflua
- Annonaceae (Custard apple family)
  - Cherimoya Annona cherimola
  - Custard apple Annona reticulata
  - Pawpaw Asimina triloba
  - Soursop Annona muricata
- Apocynaceae (Dogbane family)
  - Pachypodium Pachypodium species
- Aquifoliaceae (Holly family)
  - Holly, Ilex species
- Araliaceae (Ivy family)
  - Kalopanax, Kalopanax pictus
- Betulaceae (Birch family)

  - Alder, Alnus species
  - Birch, Betula species
  - Hornbeam, Carpinus species
  - Hazel, Corylus species

Fig. Birch Tree (Foreground) and Maple Tree (Background) in Fall.

- Bignoniaceae (family)
  - Catalpa, Catalpa species
- Cactaceae (Cactus family)
  - Saguaro, Carnegiea gigantea
- Cannabaceae (Cannabis family)
  - Hackberry, Celtis species
- Cornaceae (Dogwood family)
  - Dogwood, Cornus species
- Dipterocarpaceae family
  - Garjan Dipterocarpus species
  - Sal Shorea species
- Ericaceae (Heath family)
  - Arbutus, Arbutus species
- Eucommiaceae (Eucommia family)
  - Eucommia Eucommia ulmoides
- Fabaceae (Pea family)
  - Acacia, Acacia species
  - Honey locust, Gleditsia triacanthos
  - Black locust, Robinia pseudoacacia
  - Laburnum, Laburnum species
  - Brazilwood, Caesalpinia echinata
- Fagaceae (Beech family)
  - Chestnut, Castanea species

  - Beech, Fagus species
  - Southern beech, Nothofagus species
  - Tanoak, Lithocarpus densiflorus
  - Oak, Quercus species
- Fouquieriaceae (Boojum family)
  - Boojum, Fouquieria columnaris
- Hamamelidaceae (Witch-hazel family)
  - Persian Ironwood, Parrotia persica
- Juglandaceae (Walnut family)
  - Walnut, Juglans species
  - Hickory, Carya species
  - Wingnut, Pterocarya species
- Lauraceae (Laurel family)
  - Cinnamon Cinnamomum zeylanicum
  - Bay Laurel Laurus nobilis
  - Avocado Persea americana
- Lecythidaceae (Paradise nut family)
  - Brazil Nut Bertholletia excelsa
- Lythraceae (Loosestrife family)
  - Crape-myrtle Lagerstroemia species
- Magnoliaceae (Magnolia family)
  - Tulip tree, Liriodendron species
  - Magnolia, Magnolia species

Fig. Baobab tree in South-Africa.

- Malvaceae (Mallow family; including Tiliaceae and Bombacaceae)
  - Baobab, Adansonia species
  - Silk-cotton tree, Bombax species
  - Bottletrees, Brachychiton species
  - Kapok, Ceiba pentandra

  - Durian, Durio zibethinus
  - Balsa, Ochroma lagopus
  - Cacao, (cocoa), Theobroma cacao
  - Linden (Basswood, Lime), Tilia species
- Meliaceae (Mahogany family)
  - Neem, Azadirachta indica
  - Bead tree, Melia azedarach
  - Mahogany, Swietenia mahagoni
- Moraceae (Mulberry family)
  - Fig, Ficus species
  - Mulberry, Morus species

Fig. Eucalyptus Bridgesiana on Red Hill, Australian Capital Territory

- Myristicaceae (Nutmeg family)
  - Nutmeg, Mysristica fragrans
- Myrtaceae (Myrtle family)
  - Eucalyptus, Eucalyptus species
  - Myrtle, Myrtus species
  - Guava, Psidium guajava

Fig. Nyssaceae: a Dove Tree in Flower

- Nyssaceae (Tupelo) family; sometimes included in Cornaceae
  - Tupelo, Nyssa species
  - Dove tree, Davidia involucrata
- Oleaceae (Olive family)
  - Olive, Olea europaea
  - Ash, Fraxinus species
- Paulowniaceae (Paulownia family)
  - Foxglove Tree, Paulownia species
- Platanaceae (Plane family)
  - Plane, Platanus species
- Rhizophoraceae (Mangrove family)
  - Red Mangrove, Rhizophora mangle
- Rosaceae (Rose family)
  - Rowans, Whitebeams, Service Trees Sorbus species
  - Hawthorn, Crataegus species
  - Pear, Pyrus species
  - Apple, Malus species
  - Almond, Prunus dulcis
  - Peach, Prunus persica
  - Plum, Prunus domestica
  - Cherry, Prunus species
- Rubiaceae (Bedstraw family)
  - Coffee, Coffea species
- Rutaceae (Rue family)
  - Citrus, Citrus species
  - Cork-tree, Phellodendron species
  - Euodia, Tetradium species
- Salicaceae (Willow family)
  - Aspen, Populus species
  - Poplar, Populus species
  - Willow, Salix species

Fig. Yellow Maple in Fall.

- Sapindaceae (including Aceraceae, Hippocastanaceae) (Soapberry family)
  - Maple, Acer species
  - Buckeye, Horse-chestnut, Aesculus species
  - Mexican Buckeye, Ungnadia speciosa
  - Lychee, Litchi sinensis
  - Golden rain tree, Koelreuteria
- Sapotaceae (Sapodilla family)
  - Argan, Argania spinosa
  - Gutta-percha, Palaquium species
  - Tambalacoque, or "dodo tree", Sideroxylon grandiflorum, previously Calvaria major
- Simaroubaceae family
  - Tree of heaven, Ailanthus species
- Theaceae (Camellia family)
  - Gordonia, Gordonia species
  - Stuartia, Stuartia species
- Thymelaeaceae (Thymelaea family)
  - Ramin, Gonystylus species
- Ulmaceae (Elm family)
  - Elm, Ulmus species
  - Zelkova, Zelkova species
- Verbenaceae family
  - Teak, Tectona species

Monocotyledons (Liliopsida)

Fig. Coconut Palm, a Monocotyledonous Tree.

- Agavaceae (Agave family)
  - Cabbage tree, Cordyline australis

  - Dragon tree, Dracaena draco
  - Joshua tree, Yucca brevifolia
- Arecaceae (Palmae) (Palm family)
  - Areca Nut, Areca catechu
  - Coconut Cocos nucifera
  - Date Palm, Phoenix dactylifera
  - Chusan Palm, Trachycarpus fortunei
- Poaceae (grass family)
  - Bamboos Poaceae, subfamily Bambusoideae

History of green plants alterations in phenotype, different selective pressures on different parts of the genome and/or organism mean that evolution is not uniform for all characters of the organism – the principle known as 'mosaic evolution'. Compare crocodiles and birds to their common reptilian ancestor – one is more distinct from the ancestor than the other, and within each, some features have changed more from the ancestor than others.

Under this principle, the supposedly 'inexplicable' combination of characters possessed by Archaea is entirely explicable. Some of the features shared with one domain will represent plesiomorphies that have been lost in the remaining domain, while features shared with one or the other domain may be apomorphies of a larger clade.

To make any sense of this requires us to establish which domains are more closely related, and which is the most basalmost domain. This is where the real fun and frustration begins. The rRNA tree is, like all phylogenetic trees when they are first calculated, un-rooted. Normally the position of the root of a tree is established by inclusion of an outgroup, a taxon that is definitely known to be outside the group of interest.

Unfortunately, somewhat by definition, no suitable outgroup exists for the totality of life. Obviously, a more inventive approach was needed.The trees of these genes should be able to be used to root each other and indicate the point where Luca was to be found. The first two gene pairs used were elongation factors (EF-Tu vs. EF-G) and catalytic vs. regulatory subunits of eubacterial F-ATPases with V- or V-like-ATPases of Eukarya and Archaea. Both these studies found the root to be on the branch separating Eubacteria from the other two domains. Studies using other genes also found this pattern, and it became accepted as the standard view.

The evolution of life sat well with the supposed greater complexity of the DNA-processing systems in Eukarya and Archaea than in Eubacteria. Like all popular pictures, though, critics soon materialised to complain about itmany of the genes used appeared to be mutation-saturated at the level used, so that the points of inter-section of the paralogous trees were potentially the result of long-branch attractionFor various reasons, most researchers in bacterial systematics continue to use rRNA trees exclusively, despite suggestions they may be unreliable and increased recognition in systematics of other organisms that phylogenetic evidence should be drawn from as many sources as possible. Division into three domains, with Eubacteria sister to Archaea + Eukarya, remains the norm, though a few alternative suggestions will be examined here.

The common ancestor of all three domains was not yet a properly developed, integrated cell, but a 'progenote.' Cell design was held to be shaped largely by rampant lateral gene transfer, with genetic components functioning as interchangeable modular units. Eventually, a 'Darwinian Threshold' was passed where genetic components of individual cells became integrated enough that lateral gene transfer was no longer able to occur enough to blur genealogical lines, and standard vertical descent became predominant. This threshold was passed separately in each of the three domains. The supposed sister status of Eukarya and Archaea is actually an artefact of analysis resulting from Eubacteria crossing the threshold earlier than the other two domains.

Support for this concept supposedly came from the wide divergence between the three domains, with completely different translation systems in Eukarya + Archaea vs. Eubacteria, plus the lack of phylogenetic resolution between domains and at the base of domains in trees for many genes. Translation systems were thought to have evolved independently in the two branches, thus removing the need to explain how one system replaced another. Multiple gene trees for Eubacteria show concordance at more recent nodes, but lower resolution at older nodes, potentially compatible with a 'Darwinian Threshold.'

LUCA lacked a translation system is not possible – it must have possessed one to have functioned as an organism. Characters such as the genetic code remain reasonably constant between domains, which would not be expected if it was independently derived in them. Therefore, a separate origin for the eukaryal and bacterial translation systems does not remove the need to explain the change of translation system – instead, we have to explain the replacement of the ancestral system by each of the derived systems.

Also, as noted before, Archaea actually share many features with Eubacteria rather than Eukarya, and the differences are not as completely all-encompassing as often thought. The existence of a 'Darwinian Threshold' seems similarly tenuous – if lateral gene transfer was common in the past, there seems to be little reason why it should not still be so. The reasonable resolution in recent branches of gene trees argues against this – if anything, one would expect gene transfer to be more common between closely related organisms than distantly related ones, as there would be less chance that the newly-acquired genes would overly disrupt the genome of the recipient organism.

It seems much more likely that the lack of resolution at more ancient levels is due as much to time eroding phylogenetic signal combined with rapid radiation of basal branches, as much as lateral gene transfer obscuring it. After all, Neoaves (the clade containing most modern birds) is also almost completely unresolved as to basal relationships, but no-one is suggesting lateral gene transfer between birds as the cause. Eukarya might be basal, with prokaryotes derived from eukaryotic ancestors by 'genetic streamlining.' This suggestion was based on gene trees of slowly evolving positions of elongation factors. It was felt that this rooting 'would best explain the presence of many more eubacterial-like genes than eukaryotic-like ones in completely sequenced archaebacterial genomes.' But, as explained before, there is no problem with this fact even if Archaea are sister to Eukarya. Archaea would then have simply retained mostly plesiomorphic features that have been lost in their sister group.

A basal position for eukaryotes is also at odds with the fossil record. The earliest unequivocal eukaryotes are from the Late Proterozoic, about 850 My ago, though more doubtful examples are known from 1200 My ago. Either date is considerably younger than the earliest Eubacteria.

Paraphyly with regard to Eubacteria, however, seems unlikely in light of the aforementioned greater complexity of DNA-processing systems in Archaea + Eukarya than in Eubacteria, probably due to DNA in the former group usually being contained by histones rather than DNA topoisomerases in Eubacteria That these systems have not been 'genetically streamlined' in Eubacteria is supported by the fact that Eukarya and Archaea which lack or have reduced histones, such as Crenarchaeota and Dinoflagellata, retain the advanced processing systems rather than developing more eubacterial-like onesParaphyly of Archaea with regard to Eukarya often appears in gene trees, but if Eubacteria is basal to Archaea + Eukarya, there is quite strong 'morphological' evidence against it. Archaea possess a cell membrane composed of prenyl ether lipids, as opposed to acyl ester lipids in Eubacteria and Eukarya.

Cell membrane characters are evolutionarily extremely stable, and this makes it much more likely that Archaea are a monophyletic sister-group to Eukarya. Also worthy of consideration is the suggestion that Eubacteria is actually paraphyletic with regard to Archaea + Eukarya.). Prokaryotes can be divided into two groups on the basis of cell membrane structure.

The Monodermata or Unibacteria, containing Archaea and mostly Gram-positive Eubacteria, possess a single cell membrane. Didermata or Negibacteria, containing mostly Gram-negative Eubacteria, have a double membrane – the inner cytoplasmic membrane, and the more porous outer membrane. Cavalier-Smith made the argument that Didermata must be ancestral as loss of the outer membrane by hypertrophy of the murein wall between membranes was more probable than gain of a new membrane.

While this theory is mechanistically plausible, the problem in evaluating phylogenies with mechanistic models is that Life has often proven to be more ingenious than researchers in coming up with pathways by which evolution may occur.

Cravenly cower to the popular vote, and organise this page with the basalmost division on life between Eubacteria and Archaea + Eukarya. Names and information for divisions in Archaea are taken from, while names for Eubacteria are mostly taken from r clades not recognised or named in the former source.

A few comments need to be made on the use of names for taxa. Archaea were previously universally regarded as bacteria, and terms such as 'bacteriology' and 'bacterial' are still often used to cover both Eubacteria and Archaea. The redefinition of 'Bacteria' was unnecessary as the name 'Eubacteria' is well-recognised, and doesn't have the same potential for double meaning.

The name 'Archaebacteria' was altered to 'Archaea' at the same time, to lose the implied connection to Bacteria. This also appears to be an unnecessary name-change. Names should not be changed merely because they are felt to be unsuitable for some reason – not only is it potentially confusing, but unsuitability is often a subjective matter that different researchers may disagree on. Despite the priority of Archaebacteria, the name Archaea has become more commonly used, and at least doesn't have the same potential for confusion as 'Bacteria.'

The Diversity of Bacteria

Our tentative cladogram of the bacteria may be found, oddly enough, on the Cladogram page. Not to belabor the obvious, but the bacteria have been around a lot longer than anything else. Living species tend to be at the tail end of very long evolutionary chains; and, with rare exceptions, our knowledge is limited to living species. Consequently, there are pockets of diversity everywhere in the bacteria that don't seem to be very closely related to anything else. This makes it unreasonably difficult to summarize bacterial diversity. For the moment, we will have to make do with only the largest and most conspicuous groups

```
LUCA
|–Eubacteria
|  |–Actinobacteria
|  '–+–Firmicutes
|     '–Didermata
|       |–Cyanobacteria
|       '–+–Sphingobacteria
|          '–Proteobacteria
'–Neomura
|–Archaea
'–Eukarya
```

Relationships within eubacteria are extremely uncertain at almost all levels of divergence, and many of those that have been suggested make little obvious sense. A number of factors have resulted in this situation – one is the general reliance on rRNA trees to the exclusion of other data sources. rRNA trees have been shown in recent years to be sensitive to variations in evolutionary rates in eukaryotes, leading to such errors as the placing of Microsporidia low down in the eukaryote tree, instead of in or near the Fungi. rRNA trees also show low resolution between most branches at high levels.

The other major issue with tree construction which has received a lot of attention is lateral or horizontal gene transfer (LGT), the direct transfer of genes from one species to another. The occurrence of LGT in prokaryotes between unrelated species is undoubted – however, opinions differ as to just how prominent it is.

Some regard its occurrence as minimal others feel that LGT may be so common as to render the construction of an organismal phylogeny for prokaryotes effectively impossible. This page tends away from the latter view, of course – if for no other reason than that otherwise we might as well give up and go home. Cases of LGT might even be potentially used as characters to support clades.

The general trend of current eubacterial phylogeny:

```
LUCA
|—Neomura
`—+—Aquificae
  `—+—Thermotogae
    `—+—Dictyoglomus
      `—+—+—Firmicutes
        | `—Cyanobacteria
        `—+—Actinobacteria
     `—+—+—Caldithrix
       | `—+—Deferribacteres
       |   `—+—Nitrospina
       |     `—Thermodesulfobacterium
       `—+—+—Sphingobacteria
         | `—+—Spirochaetes
         |   `—+—Fusobacteria
         |     `—Proteobacteria
         `—+—+—Acidobacteria
           | `—Nitrospirae
           `—+—Eobacteria
             `—Planctobacteria
```

Constructed using mostly 'morphological' or physiological characters:

```
LUCA
|—Eobacteria
```

```
'-+-+-Cyanobacteria
|  '-+-+-Firmicutes
|    |  '-Thermotogae
|    '-+==Actinobacteria (paraphyletic)
|      '-Neomura
'-+-Spirochaetes
   '-+-Sphingobacteria
     '-+-Planctobacteria
   '-Proteobacteria
```

As different as these two trees are, there are some similarities. Most notably, if both trees are unrooted, the Gram-positive bacteria (Actinobacteria, Firmicutes and Thermotogae) are close to Neomura (corresponding to the Monodermata); the Didermata are mostly further away.

The relationships within Didermata are more contradictory, but seem poorly supported in both papersThe exception is Cyanobacteria, which are closest to Monodermata in both trees. Differences in positions of the Aquificae and Thermotogae are the most significant differences between the trees. Aquifex has been widely accepted as the basalmost eubacterium due to its position in rRNA trees. However, Aquifex has a double membrane, suggesting a position within Didermata. Some protein trees place it within the å-proteobacteria, and this was the position accepted by Cavalier-Smith. As placing Aquifex in its position on the rRNA tree implies multiple gains or losses of the outer membrane.

Thermotogae is the second-most basal major branch in rRNA trees, but is grouped with Firmicutes on many protein trees, by comparison of indels, and by the gene-content tree. The differences in position of the Thermotogae and Aquificae are probably due to long-branch attraction in the rRNA tree, and a high proportion of G+C in the genomes of these two taxa and Archaea.

The reposition of these two taxa has significant implications for one of the conclusions drawn from the rRNA tree of life – the supposed hyperthermophilic nature of Luca. This theory was supported by two of three domains having hyperthermophiles as basalmost members. With the eubacterial tree shown here, Archaea is the only domain that is still potentially basally hyperthermophilic, and a mesophilic Luca seems more likely. A hyperthermophilic origin of life, while thought to be consistent with widespread conditions on the young, newly-formed earth, is not consistent with the reduced stability of RNA at high temperatures. In the tree used here, the order of branches between the base and Cyanobacteria is based on the Cavalier-Smith tree, while relationships within the Didermata exclusive of Cyanobacteria are, for now, based on the more familiar rRNA tree in light of their greater uncertainty. Most of the taxa are based on clusters in gene trees, and may be lacking in morphological apomorphies.

ACTINOBACTERIA

Actinobacteria are Gram-positive and almost exclusively aerobic. Their DNA is biased towards high G+C content. Actinobacteria contain 20S proteasomes. Such proteasomes are otherwise known only from Archaea and eukaryotes. Often with snapping division or branching filaments; spores if present usually exospores.

Filamentous members of this clade are often referred to as 'fungi'. Actinomyces, Streptomyces, Mycobacterium, Propionibacterium, Corynebacterium, Nocardia, Micrococcus.

FIRMICUTES

with thick rigid murein walls containing teichoic acids and lipoteichoic acids; often forming endospores. Clostridium, Bacillus, Lactobacillus, Streptococcus, Staphylococcus. In contrast, one subclade, the Mollicutes, has lost the cell wall, and is mostly intracellular parasites or symbionts (Mycoplasma). The name 'Firmicutes' was originally coined to include all Gram-positive bacteria (including Actinobacteria and Togobacteria) and excluding Mollicutes,

DIDERMATA

These are mostly Gram-negative Eubacteria, have a double membrane – the inner cytoplasmic membrane, and the more porous outer membrane.

CYANOBACTERIA

The blue-green 'algae', probably the most familiar bacterial clade, and one of the few to be recognised before the advent of molecular data (the other was the Spirochaetes). Characterised by oxygenic photosynthesis with chlorophyll a. Flagella absent.

A single genus, Gloeobacter, is recognisably basal to all others in lacking thylakoids. The clade Phycobacteria contains all other cyanobacteria, and has the chlorophyll contained in thylakoids. Phycobacteria have traditionally been divided into five orders on the basis of morphological colony characters. Chloroplasts are derived from Phycobacteria, though from which subclade is still unknown.

SPHINGOBACTERIA

Cytoplasmic membrane with sphingolipids; outer membrane with lipopolysaccharide; flagella absent.

PROTEOBACTERIA

Largest bacterial clade – well-recognised by molecular data, but short on morphological synapomorphies. Large insertion in RNA polymerase and DnaK. While the genus Proteus is included within Proteobacteria, the division is not named after the genus. Instead, both are named after the Greek shape-changing god Proteus – in the case of Proteobacteria, to reflect the wide range of morphologies covered by the clade. Includes photosynthetic purple sulphur (*e.g.* Rhodocyclus) and non-sulphur (*e.g.* Rhodobacter) bacteria, intracellular parasites (*e.g.* Rickettsia), colonial formers of fruiting bodies (Myxococcales), and a wide range of heterotrophs, such as probably the most well-known bacterium of all, Escherichia coli. Divided by molecular data into five large clades, the á-, â-, ã-, ä-, and å-proteobacteria. Examples –[Alphaproteobacteria] Rhodobacter, Rhizobium, Rickettsia; [Betaproteobacteria] Neisseria, Spirillum; [Gammaproteobacteria] Pseudomonas, Vibrio, Escherichia; [Deltaproteobacteria] Bdellovibrio, Myxococcus; [Epsilonproteobacteria] Helicobacter.

ARCHAEA

The Archaea, or Archaebacteria have cell membrane of prenyl ether lipids. Flagellar shaft of acid-insoluble glycoproteins related to pilin. DNA binding protein 10b. tRNA modifications, including archaeosine in D-loop and absence of queuine. Tiny large subunit ribosomal protein, LX. No Hsp90 chaperone. RNA polymerase A split into two proteins. Glutamate synthetase split into three proteins. Divided by rRNA trees into two major clades, Crenarchaeota and Euryarchaeota.

WOOD STRUCTURE

Wood is a plant secondary tissue that is formed mainly in the stems of gymnosperms and dicotyledons through the activity of a growing layer, the Cambium. The cambium is responsible for the growth of stems in thickness through the formation annually of new layers of both wood and bark.

H] COMPOSITION OF WOOD

Wood is a heterogeneous tissue made up of several different kinds of cells, some that have the function of mechanical support and others that of conduction. In softwoods, or gymnosperms, both these functions usually occur in cells called Tracheids. In hardwoods, or angiosperms, a division of labor usually exists. Mechanical support is provided by the several types of wood fibers that make up a greater part of the woody tissue, while the conduction of water is by tubular cell fusions called Vessels. Tracheids are also occasionally present. Wood also functions in the distribution and storage of carbohydrate that is accomplished in theParenchyma Cells. These are the only parts of the wood that is truly living and which contains protoplasm. Parenchyma cells occur in two forms, (1) wood parenchyma and (2) ray parenchyma. The former are arranged vertically in the stem while the latter are horizontal.

DIAGNOSTIC FEATURES

Valuable diagnostic traits are afforded by the arrangement of the different types of cells in wood. Woods may be distinguished by pores, early wood and late wood, growth rings, rays, heartwood, sapwood grain and figure.

Porous & Nonporous Woods

The presence or absence and the nature and arrangement in cross section of pores that are really vessels, offer a quick way to classify woods. Conifers that do not have vessels are in the nonporous wood category. Hardwoods that do have vessels may be further divided into those where the pores are arranged in concentric circles, the outer and inner portions of which differ according to number and size of pores, and those where the pores are all small and about the same size and are scattered uniformly through the wood. The first category is called ring-porous and the second diffuse-porous. .

Early & Late Wood

In temperate climates new wood is formed annually during a limited growing season and definite growth layers result. These usually have two distinct areas within each layer. In springtime when growth resumes, the first wood to be formed contains many large and thin-walled cells as a response to the greater need for conducting nutrients. This is the early wood or spring wood.

As the season progresses a more dense kind of wood is laid down that has smaller, thicker walled cells, the late wood or summer wood. This produces a sharp transition between the cells formed at the end of a growing season and those formed at the beginning of the succeeding one. In cross section this appears as concentric rings called Growth Rings. The growth ring of one year is called an annual ring and the number of these indicated the tree's age. In the tropics where growth may continue throughout the year growth zones may occur also, but they are due to changes in weather or other causes rather than to definite growth periods.

Rays

These are thin sheers or ribbons that are made up primarily of parenchyma cells oriented at right angles to the stem's main axis. They vary in height, width and arrangement. In cross section they are visi8ble as lines that radiate from the stem's center. They are most obvious in radial sections where they can also be used to identify the tree species by the variety in their form and arrangement.

Sapwood & Heartwood

When young all wood cells are physiologically active. But in time many of them lose their activity and become skeletons that serve only to provide strength to the tree.

Eventually two distinct areas develop:

(1) A light colored outer region of varying width, the sapwood, and

Bibliography

A K Srivastava and Shyam Singh.: *Citrus : Climate and Soil*, International Book Distributing Co, Delhi, 2002.

A. Aysen.: *Problem Solving in Soil Mechanics*, Taylor & Francis Publication, New York, 2011.

A. K. Kolay.: *Soil Fertility*, Atlantic Publication, New Delhi, 2010.

A. Rami Horowitz and Isaac Ishaaya.: *Insect Pest Management : Field and Protected Crops*, Springer, London, 2004.

A.K. Dhawan, Balwinder Singh, Manmeet Brar Bhullar and Ramesh Arora.: *Integrated Pest Management*, Scientific Publication, Delhi, 2013.

A.L. Bhatia: *Handbook of Microbiology*, Pointer Publication, New Delhi, 2005.

Arun Shridhar Phadke: *Handbook of Microbiology*, Adhyayan Publication, Delhi, 2008.

Charles Ernest Millar.: *Soil Fertility*, Biotech Books, Jaipur, 2004.

Charlotte Jhonson.: *Biology of Soil Science*, Oxford Book Company, Delhi, 2009.

Ehrenfried Pfeiffer and E B Balfour.: *Soil Fertility Renewal and Preservation: Bio-Dynamic Framing and Gardening*, Asiatic Publication, Delhi, 2006.

G.S. Dhaliwal and E.A. Heinrichs.: *Critical Issues in Insect Pest Management*, Commonwealth Publication, New Delhi, 1998.

Geoff M Gurr; Steve D Wratten and Maguel A Altieri.: *Ecological* Engineering for Pest Management : Advances in Habitat *Manipulation for Arthropods*, SBS Publication, Delhi, 2009.

Ghulam Hassan Dar: *Soil Microbiology and Biochemistry*, New India Publishing Agency, Delhi, 2010.

H.A. Modi: *Soil Microbiology*, Pointer Publication, New Delhi, 2013.

H.C.L. Gupta, A.U. Siddiqui and Aruna Parihar.: *Bio Pest Management : Entomopathogenic Nematodes, Microbes and Bioagents*, Agrotech Publication, Delhi, 2010.

K. Kumutha, K.G. Anitha and K. Saranya: *Agricultural and Industrial Microbiology*,

Satish Serial Publishing House, Delhi, 2012.A C Mittal : *Energy and Sustainable Development,* Vista International, Delhi, 2008.

Asit K. Biswas and Cecilia Tortajada : *Appraising Sustainable* Development : Water Management and Environmental *Challenges*, Oxford University Press, Delhi, 2005.

B Balaswamy : *Communication for Sustainable Development*, Concept Publisher, Delhi, 2006.

Biodiversity and Sustainable Development : Edited by R.N. Pati and Atul K. Jain, Sarup, 2010.

Bruno Dorin and Thomas Jullien : *Agricultural Incentives in India :* Past Trends and Prospective Paths Towards Sustainable *Development*, Manohar Publisher, Delhi, 2004.

Chandra Shekhar Prasad : *Agriculture and Sustainable Development in India*, New Century Publications, Delhi, 2012.

Corruption - Free Sustainable Development : Challenges and Strategies for Good Governance : Edited by R.B. Jain, Mittal Publication, Delhi, 2004.

G. Narayana Reddy : *Building Capacities for Sustainable Development*, Kanishka Publisher, Delhi, 2002.

H.P. Mathur, N.B. Singh and V.K. Kumra: *Energy Resources Alternative Search and Sustainable Development*, Shree Publication, Delhi, 2011.

Madhusudan Mishra and Prabhakar Sharma: *A Textbook of Plant Genetics*, Wisdom Press, Delhi, 2012.

Mukta Bhargava: *A Textbook of Plant Diseases and Their Control (2 Vols-Set)*, Dominant Publication, Delhi, 2007.

Mushtaq A. Wani: *Soil, Plant and Water Analysis Manual*, Agrotech Publishing Academy, Delhi, 2011.

N.S. Kute and A.R. Aher: *Principles of Plant Breeding*, Agri-Biovet Press, Delhi, 2013.

N.S. Subba Rao: *Soil Microorganisms and Plant Growth*, Oxford & IBH Publishing House, Delhi, 1995.

Nafees A. Khan and Sarvajeet Singh: *Abiotic Stress and Plant Responses*, I.K. International Publication, Delhi, 2008.

P. Vidhyasekaran: *Principles of Plant Pathology*, CBS Publication, Delhi, 2010.

P.C. Ram and G.S. Chaturvedi: *Abiotic Stresses and Plant Productivity*, Aavishkar Publication, Delhi, 2010.

P.C. Trivedi: *Plant Physiology in Agriculture and Forestry*, Aavishkar Publication, Delhi, 2009.

P.K. Gupta: *Soil, Plant, Water and Fertilizer Analysis*, Agrobios Publication, Jaipur, 2009.

Index